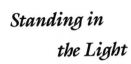

Standing in
the Light

University of Nebraska Press
Lincoln and London

STANDING IN THE LIGHT

A Lakota Way of Seeing

By Severt Young Bear and R. D. Theisz

© 1994 by the University of Nebraska Press

All rights reserved

Manufactured in the United States of America

∞ The paper in this book meets the minimum requirements of
American National Standard for Information
Sciences—Permanence of Paper for Printed Library
Materials, ANSI Z39.48–1984.

Library of Congress Cataloging-in-Publication Data

Young Bear, Severt, 1934–1993.

Standing in the light : a Lakota way of seeing /
by Severt Young Bear and R. D. Theisz.

p.   cm. — (American Indian lives)

Includes bibliographical references and index.

ISBN 0-8032-4911-X (alk. paper)

1. Young Bear, Severt, 1934–1993.

2. Dakota Indians—Biography.

3. Dakota philosophy.

4. Dakota Indians—Rites and ceremonies.

I. Theisz, R. D.   II. Title.   III. Series.

E99.DIY688   1994

970-004′975—dc20   93-50834

[B]   CIP

Contents

Illustrations

INTRODUCTION

Two Minds Working as One

✦ *R. D. Theisz*

I first met Severt Young Bear in 1963 in a small log dance hall at Wanblee, South Dakota, on the Pine Ridge Sioux Reservation. I do not recall a flash of preordainment, nor the feeling that fate had forged our meeting for some great purpose, nor any mutual attraction out of the ordinary. I remembered little about him other than his name as I returned to my studies at Queens College in New York. This had been my second year of spending summers attending powwows and getting to know the Lakota people of South Dakota and other tribes. That summer of 1963, Severt was one of the Lakota singers we had brought back east for a powwow stressing dance, song, costume, and other celebrations of traditional American Indian ways.

Four years later, in 1967, after two more summers spent traveling the West, I was able to recruit Severt again as one of the group of singers we were able to bring back to New York to provide our powwow singing. Thus, he came in twice to our powwow—once with Leo and David Clairmont from Rosebud, another time with Drury Cook of Red Scaffold—to provide the singing central to our annual celebration. Though he was considered a good singer even then, he did not, at the time, possess the leadership qualities he has acquired since.

In 1972, after two years of studies at European universities and the completion of my doctoral studies, I moved to the Rosebud Reservation in South Dakota. Having taught literature and language for seven years at universities in New York, my wife, Cheryl, and I cast our lot with the recently established Sinte Gleska College, one of the newly organized Indian tribal colleges. As a result, my professional commitment as well as our personal orientation more and more pivoted around our developing relationships with the Lakota Indian people of South Dakota. We had been interested in Lakota music, dance, and art, as well as literature, for some years, so we welcomed the chance to learn from the Lakota people directly and to be an integral part of the reservation environment. We served the community as educators, became friends with many, but most of all learned both cultural and human lessons from our friends and colleagues. We were committed not to be do-gooders or wanna-bes. In those years we formed some very meaningful permanent relationships and many more temporary and ultimately passing ones.

Our new existence at Rosebud included the slowly growing and, later on, deepening relationship to Severt Young Bear, the clear leader of the Porcupine Singers from the neighboring Pine Ridge Reservation. I had been adopted in the Lakota ceremonial way—that is, I was taken into the family as a son and brother—by the Clairmont family of singers from Rosebud, some of whom also sang with the Porcupine Singers. As a result, I also became acquainted and familar with members of the Porcupine Singers, a group that was emerging in the years 1972–77 as one of the most popular and definitive traditional Indian song groups of the Northern Plains.

We have traveled with the Porcupine Singers since 1972. I was formally and publicly taken into the group in 1974 at a ceremony during the Ring Thunder Powwow. My wife and I throughout the years since—with some diversions since our three children have in recent years started growing up with interests of their own—have followed the powwow trail with the Porcupine Singers. We ranged from North Dakota to Indiana, from Nebraska to Arizona, from Washington to Manitoba.

Everywhere the singers have gone, Severt Young Bear and I have traveled together. Our relationship gradually deepened and became anchored by our many shared experiences. We enjoyed the successes of our families and the Porcupine Singers together. We experienced mutually the consequences of jealousy from other singing groups. We lent our personal support and commitment for the welfare of the singing group. We shared the experiences of our children growing up at different stages and through various rites. My older son, Erik, formed a special tie to Severt and received a horse as a gift as part of the honoring ceremonies during Severt's wedding on August 6, 1976. My wife and I, in turn, have continued over the years to show our special support for Severt's younger son, Melvin. Severt and I have sat side by side through numerous powwows, making careful comments, and more often humorous, smart-ass jive talk about each other and ourselves. We have enjoyed countless dinners and other events, been supportive of each other at family funerals, and, in general, have grown to respect and prize each other's ideas, values, and behavior.

I have grown increasingly to admire Severt's mind and heart. His insights are generally poignant; his decisions, small or large, have been a source of conviction for me and many others. Very, very rarely have I found his judgment off the mark. His views of right and wrong, which continue to mature, are based on a culturally consistent as well as universally defensible system of caring deeply for his human relatives. His cultural knowledge and insights as well as the ability to articulate them need no further testament than these pages.

A brief biographical sketch of Severt's life and those close to him may help to provide a setting for the pages that make up the main body of this book. Severt was the second child born to William Young Bear and Sophie (Smoke) Young Bear in 1934 at Porcupine, South Dakota. His older brother, Ernest, was born in 1924; his sister, Elizabeth, in 1937. Reared in a home where the traditional Lakota language was spoken and the traditional Lakota lifestyle maintained, Severt attended the Porcupine Bureau of Indian Affairs (BIA) school from 1942 to 1948 and then seventh and eighth grades at Mission, South Dakota. After graduating from Todd County High School in 1954, Severt in 1956 married Martha Moccasin by whom he had three daughters, Mary, Lena, and Cheryl. In the same year he joined the United States Army and served from 1956 to 1959 at Fort Gordon, Georgia, as a member of the Military Police. He also had two more daughters, Ursula and Janice. In 1959, after his divorce from Martha, he first went on relocation to Cleveland for six months as part of the BIA policy of relocating Lakotas and other tribes from their reservations to the job markets of urban centers such as Chicago, Dallas, and Los Angeles. He then pursued seasonal work in Nebraska, Wyoming, and Colorado until 1963, coming home in the winters to play basketball. On May 7, 1962, Severt's older son, Severt Junior, was born to Lucille Standing Soldier, who died eleven months after giving birth. The following year, Severt began his commitment to the life of the traveling singer and became the head singer of the first of the traveling Porcupine Singers. At the same time, from 1964 to 1970, he was employed as a ranger for the Oglala Sioux Tribe. Severt's younger son, Melvin, was born on July 20, 1966, to Rachel Leclaire, who passed away in 1984.

The year 1970 marked the beginning of Severt's varied involvements in the politics of the Oglala tribe. He was elected to the tribal council, serving from 1970 to 1972, and later served as administrative assistant, public safety commissioner, and community liaison under several tribal chairmen until 1985. Severt's mother died in 1971; his father passed away in 1974. He was adopted as a brother for James Clairmont and me by David Clairmont, James's father, who also adopted me as a son at that time.

Nineteen seventy-two began a renewed period of extensive travel for Severt as leader of our reorganized traveling Porcupine Singers, who now began to achieve a national reputation for our brand of traditional Lakota singing. The same year also marked Severt's participation in the American Indian Movement (AIM) takeover of the BIA building in Washington, D.C., and the demonstrations in Custer, South Dakota—during which he was arrested—and in Alliance and Gordon, Nebraska. In 1973, Severt was heavily involved in the turbulent events of the Wounded Knee II takeover, paying for that stand by being shot at twenty-nine times by some of his own people and having seventeen of his horses and dogs killed. He spent the next two years acting as interpreter for the AIM trials in Council Bluffs, Cedar Rapids, Saint Paul, Lincoln, Sioux Falls, and Fargo. Severt passed the role of head singer for the Porcupine Singers on to James Clairmont in 1974 but remained drum keeper. On August 6, 1976, he married Myrna White Face and was appointed traditional chief of Brotherhood Community by the late Chief Frank Fools Crow. Brotherhood Community and the communities of Oblaya, Butte, Knife Chief, Rockyford, and Evergreen make up Porcupine District. The name Brotherhood was selected because several sets of brothers were among its founders. In 1976 Chief Fools Crow also designated Severt head Sun Dance singer for Fools Crow's Pine Ridge Sun Dance.

With the Porcupine Singers recording six popular albums of Lakota songs for Canyon Records in 1976, 1979, and 1988, Severt assumed his role as a traditional resource person. He taught courses for Oglala Lakota College, became a sought-after speaker, and served on the boards of directors for KILI Radio from 1979 to 1991 and the Brotherhood Community Health Clinic in 1982. In 1988 he founded the annual International Brotherhood Days held for one week in July on his land in Porcupine. He served as music and dance consultant for the popular film *Dances with Wolves* in 1989 and for *Thunder Heart* in 1991.

Along the way, Severt experienced some health problems when his appendix ruptured in 1985 and he required surgery. Two years later he underwent further surgery due to complications from the first hospital stay. In 1991 he had a silent heart attack, and in the fall of 1992 his heart stopped after he was rushed to the hospital. He was revived but remained in a coma for two days and returned home after three weeks to Porcupine, where he is now recovering nicely.

Since 1972, then, Severt and I have had the opportunity—besides sitting at the drum and passing caustic, appreciative, or terribly insightful comments on singing, dancing, costume, human nature, or other topics—to witness our mutual concern for education: his as an Indian (Lakota) spokesman; mine as a Euro-American professor who seeks to provide learning for students. In this way, we each bring our own personal perspectives to this undertaking. Severt Young Bear sings and shares his family lore and tribal knowledge. I sing, too, but I always seek to turn my understanding into meaning as a teacher and to translate that understanding into usable learning content and strategy. I rarely hear an old or new song or an expression of Lakota philosophy that I don't record and preserve as a potential learning experience within my profession. Yet, some of those privileged experiences are private and don't appear in these pages. Severt pulls forth observations from his memory or his family or tribal tradition. I try to record them, to make connections, to find meanings and linguistic insights, and to transform all of this into a learning process.

Severt and I have spoken with each other and to various audiences at funerals; in university seminars; during post-powwow, late-night testimonials; at humanities presentations; at the South Dakota penitentiary; to Indian educators; and to numerous special-interest audiences. I won't presume to state how I've affected him. But over the years I've gleaned profound cultural observations from his talks. I know how he contributes and relates to a classroom of students at any level, or to other audiences, and how I interact with his ideas and his consistently reflective presentations. We've ranged over many subjects: Lakota oral tradition, music, costuming, ceremonies, political and social systems, male-female roles, identity, values, and others.

Along came 1985. We had been seeing each other off and on to teach and share ourselves—often in tandem—regarding Lakota culture to diverse audiences. We began to realize that we had something to offer, both individually and collaboratively. That's when I said, "*Ciye,* Older Brother, how about we do a book!" I don't know what he said. Maybe he made a wisecrack or commented seriously. I think he said, "All right." We began in the summer of 1986, and what you are holding is the product.

How did we do it? We had some choices. We could either erase the traces of the compromises that are the nature of collaborative authorship, or reveal and publicly record every particular seam, every editorial wrenchhold, to make the collaboration as translucent as some thoughtful scholars or Native Americans would have it.

Our discussions on the nature of proceeding with our project resulted in the following agreement: We've known each other well for years. Nevertheless, this would be Severt Young Bear's story. Therefore, he would express himself as he chose, in the order he naturally selected and with ultimate control over the final text. Knowing of Severt's background interests and ideas, we both realized that a manuscript representing his way of seeing would obviously crystallize around Brotherhood Community, would combine a traditionalist essence with exposure to the modern American lifestyle and the lessons of many far-flung travels, and would focus on the Lakota singer. Yet neither of us realized, until we were two-thirds through our initial recording process, that we seemed to be creating a book about identity: the urgent need as well as promise of "putting things in order" for Lakota young people, all Native Americans, and perhaps every reader. Thus, as in all serious literary expression, the purely individual perspective—in this case primarily Severt's personal lens—would open up new vistas for young people of his own culture, but also ultimately for all human beings, regardless of culture, who have a thirst for understanding.

We taped for two weeks in the summer of 1986 at Severt's home in Porcupine, South Dakota, in the presence of Frank Andrews, a mutual friend. On several days we taped from late morning to two or three at night, taking time out only to eat or chat briefly with a visitor or family member. On other days we taped for three or four hours, then Severt had a meeting or I had an errand to run, and then we would tape again till after midnight. Severt seemed almost tireless as his eyes and hands traced out points of emphasis or illustration. He was always ready to crack a joke at his own, my, or someone else's expense.

Our choice of subjects each day depended on subjects he felt strongly about, or remembered when we were not taping. At other times he had said he wanted to return to something, so I prompted him. Local news events on any day might trigger his reflections and stories. At times I asked a question after he seemed finished with a subject or because I had on other occasions heard him express his views on certain points.

I felt my role to be that of an enlightened recorder. I knew much about Severt's experiences, research, family history, and opinions. I wanted to aid in bringing it forth. The interviews with Ted Means and Irving Tail—whose talents and authority Severt wanted to utilize—were governed by their availability on any certain day, not some conceived organizational plan for this book. During the taping as well as in our repeated visits and encounters since then, it has become clear that these pages do not exhaust Severt's treasury of research, reminiscences, reflections, insights, and opinions. Instead, this book merely captures Severt Young Bear at one time, in one place.

Overall, Severt selected the topics he chose to talk about as well as the ultimate order. He maintained his own English idiom, including the frequent use of Lakota terms and phrases, especially when he wished to expound on the word makeup or history of an idea.

Readers should realize that Severt's deliberate efforts at providing interpretations of the meanings of terms and the makeup of names are his own conceptions as well as those passed along in his family tradition. Historically, the translation of Lakota names into English has been a tenuous endeavor in any case, not only because of the difficulty of translating faithfully the original meaning of a name from one language to another, but also—as Severt will illustrate repeatedly, especially in the section entitled "Etymologies: Words Full of Meaning"—because Lakota names and concepts involve both a great deal of connotative flavor and also considerable associative meaning. Thus the etymology of a Lakota term may allow some freedom of translation, so that the expanded meaning of what is understood about the term may differ from one source to another.

One example may help to illustrate the issue. A captain of the Indian Police at Pine Ridge during the 1880s and one of the principal informants for James R. Walker, George Sword, explains in an autobiographical profile that he chose the name of Sword "because the leaders of the white soldiers wore swords" and they appeared to be victorious in their struggles with the Lakota (Walker, *Lakota Belief and Ritual,* 74). One Lakota version of his name, Miwakan Yuhala, Sword Owner, is offered by George Hyde as Miwakon [*sic*] Yuhala, which Hyde translates as He-Has-a-Sword (89). A briefer version of Sword's name is used in the No Ears winter count, which refers to him as Mi-wakan, stressing the "sword" aspect of the name but leaving off the Yuhala, the ownership portion (Walker, *Lakota Society,* 156). Raymond J. DeMallie and Elaine A. Jahner also list his Lakota name as Miwakan on the basis of the 1896–1904 Pine Ridge censuses (Walker, *Lakota Belief and Ritual,* 283–84). Walker himself, on the other hand, in referring to George

Sword in English, calls him Long Knife (*Lakota Belief and Ritual*, 47), which is translated by Lakotas today as Mila Hanska. By comparison, Severt's personal version of the translation of Sword's Lakota name into English will be Take Sword from Cavalry, as he seeks to demonstrate what we might call the "real" explanation of Lakota concepts.

Throughout the following narrative, then, Severt will repeatedly offer his own personal, family, and community explanations as a way of providing meaning to Lakota cultural phenomena to give them added vitality and purpose as he shares them with us. Interested readers may find some alternative as well as corroborative translations in the sources provided in the selected bibliography at the end of this text, although some of Severt's interpretations are quite novel and stimulating.

It should also be noted that Severt's pattern of organization, at least as it appears to me, was to begin talking about his name and the names of his family, using this approach—somewhat as N. Scott Momaday has done in his *The Names*—to present himself. As he explored family name history he touched on numerous other ideas—I would call them "cultural coordinates"—which in a centrifugal manner circled outward, often leading to further explication of ideas touched on briefly earlier and then recalled, broadened, and illustrated. In the original oral recording, this network had frequent gaps, spaces, and irregularities. Upon reading the initial, faithfully typed transcripts I presented to him, he recognized the need for me to revise his original narrative to a more coherent narrative, and then requested that I bring together and connect those subjects that orally had often been flung out while he was generating spoken thoughts.

In this, it should be stressed, our text is not the molded story of an illiterate narrator—as a number of classic Indian bi-autobiographies or as-told-to life histories have been—but rather the narrative of a Lakota man who writes and reads well and has read widely but, nevertheless, has made the traditionalist choice to initially express himself orally. Yet, he also realizes that a written text demands considerable editorial revising. In one of our discussions of how he saw my role in our project, Severt stated that I should "straighten out" some of his English, not to polish it up and make it seem more sophisticated or literary, but rather to deal with the oral mode of expressing oneself, which often results in forms that are unclear, repetitive, groping, and temporarily confusing or contradictory. After all, oral narrators form their speech as they think. The sequential ordering of thoughts necessary for a written narrative frequently requires the intervention of hindsight or of stepping back after initial expression to correct or expand or redirect earlier statements.

At one time Severt spoke of his concern that in previous Indian bi-autobiographies he knew of, the anthropologist or ethnographer, or who-ever did the transcribing and editing, had covered up the ideas of the nar-rator. He used his hand to envelop an imaginary object with his fingers and palm to clarify his point. In contrast, our efforts all along have been to care-fully document the steps in our project. My determination not to alter his authentic voice guided my editoral efforts at all times and I've repeatedly told him of my concerns to have his voice be heard on these pages. More-over, it might seem patronizing of the reader to expect a literate, educated, worldly-wise, modern Indian man to be illiterate in the nineteenth-century manner. Severt read through the second transcription, in which I had taken the original word-for-word transcription of thirty audiotapes and had done enough basic, primarily syntactic editing to provide a cohesive and coher-ent written narrative. I made every effort to maintain the flavor of his oral discourse for the reader but also to avoid the disturbing elements of speech which, while acceptable to a listener, violate the reader's expectations.

Severt also read this second, somewhat edited version, discussed it with me, and wrote short comments in preparation for the third and final text version. This third version of the original taped narratives, which follows below, is the result of a mutually agreed-upon process in which I would pull together scattered remarks on related topics, provide cohesion and tran-sitions between topics, and, in general, rework the second version into a cohesive and readable narrative. This process was encouraged by the Uni-versity of Nebraska Press editorial staff, who also agreed with us that an intrusive scholarly commentary in the narrative was to be avoided. Once again, Severt had the opportunity to read and edit every page of this final version to ensure that it reflected his manner of thought and expression.

We also discussed the use of family photos; the need for maps, a family tree, and certain primary documents he felt might enhance his commen-taries; and the choice of a title. When he first articulated the idea of "standing in the dark" for those Lakotas who had fallen away from cultural participa-tion and who had therefore found no meaning or support in their heritage, we both agreed to flip this idea onto its positive side and use "Standing in the Light" as a way of encouraging readers to engage with these words productively.

Chapter headings were also discussed and designed to focus and illuminate these pages for maximum accessibility. We also agreed to provide separate introductory comments to clarify our collaborative efforts for the reader.

My thanks to those who assisted in typing the manuscript: Kay Kearny, Paula Mowry, Marsha Redday, and Lavera Roether. Thanks also to Linda Winter Chaser and Thelma Winter Chaser for some of the Lakota transcription and translation. The South Dakota Committee on the Humanities and the Black Hills State University Faculty Research Committee provided released time and assistance for which I am grateful.

Mitakuye Oyasin!
All my relatives!

❧ *Severt Young Bear*

My name is Severt Young Bear. My Lakota name is Hehaka Luzahan, or Swift Elk. About two summers ago Ronnie Theisz and I recorded about thirty tapes to do a book with a goal of doing something towards education.

I met Ronnie back in 1963. The first time I met him he was singing Indian at that time, and I had just begun to sing with Drury Cook and Uncle Henry Young Bear and Irving Tail, four of us. We said we would be a traveling Porcupine Singers group. By tradition most of the Porcupine Singers never traveled except maybe to Rosebud Fair or Pine Ridge Sun Dance and district powwows. Nobody ever traveled to places like New York or California or Mescalero Apache or Sioux Valley, Manitoba, or Stony Reserve, Alberta, or Washinton State.

As I said, I met Ronnie and we went to Monroe Powwow in New York and since then we started to sing together and communicate between each other. In the summertime we'd see each other at Crow Fair in Montana or Pine Ridge Sun Dance, and later on my adopted father David Clairmont one time publicly said he wanted me and Jim and Ronnie to be brothers. So since then whenever we see each other, when we meet somewhere, we'll sing together. Around 1970 Ronnie moved from New York and joined Porcupine Singers and we became a big family. I never—when I first sang that first song with the older Porcupine Singers—I never thought I'd come this far.

For a while I had a hard time getting this introduction together because I tried a couple of times and I think I just got into rehashing the history in the rest of this book all over again, so what I wanted to do is to explain that with this book that we are working on I want to do something educational. The words that we spoke of or the songs that we spoke about or the oral history should form a kind of educational project. There's lots of oral history, especially in Brotherhood Community, that I felt should be recorded. We didn't record all of it but this is a goal that Ronnie and I talked about.

It kind of goes back to an elderly man I met one time who was talking about people standing in the dark. There's about four circles, he said, when you go to any kind of ceremony or a powwow or a gathering; there's about four circles of people around. Those in the outside circle of darkness don't know why they're there, but they're there. The third circle as you move to the center is people sitting watching their kids or their relatives dance. This circle also includes young people courting each other, trying to "snag," as we say. The people in this circle don't really know why the dancers are out there dancing, but they look on. Then there is the dancers' circle; the singers and the dancers are there. There are very few people that really actually put on their family's costumes and colors and their family tradition when they dance. The rest of them, eighty percent of them, more or less kind of adopt the other tribes' or other people's costumes or whatever. Then there is the center, the brightest part of the circles. In the center are the people that run that powwow, that community, that district, that tribe, or that college organization. Yet even some of these are on the committee just because it looks good, but most of them in this inner circle kind of know halfway why they're putting on a ceremony or powwow and maybe one or two will understand why it's going on and they'll keep the committee together.

So we're trying to orient this book towards identifying those three or four rings of circles, and the biggest part of it is we're trying to reidentify or revive the people in the dark and the people sitting halfway in the dark under the shade or in the third circle. This is why I feel that Ronnie and I, we talked about what that elderly man said, and we kind of thought about calling the book *Standing in the Light* instead of *Standing in the Dark,* as a Lakota way of reverse psychology. So we'd like to shine that light to those people that are kind of walking around that dark circle way on the outside. There's a big cultural revival in this Lakota generation, since the early 1970s. Young people are returning to our traditional songs and dances and our ceremonies, but in trying to be Lakotas again, they're often overdoing it; they're doing some things that aren't right. This is why I thought we should do the Lakota version and the white version of putting two minds together in one.

It's very difficult to do some of this, because some oral history or stories that we tell are sometimes very hard to interpret into English. But I think way back in 1963 when Ronnie and I first met, we somehow put two hearts in one and two minds in one. We've done a lot of workshops and gave lectures, and though we never sat down and carefully organized them together, whenever we got there—in Rapid City, in Brookings or Chadron or in California someplace, for university people or community people—when we do this type of work, somehow our programs kind of match each other. His contemporary or white version of talking about Indian culture and my kind of traditional way of talking about our culture, somehow the stories and things that we say or the Lakota words that we use match together. So this is why we're thinking about doing this book.

I know there's lots of books on culture and history, but what we thought about was sitting down and doing a common-sense kind of thing so our children and our grandchildren and their children can use this book and kind of do a positive thing and reorganize those four rings of people I mentioned.

In Ronnie's part of this introduction he mentioned my name and how he picked me to do this kind of book. I kind of felt good deep down in my heart. In my time I had the pleasure of sitting down with elders and talking about Brotherhood Community stories, the songs and dances of Porcupine, and Sun Dance songs. Somehow it must be a wish from the Great Spirit that I got involved in a lot of historical things.

Going back in my family history, my grandfather earned his name Mato Cincala, Young Bear, when he was fourteen years old. He was only fourteen years old. Some of my family were in the battle with Custer and part of my family went into Canada and part of it stayed in the United States. My grandmother Young Bear was shot in the back and my aunt was killed at Wounded Knee. Most of my relatives in Brotherhood Community went into the world wars, Korea, Vietnam, and then I and my father were involved in Wounded Knee II and I was in tribal government. Things kind of happened in my lifetime that I think it was kind of a gift from God that I could be part of and remember some of the important parts of this history.

And so in this book I mention some of this. A family can start to do this and start documenting and recording. All this is good history and should be recorded.

Even though that time when we recorded all of this we didn't really put down a format—this chapter will do this, chapter two will do this and that—we just sat down and started talking and things kind of fell in place. We knew we might lose some of the meanings in some Lakota story because in English it's shorter or has a different meaning to it, we went ahead. The thing that we did was that we might have to stretch something a little bit longer to tell a big story or illustrate it, so we would go in a big circle and come back somewhere to clear up the meaning of something.

Some time ago we had talked about doing a video documentary on singing, since in the Young Bear family singing was part of tradition—my grandfather was a singer, my Uncle Henry and my father were singers, then I started singing, now I have two sons that are singing—and I felt I should do this by myself. But then I talked with Ronnie and, as I said, we put our hearts into one and two minds in one and decided to write a book for future generations.

Ronnie in his part of the introduction someplace talked about how he thought about writing a book about some of this but it would be his version and might not be the traditional way of looking at some of this; some of it might lose part of its meaning. So with that we sat down and we started recording, putting things down and discussing them. It was kind of difficult to always translate and fully explain something. I think readers have to realize when things are brought up in a chapter, there's always a longer history or meaning to it. If you live a culture or even if you thoroughly study our culture as non-Indians, you realize that there's a long history behind many of the things that we talk about and if you stop and explain or break down every story, then it'll take twenty or thirty volumes. But I think that could be done later. This is kind of a beginning where we're trying to identify those four circles so people can read this book and identify themselves and which circle they stand in.

And we always talk about values, the four values for men and the four values for women, and when I was asked to do this, I did some serious thinking. There's a Lakota saying, *"tohan mate sni ehatan"* (as long as I'm alive), which says that if your family history ends, if your family name ends, if the Lakota language ends, or if the blood that runs in your family ends, your family identity, your family blood almost kind of diminishes into water. In connecting this to my life as I think about "as long as I'm alive," this book will be the way for my family and myself to go on; our traditions, our way of life will never end, because now we documented it in this book. Our songs are recorded; we retained the good side of it.

My family, and I think Ronnie's is the same way, and their life will continue as long as there's my grandchildren and their children. As long as that circle continues . . . I think that it's important that the songs we sing, the things I do, we do in this family, things we continue to do in this family, will never end. I'll give you an example. Crazy Horse was a powerful warrior, so his life never ended. They named schools after him, they named singing groups after him, they named all kinds of organizations after him, and there's even several bars around they call Crazy Horse Bar. The name of his day, his death, or his life will continue, will never end. That name Crazy Horse continues in our generation and the next generation. And that's the kind of thing that I talked about.

Somehow we lose that contact or those family traditions when we get into the tribal circle because now we get into a more politically oriented tribe. We no longer keep our traditions. I'll give you an example. One of our tribal traditions is the annual Sun Dance, that annual gathering of people. Now it's a family-oriented Sun Dance. Now we have about twenty-six Sun Dances between Pine Ridge and Rosebud. We lost that tribalness or way of keeping the annual gathering of tribes together. The only thing we do now in a tribal way is tribal council meetings or a big tribal dancing contest. They dance for one-thousand-dollar and eight-hundred-dollar prizes but it keeps up political division.

So this is why we need to bring some understanding and talk about some of these things. The other part of this is that even though I do crazy things, I was always brought up to respect; there's always respect inside. We also have a lot of non-Indian friends and most of the non-Indian friends that I have or Ronnie has are good-hearted and good-minded non-Indians that understand Lakota way, they respect Lakota way. When they sing, they respect Lakota songs, or when they dance, they respect the costume and dances. We're trying to write this book so that my Lakota people and our non-Indian friends can find better understanding. This idea also came out while we were recording till five in the morning and we started talking about having an International Brotherhood Days at Porcupine, which actually materialized because we were talking about these things. The first one took place in 1988 and was a success because we brought, for the first time in history an Indian community brought, Indians and non-Indians together to revive the Indians in their culture and explain cultural things to the non-Indians so they can respect and honor this coming together.

So those are some of the things that I feel as we're doing this book together. Sometimes it was hard, but we're doing this to be educational so that both children of Lakota people or children of white people can understand. Other times we had fun. For example, I like to tell how when I met Ronnie way back in 1963, he had a hat on with a brim about six inches wide and a crown only about two inches, black boots with white tops. He had Big Ben overalls, I think, not Wranglers or anything, but high waters too. He was really comical, so of course I had to teach him the right way.

But then I remember he was singing real high. Up to today he still maintains that, and that is kind of encouraging to other singers. If you don't smoke or drink, and take care of your voice, you can maintain your volume and sharpness. Today one of the bad parts of singing is that some think they have to drink wine or smoke a cigarette or chew to maintain it. But that's kind of a put-on or false front. You have to maintain a good clean life, and since your voice is a gift from God, you have to maintain that good life so your voice will continue.

Then we're doing this book to bring those rings of circle together. We want to orient it so people can identify which ring they stand in so that one day we'll all be centered in the bright light—the center part of it: we'll know what we're doing, we'll know why we're singing, we'll know why we're dancing, we'll know why we're having a giveaway, we'll know why we're having a dropped-eagle-feather ceremony, we'll know why we round dance, we'll know why we wear eagle feathers, we'll know why we wear those bells. I think we can do that and there'll be no time for jealousy or making fun of somebody in that circle. We all have a part in it. This is just like when during a powwow an elderly woman will get up in the third circle and she'll sing a song and wave her hand and she'll point east or west and she'll sing a song in response to what the singers sang. Or if they sang a memorial song, the woman will get up and cry and also sing a mourning song. Everybody had a place, whether it's a *heyoka,* a sacred clown, or some are doing an Omaha dance, or a *tokala,* a Kit Fox warrior society member, doing his form of the dance. Everybody had a part in it. The *eyapaha,* announcer, was a motivator; he made sure that all those rings were really involved. There was a meaning and a purpose in all those rings. I think somewhere jealousy came along so that gathering to point fingers or make fun of somebody is common. When people put on a giveaway or do a ceremony and ask you to sing a song, then you do it the best way you can and nobody should make fun of anybody else.

We didn't want to do this book because I'm a holy man or Ronnie is a most educated person. I think we're trying to orient this, like I mentioned before, from two minds in one and two hearts in one to do something educational. I think somehow the closeness between my family and Ronnie's family and his children, the respect and honoring of each other's families, produced this. We used to just sit many times and talk of these things and one day it started. We talked about the four circles in ceremonies and dances and then discussed how this book would do more than just our talking to give some kind of identity, a good identity, for those who are searching. I think we're going in the right direction and it's very important to do. At this time on our reservation, the Pine Ridge Reservation, about sixty-five percent of the children in our tribe cannot speak or understand Lakota, and we have about fifteen percent or twenty percent that speak and understand but they talk slang, and we have only about fifteen percent of our own people that speak the traditional language. So we're trying to write this book at this time maybe not to completely turn things around but at least let us step back several steps and kind of reidentify ourselves.

If you notice, on weekends the Lakota people become Lakota people. They put on costumes, sing and dance, and want somebody to tie a feather on somebody and name them, or speak Lakota on weekends, but Monday to Friday we don't live that. It's a twenty-four-hours, seven-days-a-week, 365-days-a-year type of life that we have to maintain if we want to be Lakota, not just because we put on a costume or they ask us to speak a few words.

When you do a rabbit dance, you take two steps forward and one step back, and their songs are very good and very heartwarming and they *woki-ksuye* (reminisce), kind of bring back the memories that you have in life. Those rabbit songs are made that way. If you can rabbit dance as you hear the winds tell you real good soft music in your ear, then you take two steps forward and one step back to reidentify, to continue. And the rabbit dance is in a circle. I said our sacred hoop is a circle. You dance to the left. These rabbit songs are sung in a way that makes you feel good. So if we can encourage our children, our grandchildren, to do just that, two steps forward, one step back, that way in kind of a warm feeling and at a slow pace, we can encourage our children to identify themselves as Lakota. If we do this, our generation will never end, our lives will never end, our family values, traditions, family beliefs—that world will never end. It will be continuous.

I think that I'm doing this in a way so that my Young Bear family or Smoke family and our values, tradition, and songs and dances, history—that world will never end.

I thank Ronnie for picking me to do this book with him. It's an honor by him and his family that he asked me to do this. There's a lot of other men that are also well versed in history, culture, traditions, and I want to thank Ronnie and his family and all the people that I got oral history from, whether it's Indian humor, a story or song, or way of a dance that you're supposed to dance that certain way. I want to thank them for that knowledge and wisdom that they have shared with me. I want to thank them in this book in this way. I might not mention their name, but they'll know, whether they are physically on this world or they'll know who they are if spiritually. They'll know that by sharing their values, their family traditions, and everything, that world will never end, will continue. In the Lakota way I want to thank God for that knowledge and wisdom that is shared in this book.

I would like to end in the Lakota way when they ended their talk and will say: I am Swift Elk, *Hehaka Luzahan miyelo*. And with this introduction I want to say thank you to everybody and end it by saying *mitakuye oyasin* in the traditional way, that we're related to everybody around us in this world, whether it's non-Indian, Indian, or the animal world, or the wings, or all the trees or whatever that's around us. I want to say *mitakuye oyasin* to everybody. Thank you.

Brief History
of the Sioux

Porcupine Community is located on the Pine Ridge Indian Reservation, home of the Oglala Sioux Tribe. Referring to themselves as Lakota—a term used as well for their dialect of the Sioux language—the Oglala Sioux belong to the confederacy known historically as the Oceti Sakowin, the Seven Fires. Collectively referred to as the Sioux, this confederacy includes four Santee divisions, the two Yankton and Yanktonai divisions, and the Lakota(Teton) as the seventh division.

The Lakota group is, in turn, made up of seven groups: the Oglala, Sicangu (Brule), Miniconjou, Oohenumpa (Two Kettle), Itazipco (Sans Arcs, or No Bows), Sihasapa (Blackfoot), and Hunkpapa. These seven closely allied branches of the Teton Lakota, each with its own bands, or camps, formed perhaps the central focus of much of the Northern Plains horseback, nomadic buffalo-hunting pageant from the time of the Louisiana Purchase in 1803 to the Wounded Knee Massacre of 1890.

The early history of the various Sioux bands is rather speculative. Historians have suggested fifteenth-century origins somewhere around the Ohio River with subsequent movement northwest, but Lakota oral historians— Severt is among them—propose a larger, circular pattern of migration that began centuries ago around the Black Hills, starting towards the south, then turning east, then north, and then again to the northwest, the western Great Lakes region, in a large circle.

In either case, early written documents of the middle seventeenth century place the Sioux in the woodlands of present northwestern Wisconsin and eastern Minnesota. Pressured by their Cree and Chippewa enemies and attracted by the plentiful buffalo herds of the plains, the Sioux began another set of migrations south to the Minnesota River during the latter 1600s. Acquiring horses as they moved on in the 1740s and 1750s, the western Sioux bands turned westward into South Dakota. In the process, the westernmost

Sioux, the Lakota, enthusiastically exchanged their woodland culture for that of the nomadic plains buffalo hunter.

By the early decades of the nineteenth century—after conflicts with the Arikara and Mandan and, farther west, the Crow, Kiowa, and Cheyenne, among others—the various Sioux bands achieved control over most of the territory from the Platte River in Nebraska to the Cannonball River in North Dakota, from the Bighorn Mountains in the west to the Minnesota River in the east. At the heart of their western territory lay the Black Hills of western South Dakota and the Powder River region of southeastern Montana.

The entry of Euro-Americans, with the occasional involvement of people of color, became disturbing to the western Sioux bands by the time of the 1849 California gold rush, which brought many travelers through the southern region of the territory held by the Sioux. In 1851 the United States government negotiated the first Fort Laramie Treaty with the Sioux, a treaty of peace and friendship which recognized tribal landownership on the Northern Plains, partly in an effort to stop the intertribal raids that often threatened to involve non-Indian travelers and government officials in the area.

After sporadic conflicts such as the Mormon cow incident, or Grattan fight of 1854, and the Minnesota Sioux war of 1862, Sioux resistance to encroachment by white settlers and soldiers culminated in Red Cloud's war, 1866–68, over the Bozeman Trail leading from Fort Laramie into Montana. This war ended with the Fort Laramie Treaty of 1868, which guaranteed protection from further white settlement and exploration to Sioux lands, known as the Great Sioux Reservation, in today's South Dakota from the Missouri River west to the Wyoming border. It also set aside considerable "unceded Indian territory" in parts of surrounding states. The discovery of gold in the Black Hills in 1874 led to subsequent unsuccessful efforts by the United States government to buy the Black Hills from the Sioux, and ultimately to the defeat of Custer at the Little Big Horn in 1876. In spite of this dramatic victory, the Sioux were quickly forced onto the reservations by the decimation of the buffalo, which were virtually extinct by the late 1870s.

The waning decades of the nineteenth century brought the Sioux a life of boredom, hunger, apathy, failed federal policies, and general culture shock culminating in the Ghost Dance and Wounded Knee Massacre of 1890. As a colonized people, the western Sioux were confined to their reservations by the end of the 1870s without the intertribal raiding activities or the buffalo hunt that had sustained them since their entry onto the plains. From 1879 on, their children were forcibly sent to federal and mission schools, frequently to off-reservation boarding schools.

The Great Sioux Reservation established by the Fort Laramie Treaty of 1868 was first diminished when the federal government in 1877 unilaterally took the Black Hills and portions of the "unceded Indian territory" which had been guaranteed in perpetuity in the treaty. The 1889 Act to Break Up the Great Sioux Reservation then established the present system of Sioux reservations in South Dakota. Consequently, in western South Dakota the Pine Ridge Reservation became the home of the Oglala; the Rosebud and Lower Brule reservations of the Brule; the Standing Rock Reservation of the Hunkpapa and the Blackfoot Sioux; and the Cheyenne River Reservation of the Two Kettles, the Sans Arcs, and the Miniconjou. These five South Dakota reservations west of the Missouri River were even further reduced in subsequent decades (the Pine Ridge Reservation has shrunk from some 2.8 million acres in 1889 to about 1.7 million acres today).

The federal government's intensification of its Americanization policy towards the Lakota as well as other tribal cultures after the Civil War was reflected in the assassinations of two of the great leaders of the Lakota, Crazy Horse in 1877 at Fort Robinson and Spotted Tail in 1881 at the Rosebud Agency. Concurrently in 1881, agents of the federal government imposed strictures to eliminate the Sun Dance, the centerpiece of Lakota public ceremonial life. In addition, increasing pressure was applied to make Lakotas into farmers, particularly through the application to the Sioux of the Dawes Allotment Act of 1887, which was intended to change American Indians' notions of communal tribal property to the private-property concept of their white neighbors. The Lakota of the late 1880s found themselves subjugated, in the midst of a drought, and completely dependent on government rations and promises.

In the depth of their despondency and even starvation, many Lakotas turned a hopeful ear in 1889 to the mystical promises of the messianic message of the Ghost Dance. The unsuccessful physical efforts of resistance to the white people and their government were now invested by many Lakotas in the Ghost Dance and its promise of bringing back the good old days. The devotion of many Lakotas to Ghost Dancing in 1890 caused reservation agents and white settlers such concern that the United States military was called upon to supress the "mania." When another of the great western Sioux leaders, Sitting Bull, was killed on the Standing Rock Reservation, the Lakota feared a general slaughter of their people. Their fears found substantiation when Big Foot's band was intercepted trying to reach the Pine Ridge Agency and most of its members—men, women, and children—were killed in the infamous Wounded Knee Massacre of December 30, 1890.

After 1890, the Lakota had no choice but to yield to the efforts of the government to turn them into model white Americans. Intensifying their efforts between 1891 and 1934, schools, churches, and government employees all joined in implementing the policies which had as their goal the finding of some panacea to solve the problem of modernizing and assimilating the Sioux as well as other American Indian people. This ongoing overall goal was underscored by specific federal policies that generally sought to deny Indians their cultural identity. Although the Wheeler-Howard Act (Indian Reorganization Act) of 1934 stopped the destructive effects of the Dawes Allotment Act, which had caused the loss of millions of acres of Indian land to white settlement, it could not significantly improve the situation of Indian people. In spite of its efforts at allowing Indian tribes to be governed by their own constitutions, the Wheeler-Howard Act still guaranteed that ultimate control of Indian affairs remained in the hands of the secretary of the interior and his representatives.

After a period of great patriotism during the Second World War when Indian men and women served honorably in the United States military, the next phase of policy in the 1950s and early 1960s, known as termination, encouraged Lakota and other Indian people to leave the poverty and depression of reservation life for a successful relocation to cities such as Cleveland, Chicago, Dallas, Denver, and Los Angeles. Many Lakota families left for the economic promise of the city, but most soon returned, disheartened by the alienating environment of American city life.

During the 1960s the Kennedy and Johnson administrations provided a hopeful respite to the perennial problems of life on the reservation with their New Frontier and related social programs. In spite of this ideological upswing, conditions on the Lakota reservations improved little. Friction among the Lakota of Pine Ridge even increased between conservative factions—those who supported the Bureau of Indian Affairs (BIA) and its policies of assimilation—and reformers, who sought a return to Lakota cultural traditions and a greater voice for the smaller, and often culturally more traditional, grass-roots communities. These two Lakota groups struggled to achieve their share of inadequate federal programs and self-government. When local district people requested the intervention of the militant American Indian Movement (AIM) to confront what was considered a corrupt, BIA puppet tribal government—Severt shares his participation in this process—the stage was set for a dramatic and violent confrontation.

The Wounded Knee Massacre of 1890 had festered as the tragic symbol of oppression and even genocide in the stories, songs, speeches, and hearts of the Lakota in the twentieth century. In 1973, Wounded Knee II became the focus of the violent repudiation of federal treatment of the Sioux. Some saw the Wounded Knee II occupation as the misguided outburst of urban Indian radicals leading only to further harm and disappointment, whereas others considered it a principled and necessary effort to draw attention to the conditions on the Pine Ridge Indian Reservation and in the rest of Indian country. Wounded Knee II eventually led to a gradual lessening of intra-Lakota tension. It must be acknowledged that in the decades since the violence centered around Wounded Knee II, federal policies have stressed self-determination and the choice for Lakotas to select their own identity and their own solutions for the pervasive problems of Lakota existence. Many Lakotas today will agree that progress has been made as a result, but the Pine Ridge Reservation, now home to some sixteen thousand Oglala tribal members and four thousand other residents, continues to be plagued by poverty and the accompanying sociocultural problems.

The grand flowering of these spiritual warrior people on the plains, which spanned scarcely a century, thus ended in confinement to reservations, and a life of near-starvation as well as educational, cultural, and spiritual oppression. Because the nation's hoop had been broken—as Black Elk, one of their holy men, lamented to John Neihardt in *Black Elk Speaks*—the Oglala, like the other Sioux groups, embarked on a slow, painful and often depressing search for a new identity. The abject poverty found in some of these poorest counties in the United States magnifies many of the social problems of the Oglala. Yet, as the pages that follow will attest, the love of their land, the persistent caring support of extended families, and the continuing presence of their cultural fabric for those who would avail themselves of it are the anchors that have provided a countervailing force, a source for whatever future the Sioux forge for themselves.

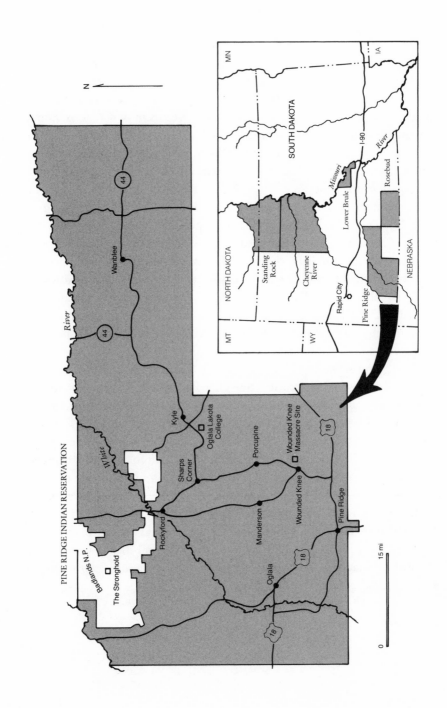

PINE RIDGE INDIAN RESERVATION

Standing in
the Light

PART ONE

Grandfather Rode through Smoke

ON THE DAY I was born, they planned to name me William Melvin. I was supposed to become William Young Bear, Jr., but my uncle George Gap wanted to change my name. Because he had given me the ceremonial Indian name Hehaka Luzahan (Swift Elk), he also insisted that he would chose my English first name. The reason he wanted to do that is that during the First World War he had a friend in the navy who was a Swede by the name of Severt from someplace in Pennsylvania. They were real good friends, I guess, real good buddies who hung around together, looked out for each other, helped each other in every way. And the day they were discharged in 1920, on a pier someplace in New York, as they were parting, shook hands, and talked, this guy said, "George, when you have your firstborn son, name him after me, and when I have my firstborn son, I'll name him after you." But when my Uncle George came back he had two daughters; he didn't have any son. So when I was born in 1934, he wanted to give me that name and they changed my name to Severt. So I'm carrying the name of an uncle's navy buddy named Severt. For a long time people couldn't understand why, they couldn't figure out why my name was Severt. Everybody else had Abraham, Joseph, Mark, Luke, George, and Lincoln. But somehow my name was different because my uncle George Gap wanted to give me that name.

The middle name Edward also came from an uncle of mine, Edward Spotted Bear, who was kind of a hell-raiser and bronc rider. My Uncle Edward was here when they had the naming ceremony and later on went into the navy and his ship went down somewhere in the Pacific; he never came back. So I carry two English names: one of my uncle's friend and that of another uncle.

My Bureau of Indian Affairs (BIA) census last name, Young Bear, has a long history behind it. My great-grandfather had an older sister who was sick, so during the winter he told his parents and he told the *ozuye itancan* (war party leader): "If my sister gets well and sees green grass, I will go on a war party and face the enemy. That will be thanksgiving for my sister being well. I will face the enemy and if the Creator wills it, I will come back alive,

Severt Young Bear / family tree

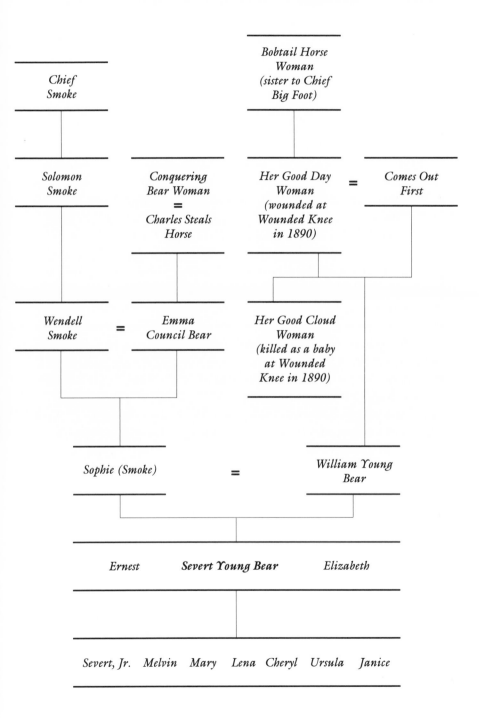

or if the Creator wills it, if the enemy will take my life, then I will replace my sister's life with mine."

He was only fourteen years old but he went. His parents got him ready and he and the warriors went southeast from the Black Hills. They came to some flat buttes and a big river. There were some camps along the river and they got in a fight with them. They tried to draw the enemy warriors out away from the camp, but they couldn't, so they laid around the camp and fired at them. When someone came out they'd shoot him. They tried to draw the enemy out but they didn't want to come out. They figured the enemy warriors were silly, so they must be Pawnee.

Finally our warriors left and were on the way back, resting on some flat buttes. They had a lookout on top of the hill and were lying on the bottom in some trees. All of a sudden, this lookout scout came galloping back and said, "C'mon, there are two guys peeking at us over the hill." So they all jumped on their horses and went up that butte and here two riders were going down a flat, down below, so they chased them. My grandfather was young and light, so pretty soon his horse started outrunning the rest and he was way ahead. He came up to a washout or gully and the *toka* (enemy) was standing with his hand out. My grandfather must have been surprised by this, because he rode up beside him, shook his hand, and then went on to chase the other one. He chased him for a distance but he couldn't catch him, so he turned around and came back. About that time the others rode up to that one guy that was in the gully, knocked him off his horse, and killed him. The war leader took off the honored parts of the enemy, a scalp or his rifle or his bow and arrows. They always saved these for the first one to count coup on the enemy, and since my grandfather was the first one that shook his hand, the war party leader took the honored parts of the enemy and gave them to him.

When they got back, they told about each other's deeds, *waktoglaka* (recounting of exploits). They talked about my grandfather. At that time the council of elders and the *tokala* chief (warrior society leader) would always think of a name that they would give to the young warriors involved. Since my grandfather was young—he was only fourteen—and was fearless, they gave him Mato Cincala (Young Bear) because a young bear cub, if you try to corner it, to approach it, it will stand up and defend itself.

My grandfather had taken that role. He was young but he was willing to stand up and face the enemy, so Mato Cincala came from that. He was given that name. After they came back and when they had their separate *tokala* warrior society victory ceremonies and dances, my grandfather put on his *tokala* costume. Whenever they sang for him, they sang his song and they would use another name, Napa Yuzapi (Shake His Hand), for shaking hands with the enemy. It is a high honor in the Oglala Lakota bands to touch the enemy physically, by hand or even with an eagle staff (for a description of the eagle staff see p. 72). So when they sang his songs, they used the name Shake His Hand and he was quite proud of that, of that *tokala* ceremonial name.

Later on my older brother, Ernest Young Bear, went into the navy when he was seventeen years old. Ernest served in the South Pacific. He was in Iwo Jima and Okinawa, all those islands. When he was discharged from the navy and came back after the Second World War, he was given that name, Shake His Hand, as his ceremonial Indian name. Right below here on the north side of this house we had kind of a picnic ground, so we had a welcome home and naming ceremony for Ernest and he was given that as his own ceremonial Indian name.

Anyway, when the Bureau started taking names down in the 1880s, when they asked my grandfather what his name was, he said Mato Cincala. They wrote Young Bear. Even though in a list of people for Porcupine District in 1881 which I once saw, my grandfather's name was listed as both Young Bear and Shake His Hand, Young Bear became the family name. So my dad didn't earn the family name; my uncle didn't earn it; I didn't earn it; my sons didn't earn this name. Instead we are carrying our grandfather's census name. In this way the tradition of earning your own name died off in that time after 1880 and the old spiritual and warrior names became set family names. Only by still giving our children ceremonial Indian names do we keep this ancient tradition. So that's how my family Bureau census name was put down as Young Bear, and so today I am Severt Edward Young Bear.

At that time, in order for you to be Christian, you had to have a first name, and also in order to be recognized as a tribal member, you had to have first names. It's funny how big a push Christianity and the BIA made in the 1900s in giving out biblical names and presidential names. You have to be a Christian to carry biblical names and you have to be a patriotic citizen to carry a president's name. So we had some Indians named Ulysses, George, Lincoln, Abraham, and on the Bible side of it we have Indian people with Bible names like Mark, Luke, John. Those types of names play a very important part in our history and those names never changed until 1973. At that time Wounded Knee II gave us a new identity, which I'll get into later.

Many of these traditional names let us relive our grandfathers' past or our fathers' past. My grandfather Young Bear came from five brothers and one half-brother, who were all part of the defeat of Custer. They were all *tokalas*, Kit Fox warrior society members; none of them were chiefs, but they were all *tokala*. So on my father's side, Young Bear, we have a long history of being fighting warriors, the *tokala*. Then on my mother's side, Old Man Smoke was the head chief of the Teton Oglala band. He had five wives, and from them he had Red Cloud and Young Bull Bear, Young Man Afraid of Horse, and, later on, Solomon Smoke and Wendell Smoke. So on my mother's side there's a long history of chiefs. Somehow I was never interested in that fact. If I'd wanted to I could have taken the name of my mother's side and could've been a movie star now or whatever. But I never really got into that side of the family because on that Smoke side, Edward and Benny Smoke are still alive. That family has long roots of heirs, a sort of royal family.

Now let me tell you the way my grandfather Smoke earned his name. He was the son of the old Chief Smoke and his census name became Solomon Smoke. I guess it was south, toward the Niobrara River. One day a warrior came back and said that while he was hunting, he saw a huge snake blowing flame, going real slow, and lights sparking all over. So they picked ten warriors to go check out what was going on. Some people who were hanging around fur-trading posts and Fort Laramie already knew about trains, but some of the Oglala bands that were around the Black Hills and towards the Little Big Horn, those areas, hadn't seen trains. So they went down in—my grandfather was one of them—and lying on top of a flat butte, they watched it go back and forth for three or four days. Finally they said, "Well, whoever is the bravest will show itself today. Let's go down and kill that snake and take it back and we'll become instant great heroes who killed a giant snake." So they got ready and went through dry creek beds and they sneaked up on it and they waited. As it was coming, they rode up alongside it shooting arrows at it. The arrows were bouncing off, smoke was coming out, and it was blowing a whistle. Some of those guys who stayed back said my grandfather rode into and then disappeared in the smoke. All of a sudden he came out again, galloping away from that great snake and came back. So when he returned home, they gave him a *tokala* name, Sota (Smoke).

Those are names that have various interpretations or stories behind them, although after you put them down in English they sometimes have a different meaning. When these names are then passed on, we choose our name or our family name or something about our family history, or about ourselves.

Recently they asked me to give a name to Francis (Chub) Thunder Hawk. I gave him the name Earth Shaker, Makoce Yuhunbunza. The reason I gave him that name was that since I came back to Porcupine, after going away to school and to the service, everything I got involved with was kind of an earthshaking thing. If I sing a song, then it becomes an earthshaking thing; if I say a couple of words that have meaning, then it becomes an earthshaking thing, shaking other people's minds or hearts. Someone in the community or beyond would get upset and something bigger would follow, sometimes trouble, sometimes something good. In this way, two of my aunts asked me back in 1973 to go after my friends Russell Means, Dennis Banks, and Clyde Bellecourt among the AIM (American Indian Movement) leaders, and they came to Pine Ridge and they shook the whole world out at Yellow Thunder, in Gordon, Nebraska, and in Wounded Knee and Custer and Alliance. I was part of the decision to take over Wounded Knee in 1973.

Many other things have happened which shook the whole world and I was part of them. Together with Cornelius Kills Small and Elijah Whirlwind Horse I started the Teca Wacipi Okolakiciye (Youth Dancing Organization) in 1978, which also became an earthmoving thing because in the past people had believed that only traditional, full-blood kids dance and sing the traditional way. We opened the door for other kids in the Pine Ridge Reservation schools and built it up to 841 dancers, some of whom were blond-headed girls with blue eyes and boys with light brown hair. Today many of these kids are still dancing and earning prize money at dancing contests.

The tribal programs that are here today and the people that are still campaigning with those programs were things that we started when I became a tribal councilman in 1970. The Lakota Oglala College and local control of federal programs by Indian contract, putting HUD housing on people's land instead of cluster housing, and turning grazing resolutions around so there would be more Indian operators on the reservation than white ranchers are all things I have done which are earthshaking things. Even singing in Canada and New York, in California, Washington, Wyoming, Texas, and New Mexico, every place I sang, we made thousands of people dance. We provided traditional songs for two films, one called *Lakota Quillwork: Art and Legend* and the popular *Dances with Wolves*. I was part of that singing group that did it and this was also all earthshaking, in a way.

Even in my personal life I've done some earthshaking things. Every time I used to bring a woman back to my home, everyone gets shaky about it. When I would ask a woman to leave or if I divorced that woman, it became an earthshaking thing to many people. Even if I would go to a local meeting of some kind and only say two words, everybody's minds and hearts would shake.

So when Chub Thunder Hawk's family asked me to give him an Indian name, I got up and explained why I was giving him that name. I told Chub: "Maybe someday you yourself, through your singing or dancing, or teaching or being a tribal councilman, might do or say things that are earthshaking for you and those around you. Hold your head up and carry this name, because one day maybe you will become a politician or singer or community leader, or even just with your family you might take up that role, that every little thing you will say will make a difference, will be a mind-shaking thing." We'll have to see if that will happen.

People can pass their ceremonial Indian names on if they want to. Once you pass it on to someone, you cannot take it back and give it to somebody else. I called my brother Ernest one time who is no longer interested in his Indian ways since he's going to live in California all his life, and I talked to him and I told him my oldest granddaughter asked me to name her. I talked to him over the phone and told him I was going to give the name Shake His Hand, Napa Yuzapiwin—the *win* ending is added on for women's names. So when I gave that name to my granddaughter I told about my grandfather's background and how he earned his name and also how Ernest earned his in World War II. Then I gave away for both my relatives and I think I gave two hindquarters of beef and some money, quilts, and other stuff (for an explanation of giveaways, see "Giving and Feeding," p. 57 below). I looked for a navy man like my brother in the crowd because as we honor a relative in a giveaway, one way we pick those who'll get a gift is to see if they have any shared experiences with our relative. For example, are they singers like my uncle, or are they on the powwow committee with my sister? So I looked for a navy man, and since Irving Broken Rope was the only one there that afternoon who was navy, I gave him all that stuff.

I think there is a right way of giving Indian names whether it's a formal *hunka* (making of relatives) or just a plain naming ceremony. At a *hunka* ceremony sacred ceremonial items are used and they sing special sacred songs and pray and go through the ritual ceremony. By comparison, a plain naming ceremony is much simpler. But either way, there is a right and wrong way. Traditionally, men had eagle feathers tied to their hair while women had plumes tied in theirs. It's too bad, but here's the thing I keep seeing: I might go to a powwow and about five minutes before a naming ceremony, they come up to me and say, "Hey, I want you to tie on a feather and give a name." Just like that. But the right way is that the year before that date on which you want to give an Indian name to one of your relatives, you take tobacco or a pipe and you give it to me and you might say: "I want you to name my son; I want you to do this for him a year from now."

In our Lakota ways I would then be a *hunka* parent, or godfather. In a traditional naming ceremony I have to dress the children in the Lakota way. I would say, "Are you cold?" And the boy would say "Yes, my *Hunka* Dad, I'm cold." I would put leggings on him, and I'd say, "Are you cold?" again in Indian and he'd say, "*Hunka* Dad, yes I'm cold," and I'd put a shirt on him or a vest. I'd keep dressing him—moccasins, everything. Then I would lead him out and as I would go through the ceremony I would tie that eagle plume in his hair. But today we often don't give anybody the chance or the time to prepare themselves for the proper adoption ceremony. So it usually should be a one-year cycle. Like last night Florentine Blue Thunder and his grandma came and gave me tobacco. They wanted me to give an Indian name to Joe Stands and his two sons next year out at Ring Thunder on the Rosebud Reservation. So in the Indian way, he said, "*Lakota ogna* (in the Lakota way), I want you to get ready," and since they gave me tobacco last night, I have to get ready for Ring Thunder next year. Now Joe will be my younger brother and his two sons will be my two youngest sons. That's the right way.

Hunka, the word *hunka*, is a secret word, an honored sacred word. They used that idea *hunka*, for example, for a very special warrior, a guy that earns all the honors of being a *tokala*. They call him *hunka bloka* (honored warrior). People don't just use the word freely, even if they pray. Once you're going to use that word, you really reverently humble yourself in using that word. It refers to very special people, for when you go through that ceremony the people use that word for you; you're a *hunka,* an honored one.

It's a very old traditional word and I never really thought about the meaning of it. The only thing I knew was that it was supposed to be a sacred word for sacred ceremonies, the making of relatives, and it's very sacred. In the beginning of the ceremony as far as I know, around 1801 or 1803, in one of the winter counts, our traditional calendars with a drawing for each winter, the first *hunka* ceremony is mentioned and is called *hunka alowan* (singing the *hunka* over someone). So at that time we probably started putting *hunka* ceremonies together as a people. Maybe we might use another tribe's corn or feathers or gourd, but we always put things together, blended our own way with those of other bands or other tribes. In this way, each Lakota band's ritual ceremonies and songs are different from each other *tiyospaye* (community). They're never the same.

A long time ago it was mostly the men who were given a *hunka* ceremony because the Oglala Lakota believe the day men were born, they were born to walk with the shadow of death and they could die anytime. This is why all the ceremonies and everything focuses on men. Because of that belief, fasting, Sun Dancing, sweat lodge, everything is geared towards the man because he was to prepare himself, and that left little room for women's roles. But there are also other things that the women are able to do, although these are limited. Each village had a few *wakan* (sacred) women, who just doctored women because there are certain parts of a woman's body that only a woman doctor can touch.

You can put names into categories, like spiritual names or warrior or even veterans' names. An example of the spiritual type would be those double animal names like Crow Eagle, Eagle Bear, or Eagle Elk which would be given through a medicine man. It all depends how that family wants to name its child. They ask a medicine man to name their son so he will always carry an aura or protection around him because he was given that name by a medicine man. He might have a vision of an eagle and elk both. But if you want to inspire your son to be a brave warrior, you pick someone who would give him a warrior kind of name. The warrior names often were based on behavior when facing the enemy, such as Kills in Water, Comes Last, Comes Killing, Stands Alone, Attack Him, and Young Bear.

In general, when you select someone to give a name to your son or daughter, you try to pick people who are honored in the community. So when you select someone, it all depends on how influential that medicine man or that *tokala* leader is, or how influential that chief is in that village or even how influential that elderly woman is in that village. A woman, for example, who is very good at tanning hides, quillwork, beadwork, or whatever, would be looked to as an influence on a young girl as she grew up. So they would ask her to give the girl an Indian name; or she might be a kindhearted woman who feeds everybody and whose house is always open to people and that girl would become like her. She might select a name like Cante Waste Win, (Good Hearted Woman) or something like that. So both the name givers chosen and the type of name that is given reflect the desire of the parents to have a good influence on their child.

You're not supposed to pass a name on over and over. One very common name for girls every place I go is Winyan Waste Win (Good Woman) and another is Ta Sina Wakan Win (Her Sacred Shawl Woman). Every place I go, the people are always giving these names, maybe because we put people on the spot. The day before or an hour before the naming ceremony, we call on a person to give a name and the only thing that comes to her or his head then is Cante Waste Win, so that's the name that girl gets. If you're going to give a name, then you should have a year of planning and maybe even time for research in your family history, your family traditions, and their family traditions and then you can find the name accordingly. It should have meaning—a story, a history—behind it.

When should your ceremonial Indian name be used? An Indian name is very important as you go into gatherings or a crowd of people and you are identified by your Indian name; that's the most honored thing. I'll give you an example. On New Year's in 1963 we were drinking outside a dance hall and just messing around. We were daring each other, "Hey, go in and sing; I dare you to sing." We started to form a little jackpot—a case of beer, a quart of Old Grandad, half a gallon of Thunderbird wine, a pack of cigarettes. So finally I said, "Okay, I'll go in and sing." But I only knew one song, so on that dare I went in and sat down with old-time singers and I sang along a little. I sang and then all of a sudden Dave Badger, the announcer, called out to the crowd of people, "This is New Year's; we have a new singer and he's going to sing a new song." And he used my Indian name, Hehaka Luzahan. *"Hehaka Luzahan alowan ahiyuyin kte lo."* ("Swift Elk is going to sing a song.")

If he had used my census name, Severt Young Bear, or Young Bear or some other name, I wouldn't have been put on the spot to sing. But when you live the traditional way of life, once they use your Indian name, you cannot refuse, no matter what. Once you go into a gathering, it's an honor for people to use your Indian name. It would be shameful to refuse. So I started a song and I didn't know how it sounded, but I sang and then afterwards my aunts and my cousins and sister all took me out in the middle and had a giveaway. As they gave away things, they used my name Hehaka Luzahan, so instead of going back out and collecting my jackpot, I stayed in and I sang. That had such an effect on me I even went and bought a drumstick from my cousin and I stayed in and sang. That's how I got caught and began devoting my life to being a traditional singer. That's an illustration of how important that awarded Indian name is for identity.

Most names tend to be positive, based on something spiritual or part of a family history. You don't just give a name so the parents know their little girl has some Indian name but they don't really understand what it means. Sure, that boy has an Indian name, but what does it mean to him? I feel a youngster should get a name around the age of six when a boy or a girl starts to understand and appreciate it. Some name their children too young and the children then don't know what happened; they are too young to understand. These Indian names play a big part in all the songs, and if you look at it—Ronnie, you've been singing a long time now—all the honor songs and traditional songs we sing put someone's name in somewhere. All the honor songs made that are used at powwows or sweat lodge, or Sun Dances leave a place for somebody's Indian name. That's because it is a very respected and honored place for people to use their names.

I have a sister. I don't know what the history behind it is, since she's a nice-looking woman, but my half sister, whose name is Helen Young Bear Tail, was given a name Winyan Sica Numpa (Bad Woman Number Two) and every time there's a gathering they would always sing for her. She would always get ready. She'd go to that powwow prepared because she knew they'd sing. She was always involved in all powwows and ceremonies and things. She was very respected, was a good lady singer too. I always think about that but I never had the chance to talk to her about the origin of her name before she died. That's the only name that I thought was out of the way, but apparently there was a good reason for such a name and she was happy about it. She always gave away when they would sing for her.

We have a name here in our community, Plenty Wounds. I talked to Pete Plenty Wounds, whose great-grandfather was a very fearless warrior; he wasn't afraid of anything. He was wounded many times and so was given that name, Plenty Wounds. Then we had another one named Wounded Arrow and that elderly man earned that name because once after a battle he had six or seven arrows going through him and they left him for dead. He broke the feathered shafts and pushed them through and he crawled to a creek and, using the black mud from the bottom of the spring, he doctored himself. They gave him up for dead but he came back, so he was called Wounded Arrow.

My aunt Julie Kills Back told still another story. Their oldest brother was killed, so their youngest brother wanted to go avenge him, to face the enemy, and he'd either avenge him or they'd take his life. When he was going to go, his older sister wanted to go also, then the other sister wanted to go;

pretty soon the whole family went. They killed a couple of enemies and they came back, so they gave them that name, Tokicun, Kills Back.

Many of the translations of traditional Lakota names are misleading and even comical. After the Bureau came and after 1924, when we were given citizenship, the Bureau used to tell us, "You're citizens now and you don't need the Indian name now. George Sword, the first police captain we had on the Pine Ridge Reservation, his real Indian name was Take Sword from Cavalry, but they just cut it down to Sword. Then today you have guys like Scout and Comes and Returns, who had their longer names cut down to just one word. When the government started recording these names as census names, we were also given first names, like I said above, usually the names of presidents or Bible names.

If we had kept on giving original names that we earned, maybe my father would have had a different name. Then I too would have had my own earned name. I'm sure my name would have been Owns Many Wives or some other wonderful name like that! Maybe I'm lucky the naming stopped.

For a long time as a youngster I really didn't know what Severt meant or what Edward meant in my family history. Later on I found out that this was my uncle's friend's name, and that was another uncle's name, and that the Young Bear name had meaning behind it, and why I had the ceremonial Indian name Swift Elk. After that I was prouder and trying to live up to each name.

So this is an overview of name giving in Lakota culture. I think we need to slow down and give names in a thoughtful, traditional way so there is a heritage behind it. For me, I know my census name is Severt Edward Young Bear and I know why. I also have a ceremonial Indian name, Swift Elk, and I know why. These names tell me who I am.

PART TWO

Butterflies from the
Mouth of an Elk

⟐ The Oral Tradition

As we are sitting here talking late into the day, it's important to remember that although we're considering making all this into a book, everything we bring up is part of the oral tradition, the *Lakol wicoh'an* (Lakota heritage). That spoken word and the memory that catches and keeps it are at the center of our tradition. When I was younger I once asked my dad to tape-record something for me because I wanted to be able to remember it. He refused and said: "Son, I will tell you all about it, but I don't want you to record it. If it's important enough to you, you will and must remember it in your mind. Concentrate and you'll remember what you're told and it will stay with you. If you record it on a machine, you'll lose it."

I think what he meant is that the oral tradition, when we really appreciate it, means more because it is so easily lost. When we record it with a machine or even in print, we get careless with it because we can always go back to it and listen to it or read it again, even long after. It requires no effort.

In the oral tradition, then—whether it's a story, a song, a joke about your brother-in-law, a prayer, or a speech—it's me telling it to you—or in public to sometimes lots of people—for your ears and mind to catch and keep. But then, in modern times, when that oral tradition gets printed as letters on a page, our oral tradition will gain horizon and importance in a different way because it will reach many more people—we hope—than just the two of us or a group of people that come to hear us.

Since I'm concerned with putting things in order again for our people, I want to talk about the way we use stories and oral language both in Lakota and English. In stories, songs, speeches, jokes, whatever, we take ideas and give them a shape, a body through the human voice. Through lively and creative language we give life and color to ideas. Through that language we make those ideas walk and fly and shine; we share our feelings and our knowledge and our memories. Our stories and songs, we should remember, also teach us lessons. Sure, dates and facts are often missing, sometimes they're not accurate in the way historians and anthropologists like it, but our oral tradition tells the truth and the heart of the meaning stays alive from mouth to ear.

I think this is where long ago I remember some of these older men talking. They would spend lots of times telling stories, good stories and bad stories, over and over. Today, though, you go to a meeting and if someone goes on a little too long, someone might say, "Geez, I'm sick and tired of that old man; he talks on and on!" What that old man is demonstrating is that in oral history your ears and your eyes are your tape recorder. The Creator gave us a mind, and our oral traditions tell us to use that mind to remember them. That elderly man is telling you those stories over and over so that you learn, you learn word for word and find out what he's talking about. He would tell about something that happened a long time ago before the reservation days and in the 1920s and the IRA (Indian Reorganization Act of 1934) days and all the way up to today. It's up to you as a young man listening to him speak to see that someplace, while he was talking, he has made his point, and it's for you to listen and identify it when he makes that half-hour circle of talking about an issue. He'll talk about everything in the world, but somewhere he has come to the point and realizing where he did is up to you.

Even the humor that old man used when he talked about his brother-in-law or made fun of himself or told a joke, all these things he says will relate to the point he is trying to get across to the people. This is why the oral history of the Lakota takes a lot of patience.

I remember an old man who died not too long ago, Frank Kills Enemy. He wasn't an educated man with a high school or college diploma, but through his Lakota mind and things that he taught himself, through studying treaties, the interpretation of the Indian Reorganization Act, the public laws that have been passed, and all the Indian policies the government has enacted, he took the time and he studied and he interpreted these words into the Lakota language. When he talked, he talked like he was way out of line. He might go way back to 1600 or that time after 1777 or when George Washington signed a treaty. He would talk about these long-ago things that come down through history and mention this treaty and that treaty along the way. He was well versed and a very good speaker. He could even speak in English if he wanted to. It was funny; around some people he said that he couldn't speak English and needed an interpreter, but then with other people he could really speak English very well.

Etymologies: Words Full of Meaning

Let me say here, although I think we'll be doing it throughout this book, that the interpretation and history of words often give them more meaning.

When you know that this Lakota word or that Lakota word is made up of these syllables or ideas, it helps to fix it in your memory. Let's start with the word *Oglala*. That word can mean different things and I've read some of the interpretations in books as "scattering their own," but then the author usually doesn't know what that really means. Here is the way I see it: The Oglalas were warriors. When a group of warriors were ready to ride into an enemy camp or ride against the cavalry, they'd sing themselves a death song. They would also get on top of a molehill; they would brush it off and get the fine dirt towards the center of the molehill. Then they would *aiglala* (scatter on themselves). That means they were ready to die for their people. They would sprinkle that fine dirt over their heads and shoulders and even on their horses between the ears, on the manes, and on the back. They didn't fear death and were willing to return to the earth. *Aiglala* later becomes Oglala, what the Pine Ridge Sioux call themselves.

Here is another example of the meaning of words as a way to find understanding. Going back to before the reservation days of, say, the 1870s, regarding the forming of large bands and smaller bands, we were given the name of the Great Teton Sioux Nation. But I think the original words for our groups held the true meaning of *oyate wicoti* (people camping together). Here are the ingredients of that: *oyate* (people), *wi* (sun), *can ohan ti* (camping among the trees)—all these words were shortened to *oyate wicoti*. But the original meaning of all this was the little longer meaning of people-in-the-sun-camping-among-the-trees. The reason behind this is that the Lakotas used to look for the ideal camping ground where there was lots of tender grass for the horses, a lot of good firewood and water for the people. A long time ago, for the inside fire or inside cooking they would prefer cottonwood trees because their smoke stings the eyes less. In the winter they would be camping into higher timber for protection and would burn pine, but that has an odor and eye-stinging smoke that lingers. When they sent out the village scout to pick a new camp, he had to find a high hill close by so they could have a view of the surrounding area and at the same time have a campground for the people with easy access, yet offering protection for the people at night. In the daylight scouts are always out, so I think this is where the word *wi* (sun) came in.

Later on, the government used the word *tiyospaye,* meaning smaller units of people or what is called the extended family. *Ti* means to live; *spaye* means a little smaller group or cutting a circle around that little *tiyospaye*. Still later the government used words like chapter, then village, then later on communities, then subcommunities, then districts—all based on district lines and reservation lines drawn on maps. It's important, then, to know that the original word for it was *oyate wicoti*, a camp, large or small. Knowing the real meanings behind certain terms clarifies their importance.

The terms for man, woman, and child are also revealing. *Wicasa* (man) is based on *wi* (sun), *can* (wood or staff) and *sa* (red). *Wi* is the highest form the Great Mystery can take; *can* refers to the staff a warrior can touch the enemy with; and *sa* (red) is the color of the sacred. In this way the spiritual Lakota warrior is defined. The word *winyan* (woman) is also made up of *wi* (sun) and then *inyan* (rock). A woman is the foundation of the home, so she combines the great power of the sun and the rock, the beginning of creation and the foundation. The word for child is also illuminating when we look at its parts. *Wakanyeja* is our Lakota word for child. It is made up of two parts, *wakanyan* (sacred) and *najin* (to stand); so for us a child stands sacred in this world, a special gift from the Creator.

When these kinds of terms are used without understanding of their makeup, they become hollow and eventually meaningless. Our oral tradition gives us the chance to hold onto ideas in the way I just illustrated, but probably much more common for our people is the telling of stories, the singing of songs, the making of speeches. These give words a net or anchor to fasten them down. Lots of times instead of giving facts, statistics, and definitions, instead of analyzing and dissecting something directly, we tell a story or we sing a song or somebody makes a speech to make people laugh, or make them cry, or make them think about it.

Sio Paha: The Medicine Hill

My father and I once talked to two elderly men, George Iron Cloud and Dave Badger. They said there is a place not far from here between Porcupine store and Evergreen Housing, right across the road from my sister's, they used to call Sio Paha (Prairie Chicken Hill). In the prereservation days it was designated as a sacred gathering place of people and of sacred things. People used to camp in the area annually; it has some springs there for water and timber. It's flat with a little hill in the center called Sio Paha. The site played an important historical role for the people of Porcupine District.

One of the events during these annual gatherings was that the medicine men always tested each other. On one certain day the *eyapaha* (camp announcer) would go around and say, "Keep all your children under cover, stay inside your tents! They are getting ready to go after each other with the sacred ways." All the medicine men would go out in the center, sit and put on their special sacred costumes and paint, prepare their medicine bundles, and shoot each other with their medicine. If they had power and had that vision, they could take the medicine shot by others out of themselves. As they did, they would get their bundles and go stand on the side. The guy that could stay out there the longest without getting knocked down won. Some of the medicines they could shoot were so powerful they could knock some of these men down. They would stagger, fall down, and roll around. Some of these guys couldn't handle it, or they knew they didn't have enough power, so they would groan and cry and roll around. There would be a respected medicine man on the side who had been picked for taking the medicine out of those guys who couldn't take it out of themselves. Then he would hold them by the hand and take them around the circle getting after them by saying, *"Nahanhcin niwakan sni!"* Don't try to fool people and go out to try your medicine, because you still do not have the ability or the power as a medicine man. Go back and go through the ceremonies, fast or whatever you have to do until you can prove to the people that you are a holy man of medicine!"

I guess one year Ikunsan (Weasel), a guy who had weasel medicine, knocked everybody down. He was the last one standing out there and nobody could get to him. Everytime somebody would shoot a medicine at him, he would turn his weasel in his hand towards them and that other medicine would fall, or if the medicine hit him, he would turn the nose of the weasel to that spot and the medicine would fall from him.

Then the next year at Sio Paha a guy with *mato* (bear) medicine was the last one standing. He wore a bear head and bear claws and started chasing people around, even people out in the tipi area. He went out there and started ripping up tipis and scaring horses away and chasing people so everybody was running around and crying, *"Nikte! Nikte!"* (He's going to kill you, run!) And *ata* (wow!) everybody was running and lying on the ground and rolling around. He was the last one. He was looking around and saw somebody out around some rosebud bushes not paying attention, not frantic or anything. It turns out this man was a *heyoka* (sacred clown), one of those medicine men who are given awesome power when they dream of *wakinyan* (thunder spirits) and then always behave in an opposite or contrary behavior. This *heyoka* had a long rope with a bell on the end and he had a porcupine quill between his two fingers and he was making out like a bumblebee. He would go to one of the flowers and say "bzzz" and he would jump up and down and do a little dance to make off like he was flying backwards and sideways and back and forth, and then go to another flower and bzzz and dance backwards and sideways. Pretty soon this *mato* guy started approaching him growling. Then he started running at him and everybody started hollering, "Run *heyoka!* He's going to kill you!" But the *heyoka* didn't run; he just kept going "bzzz" and then go to another flower and down and fly around on tiptoes and jump down, back, and sideways like he was flying to another flower and go "bzzz" again. The bear man was getting closer and everybody started crying and hollering, but the bumblebee just kept on going in his way.

All of a sudden, right behind him, the bear growled, ready to attack him, when that *heyoka* with the porcupine quill just turned around and pointed that porcupine quill towards the stomach of the bear and said "bzzz" and the bear screamed and fell over. In a while he jumped up and started running the other way and the *heyoka* still danced like a bumblebee behind him, flapping his arms once in a while and jumping up and down. The bear man was running fast, but the *heyoka* was faster. He would jump up and down dragging that bell behind him and once in a while he would point the quill at him right below the beltline and say "bzzz" and the bear guy would jump forward and run a little faster. That year that *heyoka* who had the bumblebee vision was the winner.

There are also some other stories my father told me about that Sio Paha site. If you felt bad, you could go up there and put some tobacco ties out as offerings. These are little one-inch squares of cotton material with a pinch of tobacco tied into little pouches as prayer offerings. Or even, in the Christian way, you could put out a wooden cross or something and pray. Our stories identify that place as very *wakan* (sacred). Yet, somehow, many people I've talked to don't know these oral stories anymore and don't show any interest in this place.

Another story was about this old man named Huncaje (Garter). He wore a red sort of kneeband below his knee to symbolize being wounded there in battle, so he had that name. Well, one day there was a big storm with gray clouds in a purple sky, like this one coming at us from the west right now as we're talking, the gray clouds just rolling, coming off the flat ridge on the west side of Sio Paha. It looked like everybody would be blown away, so they told the people to turn their horses loose and throw their tents down flat in the wagons and tie the wheels of the wagons together with some rope to keep them from turning and the wagons from taking off, and to go in a gully or creek bottom and be prepared. This was a big storm. Then, all of a sudden, this old man Huncaje was there. All he had on was a breechcloth and he held two eagle feathers. He ran to the top of the Sio Paha and started singing and praying and waving those two feathers back and forth, making a motion of separating. Here that storm physically and visibly came just so far and broke up in half and went around them all. They only got a few raindrops and a little bit of wind and that was it. A long time ago in crises like that, these guys had the power to do things like that. Sio Paha is where some of this happened.

Plenty Wolf's Journey

Let me tell you another story about a song. By chance I was visiting with some older men one time and we were talking about how during President Lincoln's administration they hung thirty-eight Sioux in Mankato. What happened was that after the 1851 Fort Laramie Treaty and especially after the 1862 Sioux war in Minnesota, the government started rounding up Indians. This was a punishment because some of our Dakota relatives in Minnesota wouldn't take it any more—they were starving and angry about the way they were being treated by the government—and they attacked some of the white towns in southern Minnesota in 1862. After several hundred settlers were killed and it was over, these Dakotas were to be moved from their home territories to new and different areas so they could break up their old band structure, their morals and their spirit. They started rounding up the Sioux and taking them to places like Fort Yates, Fort Randall, and Fort Thompson. They promised them rations and made all kinds of other promises. Only the Oglala resisted and half of the Sicangu, the Brule or Burned Thigh, who stayed with the Oglala around the Badlands and Black Hills and the rough country in the Scotts Bluff area of Nebraska. They didn't want to give in and move their camps. They had very powerful war leaders and so the government couldn't round the Sioux up militarily until they came in after the Little Big Horn fight in 1876. There were plans to float the Lakota people down the Missouri, but they resisted.

So after the trouble of 1862 in Minnesota, all the Sioux bands they had at the forts along the Missouri River had their influential men—medicine men, chiefs, and war leaders—taken back to Mankato. They were told, "We'll hold you prisoner until the western band of Teton Sioux, the Oglala Sioux, give up and come in." Several times they sent runners out there to tell them to come in. They didn't. So they wound up hanging thirty-eight Sioux and made it a public event, advertised it with posters. They sent runners out west again and threatened, "Come in or we'll hang some more!"

During that time lots of the men who were held prisoner were very powerful medicine men. They were stripped of everything—sacred pipes, clothing, anything that represented some kind of authority or power. They stripped them naked. They used to walk around inside the stockades and when the soldiers would throw away cigarette butts, they gathered them. This one medicine man carved a pipe out of wood. He said that at night he was going to pray for help. So he gathered enough tobacco, fixed his pipe, and got ready. That night he prayed all night and that day and that night again. That second night, even with the guards walking back and forth and guards at the gate, a spirit came and unlocked the gate and said, "Go on! They won't see you." And he told all the men to scatter, told them not to bunch up. So they came out of the gate and ran, but they all had ball-and-chains on their ankles but ran anyway. Eventually some got recaptured, some got away.

This one man who got away kept running west and ran, ran, and would hide and sleep in the daytime and then he'd run again at night. Finally he couldn't run anymore and fell down. He had sores and cuts all over his legs and ankles from the shackles around his ankles. Later that night, toward morning, a she-wolf came to him and said, "Come and follow me." So he got up and slowly followed her to a big cave with all kinds of wolves in it, a wolf den. What they did was to go to the spring and get the black dirt in the spring, bring it back in their mouths, and the she-wolf would put it around the shackles. They kept doing that until he healed up. They also brought him herbs and stuff, and since he was a powerful medicine man, he started chewing these and doctored himself.

Those wolves would bring him rabbits and other meat. They took care of him like this until one morning the she-wolf came and told him, "I will take you west to your relatives but we have to hide out during the daytime and go at night." So they kept doing that and when they finally came up to the Missouri River, she told him to get down and pray, and that wolf prayed and howled. Here somebody answered on the other side. The sand in that river came up and formed a bridge, so the wolf went forward and said, "Stay right behind me!" He stayed close behind and they walked across and got to the other side and kept going. She howled again and got an answer again and said, "We'll rest up and early in the morning I will take you as far as your relatives who are over those two ridges." He still had those shackles on his ankles but he kept going. Finally she said, "Well, this is how far I will go. You go on from here over these two ridges and in that next valley you will find your relatives."

Sure enough, he found his relatives, who welcomed him back. Even though they had a hard time at it, they broke his shackles and gathered to sing a special song for him. When they sang that song, his reaction was to act out how he ran, the suffering he went through, and how that wolf finally brought him back to his relatives and how he survived. When he came back like this, they gave him the name Has Plenty Wolf for Friend, Sungmanitu Ota. When the Bureau census names came down, they cut it down to Plenty Wolf. Afterwards for years, when they sang his song, he used to run, fall down, and crawl and go through his motions at gatherings and people would cry.

The words to this song go like this: *"Tehiya ku welo, tehiya ku welo."* (He has a difficult time as he is coming home.) *"Nitakola, ku welo."* (Your friend is coming home.) Then they mention his name, Sungmanitu Ota and then *"Tehiya ku welo, tehiya ku welo. Nitakola, ku welo"* again. People sing that song at times today, but not all of them know the story that is behind it.

The Double Woman

We also have some old stories about Winyan Numpa (Double Woman). Women who would see this Winyan Numpa appear in a dream in some way had to make a decision about their future, and if they made the right choice, the Double Woman would give them special artistic powers. My grandmother talked one time about how in her dream a wolf took her along, and as she went around one of those washouts like a horseshoe, just a little bit below them she heard some women laughing aloud having a good time playing cards. The wolf told her: "Don't go down there; that's not the right place for you. It's not the right way for you. Go, follow me!" So she kept on going and a little way down there were two women. One was tanning hide and one was painting and beading. All the beautiful work that they had done, bright beadwork and shining quillwork, was spread all around them. And the wolf said, "This is where I want you to go." So she went down. She didn't recognize those ladies but went down to where they were sitting. It turns out all these different women were the two different sides of the Double Woman. The women laughing aloud were the bad side of this spirit woman and the other two represented the side a good, modest Lakota woman should pick to be like.

Traditionally, in everything a Lakota woman does she uses her mouth and her fingers. She would chew tanned leather with her saliva, chew it and soften it with her teeth. Then to make the design she would take an awl, wet it on her tongue, and then press a moist design into the hide. Then, when she would prepare her sinew as thread, she'd run that through her mouth and roll it with her fingers. In this way she puts herself—her saliva, her spirit and love—into the things she makes for the ones she loves. A very creative woman, if she is not careful, gets close to the crazy side where she could be a *blete winyan* (loose woman). She must be careful in her dream to choose the right side of that Double Woman. In one of the songs about the Double Woman there is a real loud laugh at the end of it signifying the danger and a warning.

One of the Double Woman songs I heard about thirty years ago was sung by Lucy Swan from Cherry Creek on the Cheyenne River Reservation. The words went like this: *"Hoksi cankiyapaha tewahila ca oyate ki wamiciyankapi."* (That honored child of mine, I want the people to see him or her.) She would sing this song invoking the good side of the Double Woman as she beaded a vest or a buckskin dress or whatever for someone she loved. Double Woman dreamers have their own special designs. You never see these one-of-a-kind designs in other people's artwork. At one time these pieces were not made to be sold to just anybody. It was a special gift of love from a wife to a husband, or from a mother to a son, from a grandmother to a granddaughter. The gift of the Double Woman dream was granted only to special ones.

Elk Power and the Dream Flute

One special tradition that is almost completely gone is that of the flute. I know about the spiritual side of the flute from my grandfather. He had a dream that he was to go to a certain place and he would be given a flute. So one day he got his things ready and went. He just kept on walking till he finally came to a place he'd seen before in his dream. As he was going, he saw the the skeleton of an elk lying there with real nice teeth on it. *Pahin ske* they call it, elk's teeth. The elk is called *hehaka* based on his horns branching out. If you have elk medicine or elk love potion or medicine, if you use it, then you have your way with women. Whatever woman you want, it is said, you circle her a couple of times, or take one of her hairs and roll it up and keep it with you, and you circle her a couple of times like a male elk, and she'll soon be hanging on your *hehaka* (branching antlers). Women will be hanging onto the tips of your horns.

Those guys that are elk dreamers have a butterfly as their symbol. When my grandfather approached that elk skeleton, it talked to him. He was given certain things that he had to do and he had to have some kind of medicine. When he said that he would accept it, then four of the most beautiful butterflies flew out of the elk's mouth and flew into my grandfather's mouth and down into his chest and his lungs. Then the elk told him to turn around and look behind him, and there a piece of ash wood was lying with carving on it. The elk told him to blow hard on it and to make the sounds of music on that wood. There were no holes on it for the fingers to play notes; it was just a solid piece of ash. When he blew on it he could play music. After that, whenever he did his own ceremonies he blew this solid piece of wood.

One day, after many years, the spirit came again to him in a dream and told him that now he had to leave his wife and stay with three women. The spirit in the dream even said, "These are the women," and he turned three women to face him and he recognized them. So later he went to talk to his wife about it and she was very understanding. "Yes, this is why you are a medicine man, a spiritual man. If this is what they are asking you to do," she said, "I'll go on and raise the family by myself. If they ask you to do this, then you have to do it; there is no turning back now."

But he looked at his children and his wife and he refused; he went on a hill in a spiritual way, to leave behind the everyday world and get spiritual communication by fasting and praying all by himself up on the hill. Still he refused the elk spirit. In his dream he was again told to go to that certain place again like long ago. So he got ready and he went. He kept on walking till he found that place and he knew he was there before and here was the elk skeleton lying there. It told him again what to do, but he refused again. "No, I shouldn't do that. I can't do that. Ask me to do something else but not to leave my family." He was told that if he didn't do it, they would take the power back. Pretty soon, my grandfather said, he felt kind of a scratching inside. Things were flying around in his lungs and they were coming up, up towards his mouth so that he even tried to cover his mouth. But then with a soft flutter they came out between his fingers and flew. They were two of the butterflies and they flew back into the mouth of the elk.

So two stayed inside of him so he could still do certain things on the love medicine side of it, but he could no longer perform healing, or when people asked for various medicines there were some medicines he couldn't provide anymore. And he could no longer play into that ash. But he still had a little part of his power. So now he drilled holes into the ash wood and hollowed it out and could still blow on it so that its song, like the fluttering wings of the butterfly, appear to a woman and she can't resist its powerful melody. I know there are other stories about the love flute and elk medicine—I know that Richard Fool Bull years ago was a famous flute maker—but this is the story in my family.

The Great Migration

Ronnie, you and I have talked about migrations and where the Lakota come from. Was it North Carolina around 1500 like some historians believe and then Minnesota a hundred years later, or what? Here again our oral history gives us a different version. From what I heard over the years there was little about moving from east to west. The Oglala are very adventuresome and very spiritual people and very fearless warriors. If there's a high butte someplace, they want to know what's on top of that high butte or mountaintop. If a Lakota sees an eagle circling above him and then going east, he'd say, "Hey, there's a reason why the eagle circled around me and went east, so I'll follow him." So this is why traces of the Sioux are found in all the four directions—in Canada, the East, into Mexico and Salt Lake and beyond.

The oral history I heard said they moved from the Black Hills in all four directions. There are reasons for going in all directions. Sometimes they would pick ten or twelve warriors to go west and bring back some salt. They'd go and go until they find a salt lake or some salt deposit and they would take extra horses to load and bring it back to share equally with everybody. Or somebody might say, "There's some pretty high-spirited horses, fast-running horses, towards the south." So they'd pick ten or twelve to go and find those horses and bring them back. Or they'd say, "Up north there's a camp of warriors that's causing trouble for our people." So again they would pick enough warriors to go find out and, if necessary, fight with them. It reminds me of some of those medieval knights who were always ready to go on some quest; it was a challenge and the enjoyment of traveling out.

When an anthropologist or archaeologist digs up a grave and interprets and classifies it, nobody can dispute it. You won't catch an Indian digging up a grave and saying, "This is my great-grandmother in South Carolina" or "These are my long-ago relatives," because to us all burial grounds are sacred. So it's very hard to dispute these archaeologists and anthropologists. Let's consider this: God made people and gave everybody a different tongue, so even the Sioux Nation had *n*-speaking groups, the Wiciyela, or Yanktons; the *d*-speaking groups, the Santees; and the *l*-speaking groups, the Tetons, or Lakotas. Each of these groups has a slightly different dialect of our Sioux language. Where the *n*-speakers (Nakotas) use the *n* sound in the word, the *d*-speakers (Dakotas) use a *d* sound, and the *l*-speakers (Lakotas) use an *l* sound. So each of our dialects is a little different, the meanings of words are different, and we have different ceremonies. Maybe the eastern *d*-speaking groups went east and came back. It's very hard to really say, but all the oral history the Teton Oglala have says we were always in the Black Hills. That's not the whole Sioux Nation, because there were seven council fires plus the Assiniboine, who are near relatives of ours who split off from the Nakotas a couple of hundred years ago and now live up towards Montana.

Even though the Big Missouri winter count that Mallery wrote down in his book *Picture Writing of the American Indians* says that a band of Oglalas brought back a cedar tree from the Black Hills in 1775, that has to be thought about. It doesn't necessarily mean that this was the first time they saw such a tree or had been to the Black Hills for the first time. You see, we consider the cedar tree sacred. They used it to heal certain sicknesses that had to do with the cleansing of the blood. They would also burn that cedar and use it to offer prayers and drive evil away. They always said that there was a certain kind of cedar they would use. They would send a young man to go in a particular direction and bring it back. So there would be a special reason in that band for bringing that cedar back and making that drawing in that winter count. Maybe they ran out of this cedar and needed it for some sacred ceremonies. It's not just because it was the first time the Lakota made it to the Black Hills.

He Sapa: The Black Mountains

I think the Black Hills have always been a sacred place for the Lakota. The common term Paha Sapa means Black Hills for many people, but *paha* is only a little hill like this one right next to my house. Instead of Paha Sapa many of the old-timers would use the words He Sapa, which means Black Mountains, because they called the Bighorn Mountains to the west the He Ska, or White Mountains. Anyway, the Black Mountains or Black Hills are very sacred to us. There are even little people, sort of small spirit people, who are staying in the Black Hills who are believed to be taking care of the Hills for the people. Also, eagles have their nests there.

Then, in one of our stories about Inyan Hoksila (Stone Boy) it says, *"Tohan Inyan Hoksi takpapi na mahpiya sabya kahwoke."* That means that whenever buffaloes started charging the Stone Boy and the dark clouds are flying by, buffalo herds start to migrate into the Black Hills because they know winter is coming. The clouds they talk about are winter clouds; towards the end of fall, dark clouds blow real fast. They call them *mahpiya sabya kahwoke*. Inyan Hoksi, the Stone Boy, was born from a woman who was sitting and thinking about her husband who went on a war party. She was lonesome and as she sat up on a hill she sang an old song. I can't remember the whole story, but she swallowed a stone that was shiny next to her. She had gotten interested in the rock, so she held it in her hand, rubbed it, held it in her mouth, and then finally swallowed it. She got pregnant from that stone and had a very special boy. He grew up in four days and had special powers. No one could harm him. He was so heavy and very strong, so they called him Inyan Hoksi (Stone Boy). He defended his village and wasn't afraid of anything, not even the Tatanka Gnaskiyan (Crazy Buffalo). At a certain time of the season, some of the buffalo—maybe because of the heat or the green grass that they ate, or for some other reason—would have foam in their lungs, stomachs, and brains. They would go crazy and charge anything. So those kinds of buffalo charged Inyan Hoksi in a certain part of the fall but they couldn't get him down.

All around the Black Hills there is a barrier or rim the non-Indians call Hogback Ridge. There are certain gates around the Black Hills where the buffalo used to enter into the Hills. They would go into those canyons for shelter and remain in the Black Hills until the snow started melting and green grass started showing. Then they would migrate out of the Hills again.

I used to work as a ranger for the Oglala Sioux Tribe in the 1960s. There were twenty of us who were assigned in pairs to certain areas. Matthew Two Bulls from Oglala Community and I were put on culture and history. So we used to spend time going to elderly people like Moses Two Bulls and Bunk Left Hand, Luke Weasel Bear, Frank Fools Crow, and Dave Badger. We were trying to identify, pinpoint, and catch up on any stories about local historical sites. We have lots of historical sites here on the reservation that very few people know about.

It was brought up by some of these elderly that at one time long ago the birds and the two-leggeds had a race against the four-leggeds around the

Black Hills. It was a natural track all around the Hills. The animals did this because of the sacredness of the Black Hills and also to show their stamina and endurance, to show how animals could endure hardship, run without water and food for a number of days, how some of the birds could float through the air and some have to fight hard flapping their wings, and some animals have to crawl. But no matter how slow or how fast they went, the endurance was there. As they ran and hopped and flew and crawled, they wore a valley all around the Hills we now call the Race Track. Today there are marathon runs held by Lakota young people to honor the Black Hills and that first great race all the way around the Hills. I think that's a great thing and a way of expressing identity.

I guess before the beginning of that first race there was an annual meeting of all the animals. The birds had their own meeting and all that crawl—bugs and snakes—the four-leggeds, everybody had their own meeting. One was real comical. A Lakota story tells it that when the birds had their meeting, there was a rooster strutting around sticking out his chest: "I'm not afraid of anybody here and there's nobody more powerful or with more authority than me. I'm the best looking, and see my spurs; I can fight any of you. I'm the king!" But the other guys said, "No, keep quiet, sit down. There's an *itancan* (chief) coming, so we're waiting for him." "There's nobody any higher than me; I'm the chief!" Pretty soon they heard a whistling sound way off; it got louder and louder and "I'm the boss, I'm the . . ." All of a sudden those birds all started jumping back and formed a circle and a big gray eagle landed right in the center of that circle. When that rooster saw that eagle, boy, he took off and jumped over the other birds and ran into some plum bushes. Even today, out in the back of the house or in the front yard, whenever a rooster hears a whistling sound, right away he runs for cover in some plum bush or under a hayrack or wagon because he found out from experience that there's a bird mightier than him.

The Lakota would also go into the Black Hills for food gathering, tipi poles, herbal medicines, for fasting and doing sacred ceremonies, and they would even go into the Black Hills as a sacred home where they could die. A long time ago elderly warriors when they knew they were very sick would start to get very restless and keep moving around. They would call that *owanka iyokipi sni* (he doesn't like the ground he is sitting on). They would be so restless they would move here and there and keep moving and finally say, "Well, I might as well go into the Black Hills and prepare myself to die within the Black Hills." So after they were gone so many days, their relatives usually would go look for them in the Black Hills, and sometimes they would find them and sometimes they wouldn't. So the Black Hills are very sacred.

Let me tell you another story about the Black Mountains. This man, he must have been in his fifties, was a very brave and fearless warrior. One day he took sick, so he had a medicine man come and doctor him. It didn't work and his skin started getting very blotchy. So his parents went after another medicine man, but he couldn't do anything either. All different kinds of Lakota medicine men tried to cure him but it still didn't work and he was getting worse. He knew he was getting low. He started getting this *owanka iyokipi sni* restlessness, so he started moving here and there. He would go to one hilltop that looked good and would go up and sit or lie up there. He might spend the night up there but it didn't please him so he would go to another one, and finally on one hill he sat and he saw the Black Hills. Since he had his pipe with him, he took it out and prayed: "Well, Great Spirit, maybe this is your wish or your way that I will slowly vanish as a warrior. Maybe it's my time that I can no longer go on war parties, hunt, and protect the camps. Every place I go I don't feel right, but from this hill I see the He Sapa plainly, so I pray that I will go to the Black Mountains and find a suitable place where I will feel good. I will lay there then and I will slowly vanish away as you have decided." So he prayed that and lay down for a while and left.

He walked all that day and all that night. The next morning he was some-place in the center of the Black Hills and he kept on walking, looking at peaks and mountaintops here and there, and finally he found a place where he felt good. There in a nice green meadow with pine trees was a stream with fish flashing in it. There was a ledge with a little dug-in shelf like. He made some bedding with grass and fixed himself a place and got some water. Then he lay down there and he prayed, "This will be my resting place. I will stay here and let you take me." The next morning he got up, prayed, and he went down. He was still getting low; he knew he was and he didn't feel good. He went down and washed, drank some water, and went back up and ate a little. They had given him some medicine, so he took that also.

He lay down again and he was almost off to sleep when he heard sounds like someone singing. He sat up and he thought that this could be a *toka* (enemy) coming through. "He might see me since I didn't put any blind in front of me, but I might be far enough back." So he stayed back and leaned against the back of that little dugout. All of a sudden the singing got louder and louder and here it was some wild chickens. At that time in the Black Hills there used to be wild chickens. It was a rooster with about ten to twelve hens and he was herding them to the spring. Every once in a while he would turn his neck a little and make a sound and his head would shake, his comb would quiver, and he would make this sound. The warrior felt good, so he put his head back and closed his eyes and lay there while the chickens were all around the stream. As he lay there, every so often, when the rooster crowed, it started to sound like a song, so he lay there and listened.

The song had words in it, Lakota words. He listened to that song as he lay there and pretty soon he started singing what the rooster sang. Then he really got interested in that song, so he started to learn the sound and the melody. So he himself was singing, lying there singing while that rooster was every so often making his sound. He rounded up his hens and would go so far and then he'd arch his neck. The warrior, too, would arch his neck and he would start the song. He sang and as he looked down his body, his skin was healthy again and he was back to the natural, healthy way he used to be. He was dressed in the *tokala* warrior society costume that he used to wear. He lay there but he kept singing all day. As he would go down to get water, he would keep singing. He stayed there all day and all night and on the next morning he went down again singing and washed and drank some water. What few things he had, he ate, and was lying there when all of a sudden he heard that singing again. Sure enough, that guy was coming down the valley singing that same song. Now it sounded like a man singing that song. So he started singing it with him. Whoever was singing that song got close and came into view, and here it was that rooster again.

Now that his skin was better and he was feeling better, he prepared himself and started walking towards his village. He kept on walking and when he got back, he went to the *tipi iyokiye* (council lodge) and talked to the elders. He said, "I went to the Black Mountains to die, but I heard this rooster sing this song. By learning this song I got well, so I brought it back and I want to sing this song to my people." So the *eyapaha* (camp crier) went around and announced that at a certain time this man—he used his Indian name—was going to sing a special song. He went to his parents' place and got his best out and put it on the way he had seen himself in his dream. He went out to the center and all the people came and sat around. The *eyapaha* now announced how he got well and how he learned this song from that rooster.

That was the first song that was openly sung to the people. After that, traditional singers all put their neck sideways in a certain rooster way and they would *iyaki s'as'a* (give a high-pitched yelp), crowing like a rooster as they'd start a song. It was done in honor of that rooster who sang the first special song in the Black Hills.

Some of the elderly men that have died since also talked about the Black Hills as the center of the universe. They were born, raised, and became adventuresome, nomadic warriors. They would always go from here to the next highest point and then go on to the next highest point they could see. They would go on to see what's on the other side of that next point and keep going till they ended up someplace in a strange land and see the enemy and different animals. But they would always return to the Black Hills. There was always a center of the universe for them to return to. Many of our famous medicine men would go to Bear Butte or Harney Peak to seek their visions or dreams or their medicines. Even the movement of camps of the Lakota people always remained close, within eye vision from the Black Hills as much as possible, so they would always use them as a landscape they could identify. They could always find their way back to the He Sapa, the Black Mountains.

Lakota Public Speaking

As we keep on talking about these things, I'll have some more stories from our oral tradition to tell, but right now I'd like to talk a little bit about the role of public speaking in our tradition. I think that Lakotas are good at oratory. There are four parts to a good speaker's skills. First is the ability to speak with a strong voice and change his volume at each given point to suit the point he wants to get across. The next is the ability to blend humor in so he can have a little smile or nod of the head back from the people in the audience which, in our way, means they agree. The third is to have the knowledge of different areas or different topics that he talks about. For example, does he really know the history of treaties and federal policy, or is he really familiar with ceremonies and spiritual issues, or can he really explain why a particular song should be sung for a fallen warrior or when a horse is given away during a celebration? The fourth area is what I would call his public image. Many of our gifted speakers can really use their body language. They might have a special way of getting up to speak. Sometimes they might go way out in the center and talk; other times they just stand or walk along on the side and talk. Some use their hands for emphasis and others walk or stand with their hands in their pockets. I had a grandfather, when he would talk and especially when he wanted to get after people over something, he would put his hand behind his back, walk back and forth, and talk real loud. The way a speaker dresses is also an important part of his image. A lot of Sioux speakers wear dark glasses, and somehow these speakers know that colors affect people, so they wear bright red shirts, or yellow or even all-black shirts because they want to transmit a certain mood as they speak.

These good speakers are also known for their ability to use language, both in Lakota and English. They have a way of demanding our attention by the way they use words. Sometimes, when they serve as *eyapahas* (announcers), the person they're announcing for might briefly explain to them what they should say, and then these announcers can build that into a ten-minute speech on the subject which satisfies everybody and is effectivly expressed and entertaining as well. You know that in this way the *eyapaha* can praise the person or family he is speaking for. Out of modesty and humility they can't brag themselves up, but someone else, especially a respected speaker, can. This even applies today to Lakota election campaigns, where a traditional candidate really doesn't feel right about saying all kinds of wonderful things about himself, but an announcer sure can. *Eyapahas* even have a way of bossing people around a little at public gatherings without anybody getting angry.

I think announcers are unique and gifted persons. They are good historians of local history, good at oratory, good storytellers. They must know all the songs and dances so when they get up on the microphone, they have it all, the whole powwow schedule, worked out so it falls in place as they go. The announcer has to be quick-minded so if anything comes up, he'll come up with a way to put on that ceremony or fit in that special song in such a way that the family involved will feel proud and appreciate what happened. Our good speakers can also relate to different kinds of audiences. There might be a half *iyeska* (mixed-blood) and half full-blood audience or all of one kind or the other. Good speakers can adjust and talk differently to each one, including an all non-Indian audience. They can evaluate the mood and the attitude of the people in front of them.

I've noticed that when an old-time speaker steps forward to talk, he often follows a pattern. He usually starts with some kind of greeting like *"Ho mitakuyepi!"* (Greetings my relatives!) *"Le anpetu ki cante wasteya napeciuza pelo."* (On this day I shake your hands with a happy heart.) Then he introduces himself, both his census name and his ceremonial Indian name, and sometimes with another band he mentions his home community or band. Next he will tell a couple of humorous stories about someone in the audience— preferably a brother-in-law. Then he might go way back in history about something or tell a story that's only vaguely related to the subject. After a while he might say a few words, or even many, about the subject on the floor. Then he follows with a couple of humorous stories again, verbally shakes our hand and thanks us for listening, and then ends with a closing, either *"Ho hecetu!"* which means sort of "So be it!" or the more ceremonial *"Mitakuye oyasin!"* (All my relations!), which emphasizes our humble human relationship to all living things. The audience usually reacts to that last phrase with *"Hau!"* as a way of agreeing—at least with this closing.

Most of our traditional speakers were men. It used to be that a man talked for the family and talked for his community; a man would get up and talk for his child. But somewhere along the line the rules changed. There are often women speaking now. Some of them are very effective, too. It used to be that women were storytellers in the home, and as singers they would play mostly a supporting role for the men singers, but today women are taking on a public role and speaking out.

It's also important to recognize that the older you are, the more accepted you will be as a speaker by the people. As a speaker you're supposed to be a wise elder and have a wide variety of topics you can deal with. The elders have the wisdom to get up and have people listen to them. A traditional Lakota man would prepare himself a lifetime to get those skills and be able to use them. Too many times with formal education you get a twelfth-grade diploma or a college degree and then you automatically become an instant expert without really having a full knowledge of things. In my case, I've only been asked to pray or announce at giveaways and powwows or speak to gatherings these last few years. I began when I was around fifty-two years old. Now I'm often asked to talk at birthday dinners or at memorials for a loved one, or to be the *eyapaha* at powwows. In traditional Lakota education you have to wait patiently till you become the most respected in an area, the best at something over a long period of time: the best announcer, the best bronc rider, the best dancer, the best singer. Then you can speak with authority and people will listen.

I've tried to give you a few examples of how our stories and other oral traditions help keep the meaning of things alive. Of course, there are many more stories, songs, jokes, prayers, and speeches told among our people. I'll share some more of them as we keep talking, because, in a way, you can't separate them from any subject we'll be discussing. It's like they're the skeleton of everything.

PART THREE

The Singing Rooster
in the Black Hills

You CAN tell from what we talked about above—the importance of names and of oral tradition in Lakota life—that song as well as dance was always involved. Song and dance can't really be separated. Even though I'll talk about one or the other, they're always connected. We never dance without singing and we rarely sing without dancing. The involvement of the whole body is to us part of the balance we look for in our lives. The body and the voice are there along with the mind and the heart. We use our bodies to have fun, to pay respect to others, to pray to the Great Mystery. Our voices are a gift also that should be used to send our wishes, our feelings, and our prayers. When we use our bodies and our voice in the right way, we can express ourselves and make ourselves as well as others feel good. Like anything else, if you have a special talent, you have to make sacrifices and discipline yourself, but if your mind and heart are in harmony with your voice and body, the good red road lies at your feet.

The day I could sit down at the drum and throw my voice out in the pitch, tune, rhythm, and the words of a song, and I could see people getting up to dance, some women getting their shawls and some guys tightening their belts and fixing their porcupine head roaches and then moving out to dance, it changed me. I never thought I had that gift to make even fifty people dance at a small powwow, or twelve hundred people at a big pow-wow, or to have three hundred people crowd around my drum to record my song. That really changed me, my whole way of life. I came out of my shell. A lot of those guys I grew up with thought I was quiet and shy. But singing brought me out into the public with more and more confidence. I began to look at myself and cut down on the thoughtless side of my life.

I think that can happen to anybody. You just have to want to apply yourself and dedicate your life to something special. Whether it's running sweat lodges or Sun Dancing, there are special hardships that you'll have to put up with, but the people, after a while, will know you for that. I think first you have to earn that respect and honor. But it will have meaning and give you a positive direction. Also, anytime you dedicate yourself to something, there will be criticism; you have to expect that, but I think the right term for it is "not understanding." Over the years I've heard people criticize me at times, the songs I made, the songs I sang at Sun Dances or powwows, but nevertheless, when I realized I could throw my voice out there and make people dance, I changed.

As part of my dedication to this, before I sing a song, I always try to find out the history and meaning, where that song came from, why they sang it, and the proper rhythm, tune, pitch, and words to it. Then I can sing these songs properly and feel good because of that. I also know that most people sit around a dancing arena, maybe one thousand or two thousand people, to feel good as they listen or dance. But sadly, many of them also go there to criticize. It's really true! They go there to find something wrong: a dancer didn't dress right, or she didn't dance correctly but won anyway, or the committee didn't do this right, or the announcer didn't explain that song properly. But I think, in a way, if you learn to understand criticism, then you know how to deal with it. You can deal with it next time and it will have positive consequences. I'll push that song up a little higher next time I start it, sing it a little slower, pronounce the words more clearly, maybe hit the drum more softly. Sometimes I think about it because you can always learn from it. Other times, when it comes from certain families, it doesn't bother me because I know they don't understand it. There's always good in bad, but if you take it to heart negatively, you can get hurt by it. If you learn how to understand it, you grow as a person. If I didn't live the life I learned from my grandmother and my father or if I didn't hang onto my family traditions, or didn't understand criticism or myself, then at every powwow I'd be fighting somebody or I'd be drunk and make fun of other people. Maybe then I'd slide over to the dark circle. When you are a dancer or a singer, you learn to cope with problems by falling back on traditional Lakota skills.

The traditional Lakota word for a singer is *hoka wicasa*. The original term for it is a little longer, *hokaka wicasa* (a man who can rattle his voice), because a man who has dedicated his life to singing has practiced and developed his throat so that he can "rattle his voice" to any kind of song. Maybe the idea of a mastersinger would be a good translation. He's a *wayupika*, the best. Someone who merely sings along would be a *lowan wicasa* (man singer). I'll get back to this later.

The four important parts of Lakota singing are the pitch, tune, rhythm, and words. Traditionally, the *hoka wicasa* would tilt his head sideways a little bit—remember the rooster in the Black Hills—or arch his neck a little bit, and start the beginning of a song, which is the highest part, with *iyakis'a,* a high-pitched yelp. With his voice he creates the volume and at the same time pronounces the words in the song. If it is a prayer song, God will hear his clear words and answer his prayer. If it is a song for warriors or dancers, they will hear those words plainly and they'll feel proud or motivated, go through the motions of what they did in battle and dance with enjoyment. If it's an honor song, then they'll hear the words carried by the melody plainly and feel proud that a son, daughter, mother, father, or whole family is being honored. So this *hoka wicasa* plays an important role in the community and has special status.

People go through the traditional steps of Lakota education from their birth. If his father is a singer, he will hold the baby against his chest or have him on his knee or have him sit by him as he sings to implant in that baby the rhythm, pitch, and tune while he's young. These will be stored inside of that young boy so that later on, when he wants to be a singer, he will already have some background in singing. We call this family tradition. Still today it is an honored and proud tradition to be from a singing family within a tribe or *wicoti* (camp). The grandfathers or fathers would talk to their sons or their grandsons and say, "If you want to be a singer, you've got to learn this song." In the same way, if a woman is a good singer, she will encourage and pass on her gift to her daughter or granddaughter. This is why very early in the morning grandfathers would be singing a song; this is why fathers would be singing songs in the evening, take out their hand drums and start singing. Constantly there is singing in the family.

Just like for an opera singer there's a need to get feeling across to the people looking on, it's similar for the traditional *hoka wicasa.* He is there to satisfy the need of a family with his drum and drumstick, his facial expression, and the tone of his voice with which he puts that song across. If it's a happy-feeling song, he puts gladness to it. If there is sadness or mourning in the family, he'll sing it so there is sadness in it. And once you start, your throat—its muscles and nerves—and your mind have to be trained constantly by singing. I think of two of my grandfathers. I used to hear them every time they would go someplace; right away they'd start tapping a chair or box or the wall and there would be a sound like a soft whistling or they'd actually be singing a song softly to themselves. Even after they got to be very old men, they were still there tapping, whistling, and singing. We used to want to sit beside them at church, at Christmas, Easter, or any Sunday, because here the preacher would be preaching up there: "It's devil worship to dance and sing Indian, and you have to be a Christian in order to get to heaven, and so many Indian things are sinful, and you have to watch how you live and save yourself from the eternal fire!" He would point fingers at people and say, "Don't be sinners! Those Lakota dances and songs are for the devil!" All of a sudden Grandpa would start tapping the pew seat and be whistling a song. He used to make us kids laugh because singing was always so much a part of his life.

My dad got to talking about singing one day long ago. In Lakota singing, he said, a man sometimes hears something through a dream or in the sound of a bird or the sound of the wind. If he sits there and listens, then he might hear a song. He can make a song from this. When it has no words, just vocables, he said, they call it *olowan* (song). This *olowan* will have the first three, the pitch, tune, and rhythm, but no words, just melody. They might dance to it, or it might be a personal song he sings to himself when he's feeling bad. Once you put Lakota words into that song and you sing for somebody or about somebody by name, their Indian ceremonial name, then it's called *alowan,* with an *a.* The *alowan* plays a very important part in every category of Lakota music, whether it's sacred songs, society songs, chief songs, veterans' songs, birthday songs, or whatever. An *alowan* is dedicated to or about somebody and sometimes it is even adjusted to fit that individual.

I've come up with a classification of the Lakota man singer. The first one is the individual singer who can get up and sing a birthday song, a memorial song, or a love song. He has a real nice tone to his voice and a pleasant pitch but he is just that individual kind of singer. You put him in a drum group and he cannot sing because he's not loud enough. Then the second kind of singer is what I call part-time singers who sing once in a while just for the fun of it, just for one powwow. They get themselves ready and practice a little to be ready for the one powwow. They might really sing well and even make a song, but it's just for that one time, temporary. Then we have the third kind of singer, who is just a follower, doesn't sing loud or anything but sits with the group around the drum. He has a drumstick and hits the drum with the other singers, but he can't start a song and you can't hear him sing; he barely contributes. Some just want to be part of the group to share in the giveaway money donated to the group or to be seen as a part of that drum group. I call them drummers. The fourth group, the ones I referred to as *lowan wicasa* above, are called singers. They follow, they can sing loud, they sing well, but they can't start songs and they don't know that much about the songs. They follow the lead singer or support the two or three main singers around the drum.

Then the fifth category is the very unique singer I referred to as *hoka wicasa* above. He's the guy that can start any song by himself; he can get up and explain a song; he knows which song belongs to which family and, often, who composed it. He knows the history and meaning of songs. He has the unique gift of knowing how exactly to sing each song in the best way to bring out its pitch, rhythm, tune, and words to catch people's responses and to motivate them. We have lots of singers but very few *hoka wicasa*.

Singers can also be classified by the special kind of singing they can do. One is a man that spends all his time just remembering and singing old-time *tokala* (Kit Fox Society) songs, chief songs, or Brave Heart warrior society songs. That's all he sings. I call them traditional singers. They're older and all they do is sing old warrior-era songs. A second one is the Sun Dance singer, a guy who sings those songs from the first Morning Star song clear to the end of the Sun Dance. He'll sing these various songs in special order over and over until he gets them down pat. That's his specialty. We have one like that—John Around Him, Jr. A third kind is the ceremonial singer. A medicine man might have a singer or two with little hand drums who know the songs he needs at his ceremonies. So that's all they practice for their father's or grandfather's ceremonies. I can think of Everett Lone Hill, whose specialty was to sing for his grandfather Frank Fools Crow's ceremonies. We also have social dance singers, guys who just spend their time singing those different social-type songs where men and women dance together as partners or in a circle to the left.

Next we have powwow singers who are gifted with full and strong voices because they can throw their voices out so as many as eight hundred or a thousand dancers can dance to them. Yet this powwow singer, if you ask him to sing a ceremonial song or a Sun Dance song, often can't do that. Finally, we come again to those rare gifted, unique ones, the ones who can do it all, the *hoka wicasa*, the mastersingers.

The mind of such a *hoka wicasa* is very unique. It is almost a big song library that he has there. He has to know the meaning of the words, what song belongs to what family and how to put it together, how to get in front of people with that drum, be able to open his mouth wide in front of many people, look people in the eye and start a song. And that's very difficult.

One of the guys that I feel is very respected today in that way is Matthew Two Bulls from Oglala. No matter where you go, Montana, North Dakota, even around here, whether it's a powwow or just a small gathering of people for various occasions, people always say, "Matthew Two Bulls, come out to the center! You're a *hoka wicasa,* so we ask you to sing this song." He'll get up and start a song that will fit that place and time and that situation. There are lots of good singers around but they're not gifted like him. Everybody looks up to him with respect and honor. One of the special things about him is that his wife, Nellie, accompanies him.

She is also very gifted as a *wicaglata* (woman singer) who sings behind a man. Matt sets the rhythm and pitch of the song and Nellie comes in an octave higher to blend her voice. She herself remembers many of these songs and often sings one to Matthew to remind him. She also often sings a song by herself and has a wonderful voice that's hard to describe, so clear, high, and full of emotion. No matter where they go, it's always "Matt and Nellie." They are honored by the people and given gifts on many occasions just for being present at some doings. They are the only two around who can do that. Who's going to be the next man and wife to sing like that together?

Music is at the center of Lakota life in the old days and since the reservation days started. No matter what you do, whether it's a man singing to himself because he's a brave warrior, or because he is feeling bad, or is singing to himself because he wants to identify more closely with God, anything you do in your band or community requires singing. Music helped Lakota people survive a great deal of hardship and endure lots of pain because there was a song there. We've proved that in World War I, Korea, Vietnam, Wounded Knee II, and in prisons. Songs give you a lift in life: you sing a song to yourself, or somebody sings an *alowan,* a special song, and you can go on. Singing gives you a chance to feel good, to be healed from sickness. I think this is why long ago we didn't need psychiatrists to come and put us on the buffalo robe in a tipi and counsel us for so many hours for ten head of horses.

Singing gives you an identity. So many of our singers today are younger men and even boys for that reason. It gives them pride. Even when a guy gets drunk and sings, he's singing a song to express himself. I think the act of singing gives us a positive identity. You don't need psychiatrists. Maybe that rooster in the Black Hills brought a good message.

It helps to understand singers when you look at their paraphernalia and how it's used. First is a hat. A long time ago, my uncle Henry Young Bear, Irving, and other guys, when we went around the region singing, we always wore a western hat. Back in the 1950s and '60s, I remember my uncle Henry at New Year's or Sun Dance time would buy a felt or straw hat. He'd shape it carefully and would then put a red plume on the side. It took me a while to understand why. One time I asked him why he always wore a red plume; why not white or blue? He said: "My oldest sister, Young Bear blood, was shot and killed at the Wounded Knee Massacre while she was just a baby. Since her blood was spilled there in the snow, when I go out in a crowd I put this red plume on to honor my sister and remember."

A hat played a very important part in the traditional singer's life. He wore a felt hat, or a straw hat in summer, and shaped it all different ways. There were many different fashions in shaping one just right. They would put different shiny pins on it or tie feathers to it. Since the middle 1970s some young guys started wearing beaded baseball caps or feed-and-seed caps, or whatever you call them. But the older traditional singers still wear hats. Even in North Dakota the older singers still wear hats. Most of the Porcupine Singers still wear hats.

Then it's important to have sunglasses. They're important in a singer's ways because to sit with your mouth open and sing hard, to have people around with recorders and lady singers that come around, makes it hard to always look people in the eye. It sort of preserves our privacy and we can concentrate. Of course, we can also stare at the nice-looking women without being too obvious. All the older singers used to wear dark glasses. Talking to some older singers, I once asked, "Why do you guys always wear dark glasses?" One joked, "Well, I like to look at the younger girls, but because my wife is here I have to wear dark glasses." The younger guys often talk about "fashion statement," but I think that's just a new term for an old custom.

The third item all singers pay close attention to is the way they dress. Traditionally a singer would often buy a new shirt just for that powwow, red, yellow, turquoise, or something else bright to show that he's a singer. Some wore scarves and some wear beaded medallion necklaces. In the 1970s decorated vests with "Rocky Boy Singers" or "Porcupine Singers" printed on the back came in, and in the 1980s shiny jackets with "Badland Singers" or "Eagle Whistle Singers" on the back became popular. Now we also see belt buckles, medallions, vests, jackets to identify who we are as singers. In the 1970s and '80s ribbon shirts were popular in this area. These shirts are homemade out of calico or satin with ribbons sewn along the chest, sleeve, and cuffs and with no collars. Oklahoma tribes have been wearing these since the early 1900s, I think. But now younger singers often just wear t-shirts with designs. So clothes for singers are still changing today.

The next necessary item is cowboy boots. When you go to a powwow, you see so many guys with boots it looks like an RCA (Rodeo Cowboy Association) convention or something. Boots were part of the singer's official regalia, so that guys used to buy new boots for Bismarck Powwow, for example, and stand around in a new pair of boots as a bona fide singer. But now even the boots are going out. Now I see singers with tennis shoes, Nikes, and all kinds of flashy shoelaces. Some guys are even wearing shorts or sweat pants and tank tops to sing at a drum. So now the way a singer identifies himself through his clothes is changing.

You can always tell by a singer's drumstick if he is a respected singer. His drumstick is always nice and neat, and when he goes to Rosebud Fair or to Oglala Nation Powwow, he makes sure he gets a new one. He might even carry one with a leather head and another with a softer sheepskin head. You can tell the kind of singer by the way he takes care of his drumstick; after all, that's his main equipment. The average singer doesn't care if his drumstick is all beat up and looks like it has the mange, if the sheepskin is all chewed up or has different-color tape here and there. But the serious and dedicated singers take pride in their drumstick.

Still another sign of the singer is the drum and how the members of the singing group take care of the drum, whether it's a traditional hide drum or a bass drum. Lots of singers now have the name of their group painted on their drum: Pass Creek Singers, Red Scaffold Singers, or Porcupine Singers. Again, you can tell how sincere those singers are by their drum. Some even honor their drum after a while and treat it as if it were a person. Take our Porcupine Singers, for example. We named our drum Oyate Ho Nah'umpi (The People Hear Its Voice) in a drum ceremony in 1974 because that drum brought honor and respect to those singers that sit around the Porcupine drum. We also set some rules: We put tobacco on the drum before we start singing and we pray briefly when we make that offering. We never put food or coffee on it; anyone who has been drinking must stay away from the drum; we sing a special drum song as the first song at any gathering; and we conduct ourselves in a respectable way when we set that drum in the center of our circle. Whether it's a powwow, a Sun Dance, or a dancing contest, we treat that drum with respect.

The drum, as far back as I know, has always played a big part in public events. We have three different drums that we use. The first is the rawhide drum, usually deerhide. It is homemade, with a round wood frame. These drums are used mostly for ceremonies today. Also, some families request that you sing at their gathering but that you bring your traditional rawhide drum. Since you can't control the pitch of these drums except with heat, they are today used mostly only at ceremonies and Sun Dances. Some singing groups like Howard Bad Hand's Red Leaf Takoja Singers (Red Leaf Grandsons) prefer the hide drum on a regular basis for all their singing.

The second kind of drum is the commercial bass drum. Some singers have always liked using them because you can control the pitch with the turn keys on them. The bass drum became really popular around 1960 when Cook Brothers Singers from Red Scaffold on the Cheyenne River Reservation came around this area. They used long sheepskin drumsticks and a bass drum. While the rawhide drum has a sort of flat, solid rhythm with not too much bounce to it, the bass drum has a bouncy one to it. Since the Cook Brothers' singing became real popular in the early sixties, everybody hit the secondhand stores and talked to high school bands to try to buy a bass drum. The tone of your voices and the tone of the drum has to match up, and a bass drum, if you replaced the plastic hide with a deerhide, could be adjusted to do that at any time.

The third type is the hand drum, which was usually used at traditional social dances and some ceremonies. A long time ago, at social dances, four or five guys with hand drums would sit against the wall and sing keeping the same rhythm on their drums. Sometimes they would ask them to stand in single file in the center of the hall or wherever the dance was being held, and everybody could dance around them because they didn't take up that much room. In addition, the hand drum was always important for individual singing.

One of the things my dad used to talk about was that a long time ago the Lakota people never had psychiatrists, they never had mind problems or social problems, because every tipi or home always had a hand drum in it and somebody in the family was always singing. He would always get that drum and would sing songs in the evening, or in the morning he would sing. That kept singing in the family. Happy feelings, sad feelings, or whatever feelings that family was going through would have songs that fit the mood. But if you look at that today, that's changed also. The hand drum is no longer hanging on the wall above the head of the father or grandfather or the singer in the family.

It seems like the radio has replaced the drum in our houses. Some of the words in country and western music, or whatever you listen to, get you in the mood; you're sad, lonely, or brokenhearted, or you get lovey-dovey, or you remember an old girlfriend. Maybe in that way the radio music takes the edge off the problems since we don't have the father or uncle singing traditional songs in the family anymore. Now that we have KILI Radio, an Indian radio station in Porcupine, I think especially a lot of older people are revived by it, and if you go to their homes they always have KILI turned on. It plays lots of traditional Indian music and, in a way, I think we've brought back some of the identity for some of these older people, and even for many of the younger ones. The drum on the wall has been replaced by the radio on the dresser.

I think way back a drum was a sound *bu'uta* (hitting the drum). They would strike it to send messages throughout camp. If there was going to be a *tokala* warrior society dance, they'd hit it in a certain way. If it was another type of event, they'd hit it in a certain other way. Sometimes they'd hit it close to the ground by the ankle for a certain kind of vibration; sometimes they'd hit it up high for that sound to get out and echo. The sound of the drum would add a loud sound that accompanied your voice to give it strength and power, or for the Great Spirit to hear your songs beyond your own limits.

Old people said the drum was the heartbeat of *unci* (grandmother) earth, the sound vibrating in the earth. The word for drum is *cancega*, or wooden bucket. It was made of cottonwood and there was usually only one person in that band or *tiyospaye* (extended family) gifted in the making of drums. It was he who would go to mark a cottonwood tree and at a certain time of the year would cut it down and cut out a certain section for the drum rim. He would then thin it out to the right thickness. He'd then select the right part of the hide to get the same thickness throughout the drumhead. If the head was going to be of buffalo hide, the rim would be thick; if elk, thinner; and if deer, still thinner yet. He would put the raw hide on it and then, in his own way of tightening the hide, get the right tone from it. That was based on his dream and his gift.

What you make the sound with is the *icabu* (drumstick). We have four different types going way back. For the traditional ceremonies, they'd take a plum or wild cherry or ash stick and heat it over a fire until it dries out and tightens. For some of these ceremonies a flat buffalo hide served as a drum and this stick would make a flapping sound on it. Later on they sewed leather in the form of a small pouch on the end. Some of these old-time singers used to wrap copper wire and cover it with strips of inner tube, wrap it with cloth, and then cover it with this pouch. Sometimes they bought brand-new leather gloves and cut the thumbs off it for the drumstick head. Later on, the old Bull Durham tobacco sacks came in. Sometimes they'd stuff cotton in it for a little softer beat. In the 1960s sheepskin heads came in. Now today we prefer fiberglass sticks or fishing pole sticks because they last longer.

My brother-in-law George Squirrel Coat makes my drumsticks and for those singers at our drum. I like to balance my drumstick evenly so that my arm won't get tired over those long periods of singing. The handle and the head parts will be in balance so I can sing for hours. It's up to the singer. Some singers use lighter or shorter drumsticks; some use sheepskin and some use leather heads on their sticks. I always carry one of each with me.

There are certain ways to hit the drum, whether it's a hand-held drum for one singer or a big drum for a group of singers. When you strike it on its edge, it gives off a higher, less full sound and as you move into the middle the fullness of the sound increases and it rings more. Hitting the exact middle keeps it from vibrating.

There used to be honored drumkeepers in a *wicoti* (camp) who would *bu'uta* (sound the drum) in different ways, so that the people in that camp knew right away what kind of dance or ceremony was being announced. Also, like I said, the sound of the drum goes beyond our physical being so the Great Spirit can hear it. Still today, the drum plays an important role in our ceremonies, our Sun Dances, and even our powwows. I think young singers should learn how to treat their drums respectfully and treat their drums according to what their drum is to be used for.

I know of one drum that has developed in a special way. Back in 1963 I bought a bass drum from George Whirlwind Soldier from Rosebud for five dollars. My uncle Dick Elk Boy then put a new deerhide on it. The singing group known as Porcupine Singers traveled with that drum for many years all over the country. That drum received many honors over the years. As I said above, back in 1974 the drum received its own name at Ring Thunder Wacipi Days Powwow. Four respected singers, Dave Clairmont, Ben Black Bear, Matthew Two Bulls, and Cecil Spotted Elk, gave it the name Oyate Ho Nah'umpi (The People Hear Its Voice). They hit the drum four times and then sang four different types of songs on it while out in the center of the dance shade to give it the proper breaking in. That name made the drum a person and over the years it was given a war bonnet, a sacred pipe, and an eagle-feather staff by way of recognition. Every celebration we went to we would write that on the drum: "Mandaree Powwow June 1976," "Fort Totten Powwow July 1978," "Minneapolis AIM Powwow 1975"; you could read all over the drumhead where we had sung over the years. As one place and date faded away through use, we wrote in a fresh one.

Old people and young people have come to touch the drum to share its energy over the years; dancers have thrown money on it in appreciation for the music it helped to make. I think that drum also took care of the singers who sat around it in a respectful way. Many years later, when our drum group started to have some difficulties, which I'll explain below, one day, for no reason at all except political jealousy, someone stole the drum and we never saw it again. Maybe it was meant to be that way. We didn't know who took it; it just disappeared from my house. Months later, one day a woman in my community drove up to the house and after some heavy sighs told me that she found out that her son had taken that drum and burned it in a fit of jealousy. She felt very sorry and didn't know how to tell us but knew she had to. We thanked her for telling us and said we had no hard feelings. We would have to go on. We got a new drum and began a slightly different tradition with it, but it wasn't quite the same; we missed Oyate Ho Nah'umpi.

Lastly, you identify a singing group by its PA system. Of course, we didn't use PA systems in the old days. Singers started using them in the early 1960s. Two loudspeaker horns with an amplifier and one mike was typical. For the next twenty years everybody sang into the mike sticking out over the center of the drum. Drum groups often painted the name of their group on the horns. Now we've come into a different era where we see box speakers, big sound systems with equalizers and two amplifiers, three microphones, and a technician sitting at the controls while the singers are singing. But you can still spot the older traditional singers bacause they stay with their one mike and amplifier and their two horns.

When you go to visit a singer at home, he might act kind of casual and laid back, he might have on a t-shirt and tennis shoes and not look out of the ordinary. But once there's a powwow or the announcer's voice says, "It's grand entry time!" you'll see him walk in with his drum and you won't even know that's him all decked out with hat or beaded cap, sunglasses, and a bright shirt, a little fancy, but he knows he's a singer and the people recognize him for it.

Making Songs

Another important part of singing in our tradition is making up songs. It takes many years of singing or a long tradition of singing in the family. Sometimes you just hear a melody on the wind or in your memory, or an emotion causes you to start humming, or you're looking at clouds or some hills and a pattern in them gives you a melody. The words, by comparison, are provided by something that's already happened or is going to happen that you're aware of in advance. In both cases you know that you won't have that many lines to say something because most of our Lakota songs are short. So you have to try first to cut the expression down to just a couple of lines, but those words still have to tell a story of some kind. Making up a song for yourself to use at a powwow or for a social dance is different from when some family comes up to you and asks you to make a song for their son or daughter for next summer and then explains the occasion. I might ask about a couple of things related to it so I have the necessary information, and I ask what the ceremonial Indian name is that I will be using in that song. Then I usually create a new melody or use one I've made up before and haven't used yet. If it has the right tempo, spirit, and emotion, then I begin to put in the words: sometimes words of encouragement, sometimes sad words to make family members cry but at the same time help them to wipe their tears, sometimes strong words to praise someone or give thanks to them for their courage or generosity or for being a leader, sometimes romantic courtship words for a rabbit song for couples or a round dance, and sometimes even sassy or humorous words. It all depends on the occasion.

When you make a song, unless it's just a powwow song for dancing with no words in it, then you have to tell a story. You have to tell a story about the person you're dedicating it to. Maybe it's about a veteran and how he was wounded in battle or that he was killed overseas, or how he came home after hardships. You select some words that capture the heart of the story of the person you're singing about or for. For example, a few years ago my adopted mother, Nellie Menard, came up to the drum, gave me some words that were composed for her, and asked me to put a melody to it for later on in the day. So, at the drum between other songs, I started humming a melody and fitting the words to it in a rhythmic way so that everything blended together. Then I would keep singing it till I was familiar with it and it stayed in my mind. Today sometimes, of course, once we think it's ready, we record it on tape so we don't lose it. That was always my way of making an honor song.

It's funny that these last few years some of the younger singers are making songs with words in them that don't tell a story of any kind. Francis Menard, who passed away a couple of years ago, and some of the other older singer used to get mad and say, "Those are not songs!" "Those are not songs!" he used to say. Some of these songs would just say, "Mani, mani, mani" (Walk,

walk, walk) or "Waci pelo" (Dance) over and over again. Now, in the real traditional songs these words might often appear, like the word "walk" showed
up in warrior songs because the warrior was walking among the enemy, or
his comrades were walking with him, carrying him, out of the battle, but
these words were part of a longer text that told that story in shorthand form.
Now they make these songs with a couple of Lakota words in them but
no real meaning. They might have a good rhythm and nice melody but the
meaning isn't there. Maybe today's way of honoring people is less personal,
just putting some words together.

It's a unique gift that after a family asks you to make a song, you can sit
down at a drum, or while you're riding along someplace or just spending the
evening under the pine shade in back of your house—with a gift from the
Great Spirit you have the abilty to put a song together and fulfill that family's
request. I had that happen to me a few times over the last few years. I'm not
real gifted at making songs, but I had occasions of putting songs together
on request, and sometimes even on short notice, to fulfill someone's request
for an honor song or a memorial song or a graduation song. As Porcupine
Singers, we've made lots of songs over the years. We've had three or four
members in the group who've made songs. Sure, some of our singers have
claimed to make some songs but it's open to question. Some of these songs
might be very old and someone takes one and changes it a little and then
claims that this is a new song, but sometimes it's doubtful.

When you honor somebody with a song, you make a song for dancers
to dance to. You should then give it as a gift to those dancers and to other
singers so that they, too, can sing it. When someone else sings it, you should
be glad and honored that they like your song enough to sing it, and not say,
"Hey, that's my song and you can't sing it, because I made it and I gave it
to that person or that family." I like it when a song maker hears one of his
songs sung by somebody else and donates some money to them and says,
"I'm happy this group sang one of my songs and want to thank them with
this monetary gift." I've heard in some places that I've gone that certain
singers claim certain songs and don't like to have others sing them, but I
think the traditional belief is that once you make something, you give it to
people—as long as it's not a personal sacred song or a restricted one because
it's someone's family song. But then even you as the composer should only
sing it for that family or when the proper time arrives.

The Bad Hand family, my brother-in-laws from Red Leaf Community
on the Rosebud Reservation, are really gifted in putting songs together.

One of their songs is a little humorous. My brother-in-law Willie Bad Hand was on a big party tear one time and went all around Rosebud asking for money so he could buy another jug to get over his hangover, but everyplace he went, they turned him down. Everybody—the tribal chairman, the BIA superintendent, councilmen, and his own relatives—they all said no to him. So he started up the hill towards Saint Fancis. He was walking up the hill just shaking his head, and with his hangover he was kind of sick and said, "No, everyplace I went, they said no to me, no, no, no!" and as he talked to himself like that, a song came to him and later on that dancing song was called "No, a Thousand Times No." The choppy rhythm of the song reminds you of these words. It became really popular that summer; every powwow we went to, that song was sung by some group.

That Bad Hand family tradition of making all kinds of songs is being carried on by one of their sons, Howard Bad Hand, and some of his brothers who compose lots of good songs.

I would like to stop talking now for a while and let my *tahansi* (cousin) Irving Tail say a few things about how he makes songs. He's made many of them over the years.

IRVING TAIL: Well, Ronnie, sometimes when you're by yourself, you're in your room or you're traveling, the melody might possibly come to you first. Then, after you get the melody sort of lined out so it's new and appealing, then you add the words to it. That's how I make my songs. It takes quite a bit of time, sometimes three or four weeks. You know, now that we have tape recorders, we can tape it to remember it and then pass the tape around to the other singers so they can listen to it and learn it before we try it out in public. Then we'll practice it together before we sing it for the dancers. People can usually recognize a new song and are eager to both listen and record it.

The melody is important to a singer because a lot of people don't care about the words. When there's hundreds of dancers making noise in that arena, you can't hear the words too clear anyway; dancers from other tribes and some of our own people don't talk our Lakota language either. Sure, we try to keep the drum down to let the words come across, but once we pick up the beat louder and faster, the words aren't as important as the melody and its rhythm. Like with much white music, they like the melody first. So that's what we try to do, what I try to do anyway. I'm not making that song for me; I'm trying to make that sound for the people and for the dancers—

to make that sound good, you know. Ever since I started singing many years ago, I'm still learning. I've sung many years with my *tahansi* Severt, and we both make songs. We usually get together and we listen to each other's songs and if something needs changing, then we go ahead. You know, there's no man who's got knowledge of everything. So we get together to make songs; we love to get together. But I've been lucky and I made some songs a while back that became popular and are still sung a lot. I know how we sing, so I don't try to make the songs too difficult, with a lot of steps and jumping around. I try to make a song smooth and easy to sing, understandable and easy to sing. That's the whole thing.

Severt asked me to come back again later to talk about some special songs and record some of them, but now I'll let him go on with the history of our singing and the history of Porcupine Singers.

The History of Lakota Song and Dance

Each village used to have a *hoka itancan* (head singer). Then there was also a *cancega wanka* (drum keeper) in each band who took care of the drum. There was always something going on in the way of festivities and they would ask the drum keeper; he would get ready and *bu'uta* (strike the drum) to tell the people what was going to happen. The *hoka itancan* would then come into the dance shade or dance hall, set up the drum, and start singing softly until all the singers got there and the powwow or whatever started. He would usually make the choice of songs. If he knew the song, he would lead it off, and if he didn't, he would point to the next singer to see if he knew it. In this way he would control the whole singing group by leading or designating who would do so in his place. Today we have head singers who control the group but often others who start off the songs, and still others who sing along in a supporting role. In this way some groups today share the authority, whereas in others one guy controls the whole drum group.

Until about thirty years ago traditional Lakota singing was high-pitched and choppy, with a lot of *akis'a* (high-pitched yelps) thrown in. The beat was more of a galloping beat with a little bit of an accented double beat to it. In the 1960s the pitch went down a little bit and the beat has slowed down a little bit with an even rhythm. Those former high-pitched singers would also pronounce their vowels more like an *o*, whereas since then it's become more of an *ah* because of northern tribal influences. There were a lot of songs in the 1960s which came down from Canada and the Mandaree Singers from

Fort Berthold in North Dakota, who were also very popular in the 1960s, so their vocal style affected ours. Their songs were medium in pitch and had more stretchy notes, so their voices sounded a little smoother and everybody liked to dance to their bass drum beat. For a while in the 1960s everybody forgot about the traditional Lakota singing style. I think Fort Kipp Singers from Montana and Porcupine Singers were the only ones singing old-time Sioux songs. They kept on singing the old-style songs but everybody else sang with those bass drums to the medium-pitch and -rhythm songs that Mandaree Singers used. Now, although today we're back to singing many of the old traditional Lakota songs, the voice styles are still the smoother, stretchier pattern with very little high-pitched *akis'a* to it.

A long time ago when there was any large gathering of dancers, they didn't do a grand entry like they do today at powwows where they come in to a special song after lining up outside the dance arena. They dance in lines and all dance in a circle till everybody has entered and forms a big circle out in the center. I think this grand entry is based partly on some of the old warrior society parades but is really a result of Wild West shows and rodeos. Also, at dancing contests, which started in the 1960s, it allowed the committee to give points for coming in as part of the grand entry and to make sure all the dancers are out there to put on a good show for the audience. Instead, the traditional way of people coming into the dance circle or arena to dance was called *Omaha gli otake* (Omaha dancers coming and sitting). A long time ago in the tribal camps, they camped by bands. When they got ready to come into the dance grounds, they would have their own singers bring their chiefs and Omaha dancers towards the entrance of the arena. They'd stop four times before they enter the arena, then they'd go out in the center and they might do four or five different series of songs and then sit down.

When dancing contests started making grand entries popular as a parade-in of the dancers, dancers would dance in grouped as traditional men dancers, men fancy dancers, traditional women dancers, women's shawl dancers, and then the little kids. Also, the honoring of various princesses like "Miss Rosebud Fair" or "Miss Black Hills Powwow" became popular, and today the men's grass dance and women's jingle dress are new categories which also come in by groups. It puts on quite a show having everybody come in grouped together like that.

For a long time there was no set grand entry song for that. They used any kind of song for parade-dancing in. Finally, I think it was back in 1972 at

Milk's Camp by Saint Charles, South Dakota, our Porcupine Singers made a grand entry song. It became the original grand entry song and everyplace we went for a while, Sioux Valley, Manitoba; Fort Totten, North Dakota; and other places, they would ask Porcupine Singers to sing that grand entry song. It has a kind of humorous beginning, though. We arrived at that Milk's Camp powwow early, so we partied a little before the powwow was supposed to start. We hit on the idea of composing a special grand entry song to use. We started putting some motivating kinds of words to different kinds of melodies and had a couple more drinks as we sang. Of course, as we got warmer after our drinks, that song started to sound better and better to us. When we had it down pat, we'd sing it over and over in front of our tents. Unfortunately, in the morning when we woke up with a headache, we couldn't remember that song. And we had a hard time remembering it, but it turned out to be a big hit to go with this new idea of the grand entry.

Back in the days before the reservations were set up, our dances were mostly part of the warrior societies that men belonged to, or the different ceremonial dances we used to do. Starting in the 1880s the BIA started to outlaw these old dances, so we had to get permission to dance and we soon figured out that if we picked non-Indian holidays, we were allowed to have some dances. Here in Porcupine they went to the BIA superintendent or boss farmer and said, "You outlawed traditional dancing and singing, but we want to honor the New Year and have masquerades for good health and so that our cattle and horses and produce will grow well for the next district fair or tribal fair." And the agent said, "All right, that's a good idea." So then we had some on New Year's, and Washington's and Lincoln's birthdays, and Memorial Day and Flag Day, July Fourth and Veterans Day. I guess the BIA agents thought those weren't dangerous occasions, so we got to dance. We also were allowed to dance at fairs in late summer or early fall because there would be displays of vegetables, rodeos, and other signs that we were becoming good modern citizens instead of sticking to all that old ceremonial and warrior stuff. But we still got to dance.

We developed special songs and dances for these different holidays. For New Year's there would be lots of masquerade songs and honoring songs, and for the patriotic days we would have many veterans' and warrior songs, while for the fairs we would have race-horse songs or bronc-riding songs and honor songs too.

At the same time, though, in the early reservation days, *Omaha wacipi* (Omaha dance) came on strong. It was called that because we learned some of the ways of dancing and dressing this way from the Omaha tribe. For example, the Omaha used *u*-shaped or butterfly-shaped feather bustles. By comparison the old Lakota *tokala* (Kit Fox Society) warriors wore a small, round bustle all mashed together made of rows of eagle, hawk, and owl feathers. The Omaha style added more coloring with plumes which looked more attractive to many. They also wore louder bells to dance and had brighter shirts. The Omaha Dance Society wasn't a real warrior society but more of a dance society and became very popular.

Our Lakota grass dance is called *peji wacipi* (grass dance). Some dancers would go out and pick some tall grass, tie it together, and put it on their backs at the waist. Some even braided the grass and wore it like a sash across the chest. They have their own set of songs and their dancers do a lot of fancy footwork. They dance backwards, cross their legs, and go in circles. By comparison, the *Omaha* and *tokala* dancers were straight dancers. They might go down low, but not like these grass dance guys, who were a little bit fancier and somehow identified with grass. Some say it represents scalps and others say it symbolizes generosity.

Originally, Omaha dance and grass dance were two different dance customs. Later on, I think in the 1880s and 1890s, they came together in their songs and their costuming. I remember a dance in White Clay a long time ago. Some of the dancers would dance with long-stemmed sage. They tied ribbon on it and made a fan and danced holding it in both hands. Even though we use sage in ceremonies to keep evil spirits away, I didn't know what the sage was supposed to represent, but I saw some dancers with that. So, over time, Omaha dance blended with grass dance and the *tokala* dancing too. *Tokala* songs were only sung for *tokala* members in the old days, but then everybody started to dance to them, even little tiny girls and ladies. All three are now pretty well combined into what we call traditional dancing.

In the early days when the grass dance and Omaha dance and warrior societies were just coming together, men wouldn't dance around in one direction, but would go in all directions.

Women would pretty much stay on the edge of the arena as they danced. Then around 1900, men started to go in a counterclockwise direction and women started stepping out into the arena and going the opposite way. So today, when you watch our dancing, men and women will go around the arena in opposite directions. I once asked this elderly lady why men dance in one direction and women in another. She said that at one time the women from respected families had buckskin dresses on when they danced. Their father and mother used to fix their hair and faces and then prepare a chair in front of them where their daughter would sit. When a certain song was performed, she would get up and dance in front of them and then sit back down again. They would not dance around the arena. They used to call this *han wacipi* (night dancing). When the newer courtship kinds of dances came in, both men and women danced out there and they smiled at each other and bumped into each other as the women went clockwise and the men counter-clockwise. But these were the younger dancers and maybe they didn't really come from a respected warrior's or chief's family. So these guys would dance out there to try to snag a woman.

Giving and Feeding

Dance, song, and dress are the elements of the performing side of our Lakota powwow or celebrations tradition. But the foundation beneath these performances has to be understood. The values we have tell us that once we put on a powwow, when we bring people together, two of the most important things that are supposed to happen are the feast and the giveaway.

Over the years these people here in Porcupine have had some big give-aways. All kinds of material things are spread out in the arena during the honoring ceremony and then are given away: cows, horses, money, quilts, blankets, clothes, dishes, beadwork, etc. Some used to drive a live cow into the arena and have the announcer say, "Okay, the visitors from Rosebud come and kill this cow and divide the meat among you!" They might re-lease a colt *iyuskia* (turning a horse loose) and have all the young boys try to catch it, or they would give a quarter horse to someone. They might also tie money to the mane and tail or put quilts and blankets on it.

Why do all this—give so many things away to people, sometimes hun-dreds of dollars' worth or even a couple of thousand? The traditional way of thinking tells us that when you have material possessions, the best thing you can do with them is to give them away, especially to those who are without or are having a hard time. A leader is not the guy who can store up and keep lots of things, but instead someone who will share them with the people. We are taught as young boys and girls that in order to honor ourselves and our relatives, we should always be ready to share. One of our Lakota songs tells us: "There isn't anything I won't give away because my parents are still alive." The ones we love are so much more important than material objects. Also, we believe that when you give, you create good feelings and harmony in your community. If you keep everything, you are inviting envy and jealousy.

It's funny, when you think of the Christian principle of charity, that once we were put on reservations, both the missionaries and the BIA opposed the sharing of material goods because it kept us from becoming modern, self-supporting American citizens.

I think that the most prized possession to be given away was a horse. It showed our respect for the person we gave it to and also our willingness to give not just little things but also things that meant a lot to us, to give all that we could. There is even a special honor song for a guy who gives a horse away called *sunkah'abiya* (giving a horse). Also they would sing a *wopila* (thanksgiving) song like this one: They would start with the giver's ceremonial Indian name and then, ". . . *taku ota luha kte, ohunkesni wicak'uwo, toksa ake luha kte!*" (. . . whatever you possess, give it away to the needy. You will have it again!) Those are powerful words that encourage people to give away shawls and material, wagonloads and pickuploads of goods, or a team and wagon, horses and saddles. There are always special honor songs for those kinds of people. The singers involved might actually sing three or four songs before the giveaway is finally done. And they, too, would get gifts and money as donations from the family. This is why long ago during traditional powwows, the *eyapaha* (announcer) did a lot of speaking, explaining the reason for the giveaway, explaining the person's Indian name and the song sung, praising the person being honored by the family doing the giving, and calling out people to receive gifts. So a traditional giveaway is pretty time-consuming. But people knew that and prepared themselves to stay a long time.

But like everything else, the giveaway tradition is changing. We've got brand-new pickups and new cars and can easily drive a couple of hundred miles and stay for just a couple of hours after the seven o'clock grand entry and then head home again. The holding of giveaways is also changing for the worse. The feast and giveaway is one of the family traditions that teaches your child respect and honor. His conduct in a crowd, the things he has done so far even as a small boy, that is what the family is honoring him for and the people will recognize him for.

We believe that if something good or bad happens to a family and the family honors that publicly, then that family should pay for the public time and support they receive. This could be for graduating from high school, going into the service, getting an Indian name, being honored as a committee member, or because of something bad such as a death in the family or remembering a deceased veteran. You don't just celebrate or bring something sad before the public and forget your obligation to say thank you to people—with words, by feeding, and by giving away. If you do the best you can, the people will then remember that child in a good way because they'll think of that feast and that giveaway. In this way the parents have paid or provided for the child's status in the community. Their preparation and their willingness to plan for this day and sacrifice what they can shows their child as well as the community how much they love and think of their child, but also what they think of themselves. If they're well off and do very little, that says something. If they are poor and still do the best they can, that also says something about them.

My grandmother Emma Smoke was a real role model for me in these things. She always said: "When you give away, no matter how big or little, give it away in a respectful and honorable way. When you lay things out in the arena and announce that people can come out and get whatever they want, then it's like you're throwing a bone out there and letting the dogs fight over it."

Her way was that you hand things out personally, whether it's a quilt or a small towel, whether it's a trunk or a little plastic cup, give it away in a respectable way. The things that are displayed out there on the ground at the beginning of the giveaway should be picked up and handed to the person called out by the announcer. When they shake the hand of your son or daughter or your father, then you hand it to them. If there's not enough time for some reason to hand out all the things lying out there, then you gather them up and hand them out as you go around the arena. You're supposed to be saying *wopila* (thanks) because they came to your feast and the honoring of one of your family members.

It's also important to remember that since your family is the host for these doings, you shouldn't give to members of your family. When that happens, even accidentally because sometimes younger people forget who they're related to, then there is a lot of criticism. One of my aunts got sore one time when at a giveaway they kept giving to some of the relatives, and said, "If they were going to do that, they should have stayed home in their house and given each other gifts instead!" She was upset about that. It's most honorable to give to those who are elderly or can't give you anything back, or those who are having a hard time or are in mourning.

Sometimes what is given to you in a giveaway is yours to do with as you will. You can sell it, give it to one of your children or a friend, or give it away yourself. But at other times the family might tell you that this item was especially for you. "This was our father's sacred pipe and we want you to keep it and use it," or "This was our son's favorite blanket and since he thought a lot of you, we want you to keep it."

There are only a few powwows these days where all that honoring, giving away, and name giving still takes place. In days past, there used to be at least one feast and giveaway going on here in Porcupine every weekend for a birthday, a wedding, or for somebody coming back from military service. At that time our only hall was small and the dance floor was only about as big as the deck we're sitting on as we're talking. Now we have four gymnasiums and two outdoor powwow grounds and nothing is going on. Now we get into all the big-money dancing and singing contests. In these, even if they put you on the committee, you don't prepare yourself the way you would have when you were being picked for a traditional powwow committee. Big thousand-dollar cash prizes give the committee excuses like "Well, we're giving out big money, so I don't have to have a giveaway." So we don't prepare ourselves and don't feel an obligation to give away like we used to. Now you go to a dancing contest and if certain singers sing you a special honor song, you give them twenty dollars or so and that's it. Traditionally if you were going to be honored, you would get ready ahead of time for a whole year and give gifts to the singers and share your goods with others as well.

That's something that we should have youth understand if we would like the young people to come back to the inner part of that circle with commitment. They should understand why you give away; why you have a feast; why you sew all fall, winter, and spring; why you collect things; and why, every time you go shopping, you spend eighty dollars on your family and with another twenty dollars you buy something to prepare for that giveaway. This is the heart of the *maza sa* (to have a penny) tradition. It reminds you that even just a penny should be put aside to get ready to honor someone in your family. They need to understand what's going on out in the center and how to do it properly so they don't do the wrong things.

The purpose for feeding is based on similar values. The feast and giveaway go together. First you feed everyone, then the announcer and singers honor the person it's being done for, then that person's family shares what it can and wants to with all the people there. Butchering and feeding are done by the family members themselves or they have someone who is good at it do it for them. One of my grandmother Emma Smoke's ways was that if you're putting on a feed, you're going to kill a cow, you butcher from the knee up and from half the neck down. She always said only a stingy or lazy person cooks the bone and all. "It's a disgrace to put a big knee joint with a little piece of meat on a plate for an elderly woman. That's a disgrace because soup and good meat is what you should feed the people." She would say that only the *tawacin sica* (selfish people) keep the bone in the soup. So she used to have my mother and aunt and all our relatives cut all the meat off the bone so there would be no big bones in the soup, and she measured the meat to be about two inches square. That way the people would be sure to get a nice piece of meat in their soup. Also, she said, you shouldn't cook the muscle below the knee because that meat is too hard. And finally, after the soup was cooked just right, she had us dip the fat off the top of the soup. I remember her saying, "They are hungry for meat, not for bones and grease."

As the head of the family or part of the family it is another one of the traditions that you don't eat when you are doing the feeding. You might drink a little soup or something, nothing solid. If anything is left at the end, you can eat it. In this way you're saying: "Hey, I'm the provider, I'm the hunter. I brought and am offering this meat, but I want to feed the people on this special day, so they will eat first. Whatever little pieces or crumbs are left over, that's what I will eat."

My grandmother's interpretation was that by doing this in the right way, the next time you have another feast and giveaway, you will have plenty again. That's the way of the Great Spirit blessing you because you held nothing back. My mom and my aunt carried on my grandmother's ways of doing the feast and the giveaway. Now that they're all gone, I try my best to do all that properly in their spirit.

Traditionally, when they feed the people they let the men eat first. Why do they do that? A male Lakota, from the day that he's born, was supposed to become a warrior who is ready to die anytime. So even in a tipi, a *catkuta* (honored place) on the wall furthest away from the door was kept for the man. Once the men would get done eating and wipe the grease from their chin and leave, then the womenfolk would sit down and eat. Whether in the old warrior days or in the First World War or in Korea, men went to war and were ready to give up their lives. So this is a way of honoring them. Many of the families that hold a feast might say, "Okay, we want the American Legion and other veterans to go through the dinner line first, then men traditional dancers and the singers, all first." Then they let all the women and the general public go through after that. Another traditional way is to put the elderly first, then the veterans, then the singers and dancers, then visitors next, and finally the local people. Still another way, maybe the most traditional, is to *wakpamni* (distribute) the food. This way as all the people are sitting around, the family members bring the different foods and drinks around to serve everyone. In those days also people would always bring their own dishes. Today they often give out paper and plastic dishes and silverware. So all this is not really a set pattern, but rather it depends on family tradition. As long as you do it in a respectful way, you are honoring your brother or father or daughter in the right way.

When a family had a small gathering only for the purpose of honoring one or more of its own members, the family took care of all the details, including the hiring of an *eyapaha* (announcer) and cooks. For celebrations sponsored by the community a committee was formed. The elders or leaders in a community would select a committee for the year. The most important person on a powwow committee is the head committee. He makes sure everything happens as it's supposed to. He makes sure the arena is clean, makes sure the dance shade is up, that the lights are there and working, makes sure the food is ready on time, organizes the different families who pledged to feed, and keeps the dancing going. The other important one is the president. He's the one who keeps the committee together through his leadership, is active in fundraising. Then there's the treasurer, who takes care of the money. These guys and the rest of the committee work hand in hand for a good *wacipi* (dance celebration). Then during the last evening the committee gets time for their giveaway. Towards the end of that last evening, this year's committee together with the community leaders would pick next year's committee. Once you have selected new committee members, they get ribbons and a *mazasa yuha* (penny) to make it official. Then, to honor the new committee, some singers would sing a *mazasa yuha olowan* (penny song) and they would have different songs of this type with specific wording for different kinds of people such as cowboys, tribal chairmen, for a guy who gives away a horse, or an athlete.

So the feast and giveaway were the heart of it all and the committee made it happen and was centrally involved. I think if we are going to revive that inner circle and have our youth identify with that inner circle, we should bring back the traditional way of giving ribbons and pennies and say in a nice way: "Okay, grandson, I give you this ribbon and this penny because you have an Indian name. They gave you that name in a *hunka* (making of relatives) way, so now you are on this committee. We want people to come, so prepare yourself for a feast and giveaway so you can properly feed the people, give something to them, and help them have an enjoyable time during the next celebration." In this way, they would learn to understand that in the Lakota tradition responsibility and honor are intertwined.

The History of Porcupine Singers

Singing has been an honored part of family life in the Young Bear family over a hundred years. My grandfather was a singer, my father, and my uncles. I started in 1963, as I told you earlier, on a dare from my friends, and then when they called out my Indian name, I was obligated to do it. Once that happened and my dad saw that something had happened inside me, he talked to me: "If you're going to be a singer, you have to get out on your own and learn songs, and then you have to sing often and long, and you need to learn to start songs, and if you want to be a *hoka wicasa* (mastersinger), you have to learn to make songs, to be a song maker. One of the hardest things is to get in front of people and sing a song and maybe make a mistake, and make that sort of funny face when you start a song and your throat might be sore. Then you have to be able to sing with your mouth wide open with two or three hundred people sitting there looking at you. To open your mouth and start singing by yourself is very hard. Most of us feel like turning around and hiding behind a wall.

"Your image is also important if you want to get up in front of people to sing. The tone and authority of your voice are very important. That's how the people judge you to see that you know that song well, that you know the history and meaning of that song. Then they'll stand up and respond to your singing. But if you hesitate or miscue on a song, maybe select the wrong kind for the occasion, they'll know you're not sure of yourself and don't know what you need to know, and they'll respond to you accordingly." My dad provided much support for me while I was beginning my way as a singer.

In my life as a singer since 1963, I sang in lots of places and at first I was a follower. I was learning the ropes from different singers. I followed Drury Cook from the Cheyenne River Sioux Reservation, my adopted brother, who is dead now. I also learned a great deal form my uncle Henry Young Bear, who is also gone, and from Irving Tail, who is sitting here drinking coffee with us but doesn't look so good right now. Ha! Our brother Frank

Andrews is hanging in there with us too but keeps dozing off. It's past midnight.

Anyway, after I spent some time singing along with different singers, I thought about my dad's advice and started out. If I was someday going to be a *hoka wicasa*, I would have to learn to take a leadership role in singing. If the other singers don't know a song, I'll have to. I'll have to sing it clearly and loud enough so that they will eventually pick it up and sing along. After learning quite a bit from the people I was singing with, in 1964 I took a drum and an amplifier and some small speakers my dad bought me, and I went out. I had to test myself to go out and sing. In some places I sang all by myself—in Chicago; Minneapolis; Greenwood, South Dakota; in lots of places, large and small. I was testing myself to see if I could be a *hoka wicasa*. Are you going to learn all those songs or are you going to just be a follower? One of these days will you become a *hoka wicasa* so you have that social standing among the people and be a song maker, one who can put words and melodies together to fit the mood and the right situation? And I kept testing myself and inside myself I felt good and I was happy with myself. For the next few years I traveled all over the United States and Canada. I met lots of people and I made many friends.

Then in 1970 we formed the Porcupine Singers as an official traveling singing group. Ever since that beginning I have gained a big family, adopted daughters, brothers, and other family who identified with me in a good way as a *hoka wicasa*. As I did, I had to change my whole way of life so I wouldn't bring any kind of embarrassment or dishonor to myself or the families who looked up to me as a singer. I'm telling my side of this because the singer in my life I know very well is myself. I quit drinking, went through many things, and I changed my life.

As part of it, I got involved with the people who knew more than I did—our elders. I talked to many old people doing research on songs and their meaning, on ceremonies and why they did them. In 1976 at Chief Fools Crow's Sun Dance I was made head Sun Dance singer. So I took time and went out trying to collect any Sun Dance songs that I could, from some of our older singers, from old recordings, anywhere I could find any. Before 1973 they used to sing only about five songs over and over at a Sun Dance because they were lost slowly after the Sun Dance was outlawed by the government in the 1880s. I tried to encourage the recovery of the many Sun Dance songs and tried to help bring some of them back to the ceremony.

Everything I've done has changed since I started to strive to be a *hoka wicasa*. I've been naming my children and honoring my brothers and all my other relatives. Any time I was selected powwow chairman, I tried to pay the people back, to give something back in return for the honor. I had many giveaways, naming ceremonies, ear-piercing ceremonies for young girls, adoption ceremonies. My grandma Emma Smoke always said that you have to give something back in return when the people honor you, so I've tried to do my best to do that. I've butchered one to four cows on each occasion, and since that time in 1963 when I got started and tried to keep the commitment of a *hoka wicasa,* I butchered and gave away ninety-seven head of cows. Now, that's just a way of keeping track, because each time I also tried to share whatever material goods I had: quilts, horses, money, blankets, dishes, and so on. If I were to look at the monetary side of it, if I were a greedy man, I could have a big ranch if I had kept all those horses and things I gave away. In a way, this might sound like I'm bragging myself up, but I'm the singer I know real well and can talk about. The life of the *hoka wicasa* opens you up to many people and honors but also responsibilities and giving of yourself.

The other singers I know fairly well are Irving Tail, my uncle Henry Young Bear, and Drury Cook. We traveled together many times and were very close. I spent a great deal of time with my Uncle Henry. He used to come and stay here at my house and we'd sing and visit, visit and sing, eat and sing. I also used to go visit him and we'd talk about songs and ceremonies; he might remember a song and say this is an old song and this is why they sang it, here's the rhythm of it.

Then, by accident, I met Drury Cook. In January of 1963 we went to a New Year's powwow in Gordon, Nebraska. After a couple of hours of dancing and singing and some drinking, the dance ended and we got ready to leave. As we drove down the street, we saw this big, tall guy standing on the street corner under a light all by himself. The wind was howling, snow was blowing, and everybody was gone. We picked up some gas and were coming back and still saw him standing there all by himself. I slowed down, made a turn, stopped beside him, and asked, "What's wrong *kola* (friend)?" He came over and said, "I came with some guys; I'm from Red Scaffold. They left without me because I wanted to stay. I don't know anybody here and I have no place to go." So I said, "Get in." I think there were about seven of us in the car already. We started back to Porcupine and he introduced himself. I had danced to his singing before. I had seen him around but I didn't know him. He sang as the lead singer for Cook Brothers Singers. They started coming around the Pine Ridge Reservation after 1960 with a bass drum, sheepskin drumsticks, a little different rhythm, and a little lower pitched voice in their songs. They were a little different from our local singing groups and were very popular at the time. So he came back with us. Since we did a little drinking, it took us a while to get back home. After I dropped everybody off, he came back here to the house. It was snowing hard now and about two or three days later while we were sitting here eating, he told me he wanted to be my friend and stay here with us and sing.

That was in January. I had started singing that New Year's weekend. I was still hyped up from that singing debut and was trying to come up with a new song, humming and singing around all the time. Drury started singing too and then Irving Tail came back and stayed here too. Uncle Henry Young Bear would come over and we used to sing almost every night. On Sundays we would sing all day long; it was wintertime, so we'd sing all day long. Finally I said, "This spring, let's form a traveling Porcupine Singers." So we made a kind of homemade bass drum with tire chains for tighteners and turn buckles on the side. The four of us started traveling to sing. It was a time when nobody really wanted to identify as being Indian and even less as being proud of it. Also nobody cared to bring back the singing of old songs, those traditional Lakota-word songs. We were the only group that went around singing traditional Omaha songs, warrior society songs, World War I songs, and we also made other songs ourselves we sang in between. The four of us always tried to learn four songs apiece. Then during the week, when we practiced, we would talk about the place we were going the next weekend, who the people there were, what their customs were, what the occasion was, and in this way we'd pick songs that we thought would fit the community and the event. So we'd pick different songs for that weekend and practice, practice them and remember them. Like, "Okay, Irving, you remember the warrior songs, and Uncle Henry, you remember these honor songs, and Drury, you remember these three new songs, and I'll remember some round dance or rabbit dance songs."

It always helped that we practiced so much and asked each other to remember songs, because anytime the *eyapaha* (announcer) said, "Okay, Porcupine, sing this next song!" we were sitting there with a song ready. We didn't have to hesitate and think of a song; right away we'd hit the drum and started the song out. So as a new singer what I learned from those three guys is that you prepare yourself. Each community you travel to has a different way of doing their cultural things, so it's not good to go to a bunch

1. *Chief Smoke, Severt's great-great-grandfather*
(Courtesy of the Young Bear family)

2. *Conquering Bear Woman, Severt's great-grandmother on his mother's side* (Courtesy of the Young Bear family)

3. *Severt's great-grandmother Conquering Bear Woman,*
his mother, Sophie Smoke (standing), and his aunt Elizabeth
(Courtesy of the Young Bear family)

4. *Three performers, with Wendell Smoke,*
Severt's maternal grandfather, on the left
(Courtesy of the Young Bear family)

5. *Wendell Smoke, Severt's grandfather, in 1899*
(Courtesy of the Young Bear family)

6. Clockwise from back left: *Severt's grandfather Wendell Smoke with his wife, Emma Smoke, and their daughters, Sophie (Severt's mother), Elizabeth, and Lena; taken in Boston as part of a Wild West show* (Courtesy of the Young Bear family)

7. *Severt's grandfather Wendell Smoke and aunt Elizabeth Smoke*
(Courtesy of the Young Bear family)

8. *Two traditional dancers, from Severt's family photographs*
(Courtesy of the Young Bear family)

9. *Severt in 1941*
(Courtesy of the Young Bear family)

10. *Severt's uncle Emil Smoke with Severt in 1941*
(Courtesy of the Young Bear family)

11. Opposite page (top):
*Dancing at the 1974 Saint Francis New Year's celebration,
from left to right: Bill Means, Francis Menard,
Severt, and Jonas Swift* (Courtesy of Zambrano Photos)

12. Opposite page (bottom):
*The Porcupine Singers celebrating a singing contest
championship in Lincoln, Nebraska, in 1975. Left to right: Jerry
Fallis, Drury Cook, Severt, Jim Clairmont, Francis Menard,
Ronnie Theisz* (Courtesy of Zambrano Photos)

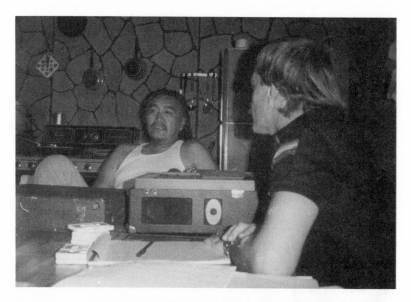

13. *Severt and Ronnie beginning this book project by recording in Severt's kitchen in 1986* (Courtesy of Kristian Theisz)

14. *Ronnie recording Severt's reflections in 1986 on Severt's porch in Porcupine* (Courtesy of Kristian Theisz)

15. *Ronnie and Severt clarifying ideas in 1992 in
Spearfish, South Dakota* (Courtesy of Erik Theisz)

16. *Severt and Ronnie on the back porch of Ronnie's home
in Spearfish in 1992* (Courtesy of Erik Theisz)

17. *Severt in 1992 wearing the vest his wife, Myrna, beaded for him.*
Three child-sized copies of this vest were also beaded by
Myrna in Severt's honor for three of his adopted sons,
Red Boy Means, Luta Jim, and Erik Theisz
(Courtesy of Rand's Studio, Spearfish, South Dakota)

18. *Severt and his wife, Myrna, in 1992*
(Courtesy of Rand's Studio, Spearfish, South Dakota)

19. *Severt in Spearfish in 1992*
(Courtesy of Rand's Studio, Spearfish, South Dakota)

of powwows in a row and just sing the same songs in the same way every time. You plan it out and then fit your songs to that community and the appropriate mood. So today I've been pretty lucky in picking songs for different tribes and to avoid some songs that would not work. I learned how to pick songs that work well from some other singers I've sung with like Dave Clairmont, Leo Clairmont, Leonard Metcalf, Ben Spotted Elk, Saul Dupris, and Ben Black Elk. I also had the chance to dance to the singing of Ellis Chips in his prime in 1964–65. He knew lots of old-time songs. At some of the Sun Dance powwows here at Pine Ridge, when the Sun Dance was held in the morning and then the powwow in the afternoon, when I was traveling alone, I would sing with the Oglala Juniors Singers, who were Matthew Two Bulls' and Harry Jumping Bull's group.

So I had the good fortune to learn from many good singers: how high you can take your voice, how to take care of your throat, how you sing each song in a way to fit the needs of its rhythm and melody, to pick songs that will fit the needs of the family who requested them. They also caused me to remember that whenever I sit down with another group of singers, I need to respect that this is their drum and I wait to be invited to join them. Just because I'm a Porcupine Singer, I never try to take over their drum, determine the rhythm, or start selecting their songs. I just try to help them sing and I always thank them for inviting me. I also never ask for a monetary share; it's up to them if they want to offer it to me. You have to respect yourself, respect other singers, dancers, and people in general; then they, in turn, will give you their respect. Over time I've been asked to talk about singing and dancing at many gatherings. Yet I know enough that there are still lots of ceremonial songs, honor songs, and related things that I have yet to master.

Even today I don't claim that I'm the best singer or that I know all the old songs and the right way to sing them. I think I'm still a little behind Uncle Henry Young Bear. Uncle Henry was a really devoted singer. All my years I was influenced a lot by my different uncles and some by my father. But I was closer to Uncle Henry than any of them. Ever since I came back from the service in 1959, I spent a lot of time at my Uncle Henry's place. I danced at that time and he spent more time telling me and others how to dance and what his view of traditional dance was. Then after 1963, when I started singing, he spent many weekends here. We'd be singing and we'd sit and listen to tapes for a while, then we'd sing again and we'd watch tv and then sing again and tell jokes. I spent much time with Uncle Henry trying to be that *hoka wicasa* (mastersinger), the best. I tried to change my voice to render different songs, to be ready to sing any song that was requested of me, to sing ceremonial songs in the right order. I practiced singing high and loud and steady all the way through to the end of the song.

As Porcupine Singers, in the early 1970s, we once got after each other a little because it seemed like we sang very well on the early high parts of a song but then towards the tail end of it, maybe only one singer finished out the song. The others were all getting themselves ready for the next rendition. So one of our elder singers reminded us that we needed to sing songs all the way through the rendition, not just the beginning. In this way, too, Uncle Henry said, "As singers you sing together so that you learn to blend your voices so that each one has his part. Even if one of you takes a deep breath, the other guys are covering you, so there's not a complete break." So at that time we needed to learn some of the things about singing that my Uncle Henry talked to me about quite a bit.

I think the whole thing changed for me around 1979. I'd be going to different reservations and all of a sudden people would come to me about a song or about singing in a certain way. "I want your Porcupine Singers to come to this powwow and I want your guys to sing this song the right way, the way it's supposed to be." Or else they'd say, "I want you to get up and explain why people should take their hats off when they sing a traditional honor song, and why, when they drop an eagle feather to the ground, they sing this special song and pick it up in this way." I think at that stage in my life I was being asked by people to do things like someone who is respected for what he has done, for his experience and his opinion. I think the Lakota are a very people-oriented society. We always try to consider the people and they, in turn, relate to us and will help us from stage to stage in our lives.

I have found through my own career, that being a *hoka wicasa* is both a good and a difficult life. It can elevate you, but if you abuse it, if you're only singing for personal or material gain, it will turn against you and hurt you in return. The *hoka wicasa* needs to have the patience of the old Lakota leaders, to make careful decisions and ponder his actions and take his time to produce a good sound so people will love to dance to it.

Before the reservation days, there was only one annual large gathering of people. They would annually pick a site someplace kind of central for all the bands to go camp for a couple of weeks and do all their sacred ceremonies, Sun Dancing, naming ceremonies, their *wacipi* (dances), their courting of young people in other bands. Once we were put on reservations we were restricted. We were told to be farmers and ranchers and not to do much traveling. In order for us to leave our reservation, we had to get a special permit signed by the agency superintendent. You could go visit your relatives at Cheyenne River or Standing Rock but you could only stay for three days, and since it was the horse-and-wagon and horseback days, traveling was very limited.

Many of the songs they sang at that time would only spread so far because of the limited travel and because it was oral tradition. You caught the song and learned it if you were good at catching songs by ear and mind, and you could even store a lot of songs away in your mind, but with traveling being limited, so was the spread of songs. But by the 1960s people were getting faster and fancier cars and pickups, big shiny vans, Oldsmobiles, Chryslers, and traveling covered much greater distances. The spread of tape recorders since the early 1960s made songs more accessible so that different tribes were recording each other's songs and singing them in a quite different area of the country right away. The tape was their memory now. Then, since 1973, dancing contests and big reservation powwows came in and often started using host drums, some of the top-name singing groups, to start attracting dancers. So dancers and singers started to travel ever greater distances. The prize money for both got lots bigger too. If you wanted to be a widely recognized *hoka wicasa,* you had to do lots of traveling.

Since the 1960s, if you were a popular singing group and you were in big demand, you traveled. This is how Porcupine Singers traveled maybe fifty weeks out of the year to places we were invited to. Sometimes they would even call us just two or three days before, say, "We want you there Friday at seven!" and send us a money order. So the life of a singer was hard. It was bad form to refuse unless you had a very serious reason. You couldn't really plan your life because one day you were here at home and the next day you were in Chicago, Denver, or L.A. It's very hard to make a living for a family when you want to be a good *hoka wicasa.* I think this is why many singers have marriage problems. I have been singing for over twenty-five years and out of those years I have often been single. It's very demanding, but people expect you and want you to be there. You and your group have earned a good reputation but that honor is very demanding.

This is why at some powwows only four of our members might be able to go, at others ten or twelve. It depends on time off from jobs or family obligations, and I think this is why I stayed single so long in the 1960s—because I wanted to be a good singer. I wanted to make sure I didn't have job or family complications to keep me from going to powwows. I was lucky at the time to have the kinds of jobs, especially in the summer, where I might just work two days a week and then spend the rest of the week singing and traveling.

Once you achieve the rank of being one of the *hoka wicasa* around your drum because of your commitment, skill, and talent, you might receive even another honor, that of being a *hoka itancan* (head singer). He starts most of the songs, he has to know most of the songs, he has experience and a good reputation, and he is always the first one there to sing, to get things going even with just one or two others to help him set up and sing. This head singer is usually picked by the rest of the group. When we started out with that 1963 group, Henry, Drury, and Irving agreed that I would be the head singer even though I just started singing. But I had the car, the drum, and the PA system, and I guess I had their confidence, so I became the head singer for Porcupine Singers for a long time. Then later on, in 1974 at Ring Thunder Powwow on the Rosebud Reservation, I passed it on to Jim Clairmont. It was now his place to make sure that our singers got to the powwow, that everybody was taken care of when they got there, that the singers got out into the arena on time, that they were organized to sing together.

When I was head singer I spent a lot of my time and money to get guys to powwows, I paid for gas for three cars to get there and back and was often broke while other guys might have money. Because I was head singer they expected me to pay for gas, food, or whatever. It caused me marriage problems at times because I often ended up with nothing. The role of an *itancan* (leader) in the traditional way is to take care of his people. I felt it as part of the commitment and responsibility of a head singer that whenever we got a donation or won prize money, were hired as host drum, or got paid for recording albums, it should be divided equally among all the singers. Whether someone was leading off songs, really singing hard, or just following along, all were part of the group and got equal shares. Sure, some singers might say, "It's not fair that I who sing the highest and the loudest am only getting the same share." That's not the way a Lakota singing group or the head singer should talk. Yet I've seen it happen in other groups. Once, I wound up bringing some members of a singing group back from Denver because they got stranded there. Their head singer had charged them for using his drum and the drumsticks and made them pay for their gas and meals and their rooms. After the head singer got all his expenses out, the rest of the singers got six dollars apiece. Then he left them there because they couldn't afford the costs for coming home. Even though I didn't have enough room with the four guys I was bringing back, we crushed everything in the trunk and the corners, fit the guys in, and came back. This also shows that many times singers don't make a great deal and often don't even meet expenses. If a dancer gets a donation or wins some prize money, it's all his. When a singing group gets the same thing, the members might have to split it six, eight, or ten ways, so it's rarely enough.

My father also talked to me one day about how difficult it would be to be one of the top singers or one of the respected singing groups. He said, "Once you've reached a high level, you always look for a higher one. Two things will bring you down, all the way down—chasing women and liquor," he said, "and maybe the second time you try to make it back up, you won't make it. All the people want you to get back up there again, let you get so far, but then they'll forget about you. Look at all our tribal leaders and those that want to be leaders. Everyone who gets up there and could be a very good leader will drop down due to women and liquor. Once you're bottomed out, it's very hard to get up there again!" So his advice was that once you have managed to reached the high levels of our Lakota society, be careful. The fastest way down is you'll either start chasing women because of your new, higher role, or some women will chase you because you're in a high rank or have a little bit of celebrity status.

After many years of going through some of these problems, our Porcupine Singers also started being affected by these demands. Once you've sacrified for a time and you see the big money there, your attitude and mind changes. You're tempted to say, "I want more money because I sing the highest and loudest; I'm the head singer or the drum keeper; I'm always sitting at the drum everyplace we go and I'm the one who remembers all the old songs; I want more." A couple of our singers started to get greedy. Everybody sang together all weekend, smiled, and was happy, but the last night of the powwow, when the money is given out, then everybody's mouth gets dry, and some get greedy.

Some of us, especially the head singer and the drum keeper, have to set an example for the rest. I still maintain the role of drum keeper for Porcupine Singers because I still have the responsibility to get our singers organized; I still pay the gas for some of our guys, feed them, and get them where we need to be.

So it's a hard and difficult life to be a singer, but it's still a good life.

There are things that will get into you anyway, sometimes cause problems, but if you're man enough, you can sit down and work it out with the others. Sometimes that's very hard.

When we first started out as the traveling Porcupine Singers back in the 1960s, Uncle Henry, Drury, Irving, and I, we were very intense. We started out as four guys singing and each one of us gave our all, our very best, as we sang. We carried that load of being a *hoka wicasa*. We weren't just sitting around smoking or taking pictures; we didn't take our drumsticks away from the drum and visit around with other groups or dancers. We focused on our singing. But after a number of years we scattered. Drury left to get married, Irving went and got married, and Uncle Henry started getting too old to go so much. I was still traveling, but by myself, and I started singing with many younger singers.

But then, in 1970 at the Sisseton Powwow, a group of us singers from Rosebud and Pine Ridge sang together. As a result of this, we decided to reorganize and decided to form a new Porcupine Singers. I think Jim Clairmont came on, Clement Whirlwind Soldier, George Squirrel Coat, and then the older guys, Drury, Irving, and Uncle Henry. We began to travel widely again, and as the years went by we were given more and more honors. One time a guy came over to the drum, it was my brother Frank Andrews, and donated a special sacred pipe to our drum. He had liked our Porcupine Singers and often traveled with us, so he gave us this special pipe. Then, later on, Calvin Jumping Bull joined the Porcupine Singers, and because he enjoyed singing with us, he gave our drum a war bonnet that was over a hundred years old and had belonged to Amos Bad Heart Bull way back. Then, in 1974 after Francis Menard, Philip Wright, Jerry Dearly, Henry Green Crow, and Ronnie Theisz joined us, we started really traveling. We traveled fifty weekends that year and close to that the next few years, all over the United States. We won twenty-four singing contests in twenty-four states that year.

One day we were talking about it, and I talked about the traditional eagle staff, how warriors would carry this staff with eagle feathers all along it, and how they would touch the enemy with it. It was a way of counting coup and coming back to be recognized for it. I thought that instead of tribes going against each other in battle, we were today using our drumsticks and the drum, using our voices to compete against each other through songs, the traditional songs of our tribes. Even though now we shared songs with each other and even sang together at times, we were still competing. So, after that, we made the staff that belongs to our drum like the pipe and the ceremonial bonnet. The twenty-four black and white eagle tail feathers on the staff represent the twenty-four contests we won in twenty-four states that year. So we've been carrying that staff ever since.

Now after Clement Whirlwind Soldier died, we added a ceremonial medallion hanging on it with a feather for the deceased. Later on, Drury Cook died, so we added a feather for him. Then there was a warrior who was inside Wounded Knee in 1973 from Oklahoma who liked Porcupine Singers' style of singing. After Wounded Knee he went around singing and then organized a singing group called Brave Scouts from Oklahoma, the first singing group from Oklahoma that publicly sang northern style. Terry Williams was his name. When he passed away, his family wished to put his memorial feather on our staff. Then there was Ellis Head, a supporter who loved to dance to Porcupine Singers. He was a highly respected traditional dancer. At every powwow when he put on his costume, the first thing he did was to come over to the drum and shake hands with us. Wherever he went people liked him because he was always friendly and humble. His wish before he died was that at his wake and funeral he wanted Porcupine Singers to sing for him. So at midnight during the wake we sang all the songs that he used to love to dance to. At the funeral the family took one of his feathers and tied it to our medallion, so his is on there too. Later on, feathers were added by the families of Cecil Spotted Elk and my uncle Henry Young Bear.

During that time there was a young lady from Black River Falls in Wisconsin who made a five-inch beaded medallion with "Porcupine Singers" on it. The reason that she did that was that her father or uncle, I can't remember which, P. J. LaPointe, sang with us for a time. She made these medallions for us in different colors. Then some families made vests for us with our group name on them, and Eddie Peters from Laguna, New Mexico, bought all our singers Stetson hats because he and his daughter enjoyed our singing. One of our identity symbols as old-time singers who still believed in traditional ways was the wearing of hats with plumes or eagle feathers on the side and beaded hatbands or metal pins of coyote, the Lakota symbol of the singer.

Our singers were also taken as brothers by Dick Lyons and his family from Thunder Bay, Ontario, because they liked our style. He's always glad to see our singers and has been very good to us when we go there. We also have good friends in California who asked to sing Porcupine Singers' songs in our style. They wanted to learn to sing our songs with the right words and in the right way. Then later there was a young girl dancer named Messabi. Everywhere we went, she was there to dance to us, so she adopted our singers as her uncles and called us her uncles. Another girl from Window Rock, Arizona, Blanche Ellison, enjoyed the Porcupine Singers so that wherever she saw us, she invited us to her place, fed us, and put us up. Even in Sioux Valley, Manitoba, we have friends who invited us up there; we shared our songs with each other and became close friends.

In these ways we've achieved an identity as respected singers. We tried to do things in the right way and according to our Lakota tradition. Part of those years of singing and traveling are some of the stories we can tell about each other as singers. I'll give you an example. In 1969 or somewhere around there, Dennis Banks wrote to me, sent some gas money, and invited us up to sing in Saint Paul as host drum. When we got there, our brother Eddie Benton had room for us, so we stayed at his house. On our way to the powwow, Irving, Drury, and the rest of us put a new song together. Saturday night, we said, when there's a lot of people and dancers, we'll sing that song. We all sat around the drum and when the announcer said, "Porcupine Singers, intertribal, take it away!" I said, *"Hoka he!"* (Let's go!) and Drury hit the drum to start the song. Right away people must have known it was a new song. Tape recorders and lady singers crowded all around the drum. Pretty soon there was two rows of lady singers around the drum singing along. Then, all of a sudden, Hubert Humphrey and Dennis Banks and Clyde Bellecourt and some other guys came up and Hubert Humphrey was smiling and waving his hands. We kept on singing again and again.

With all these women singers, my Uncle Nelson got excited and halfway through pushed the song up real high and kind of lost control and a tooth popped out. It fell on the drum as we were beating on the drum and singing and laughing. He was trying to grab it but the tooth was dancing up and down and finally fell in front of Drury. We just kept on singing. When we got done, Drury picked up the tooth and said, "This is the University of Minnesota and there must be a museum upstairs." He held up the tooth in his fingers, yellow brown, about four inches long. "There must be a museum upstairs because one of the dinosaurs lost his tooth and it fell on our drum." He got a big laugh out of that and Uncle Nelson got his tooth back. He tried to shove it back in the hole in his gum but it wouldn't fit anymore. He lost a tooth singing that time.

There's another story about a time we were coming back from a powwow, the moon was full, the summer night was real nice, and we were drinking and singing. Finally, west of this little town of Vetal, Drury said, "Stop the car, stop this car; no, back there, I wanna stop at that spot." So I backed up about fifty-six feet. He got out with a pint of brandy. He said solemnlike, "Stand in a circle; I wanna do something honorable, to honor somebody." He said, "Everybody take a drink." So we all took a drink. "We're going home safe and we had a good time and enjoyed ourselves, we're singing and feeling good. I wanna honor somebody, but before I honor somebody, I wanna say two short words." Everybody quieted a little and he said, "Irving Tail." You see, Irving is short, so we laughed. Then Drury said that he wanted to give Irving an Indian name. When we traveled at the time, everything he and Irving talked about was *ta supa* (baloney). Any Lakota word they used, they added *ta supa*. If one of them started a song, they put the name *Ta Supa* in it, and they were kind of silly about it all weekend. Drury went on to say that the name *wanbli* (eagle) was used all over, and that since Irving flew all over, he traveled all over just like an eagle. Drury then said, "Tonight I want to name you Wanbli Ta Supa (Baloney Eagle)." Then he passed the jug and we drank and all sang an honor song for Wanbli Ta Supa. Then we got back in and drove home.

We had lots of good times traveling, serious and humorous ones. Still, sometimes I got upset. Here we now had eight, ten, or twelve guys sitting around the drum but some didn't make the effort to really know the songs, so that maybe only two or three of us had to sing the traditional wording. The others weren't *hoka wicasa*, just singers or drummers. As our new Porcupine Singers formed in the 1970s and started to get quite a good reputation, it still upset me that this attitude of not giving your best to your singing showed a lack of real dedication. Some of our guys liked the glory and prestige of being part of the Porcupine Singers, but they only looked the part. They would strut around with the belt buckles, medallions, vests, or whatever they had to show people they were a Porcupine Singer, but they didn't take the time required to learn all those songs, they didn't take the time to learn how to respect the drum, and they didn't take the time to train their throat so that at some time they could lead off a song or make real contributions to our group sound. They also weren't quite willing to make the sacrifices necessary. In our Lakota way, if you are honored or get public attention and a following, you pay for it by your own generosity, by making donations in return when you are honored, by giving of yourself rather than just getting. Instead they would think, "He's the head singer, so he'll have to pay for my gas," or "Let him make a donation; he's our leader, not me." That was kind of their attitude.

For some of our guys the honor and glory came too fast and they couldn't handle it. Recognition and being in the public eye can twist your values so they got out of hand. After a while they began to overdo things, to go beyond the limit. Once you go beyond those limits of reasonable behavior, your pride, your vanity, your disregard of others takes you so far you have a hard time returning because of shame and embarrassment once you see where you've come. It might be the words you say, it might be your facial expression, it might be your body language, or it might be how you treat your family. Your excess, your going past the limits, shows itself somewhere in those areas. Being a real *hoka wicasa* makes you go through many mind-bending things. But your dedication to your singing can't make you so one-sided that you neglect your job, your wife, or your family. Some neglect those things and make themselves look bad. They might tell a big lie or some false story and then cannot turn themselves around and come back to the drum. It's hard for them to return, so they tell a bigger false story to cover the first one, and the lies get bigger and bigger.

At one time I thought that the Porcupine Singers were a big family. I thought of all the people who had become close to Porcupine Singers throughout the plains states and all over the country. We were welcome and invited to many places, won lots of singing contests, we started to make recordings of our songs that were very popular. One of our gifts was that we were pretty good at singing old traditional songs. Even today, when Porcupine Singers are at a powwow, other singers get their tape recorders ready because the Porcupine Singers will often come up with some special old traditional song. We seem to sing it in a right way for the right occasion to get people motivated and raise their spirit. For many years, many dancers really liked our music. Ellis Head and Dawson No Horse were two of the biggest supporters of Porcupine Singers. Ellis, who was a widely recognized traditional dancer, would get out there and put on his best moves when we sang certain traditional songs he especially liked. And Dawson, who was both a traditional dancer and respected spiritual leader, would often get up in public and say good things about Porcupine Singers, or say words of encouragement to us. Now they're both gone.

There were many others who responded like that to our songs. One time, for example, we were at Fort Duchesne Powwow and one of the dancers came and touched our drum by placing his flat hand on top of the hide for a moment and then rubbing it on himself and then he shook our hands. Young kids and elders would come and shake our hands as singers, or they would come up and touch our drumsticks or touch our group feather staff sort of as a tribute. One other time we went to the Yakima Reservation and their chief, his name was Tortoise, an old man, gave a talk to the whole crowd at that celebration and he prayed and then he said how happy he was that Porcupine Singers were here. He said, "They're legends in our time. They're a singing group that got into our people's mind and hearts. They're a legend during our time and here they are amongst us! I'm really happy to have them here!" He then donated two hundred dollars to us. Even though that old man never met us before and was a chief, higher in traditional rank than all of us at that drum, he wanted to express his appreciation and respect towards us.

All that support and honoring came from singing around our drum. If we didn't sit around that drum *Oyate Ho Nah'umpi* (The People Hear Its Voice) and sing our best to make people respond, to make their hearts and spirit happier, we would have never developed this large family. We now have family in Los Angeles; Warm Springs, Oregon; Nespelem, Washington; Browning, Montana; Fort Duchesne, Utah; Mandaree, North Dakota; Minneapolis; Chicago; Albuquerque; and Hopi country.

But while we were enjoying those good times, the friendship and following of our group by so many people, the pressures put on our members got to some of them and they exceeded the limits. We traveled together to many places, laughed together, ate together, named each other's children, partied together at times, and were caught up in the rush. Most of our singers were able to keep it in perspective, some couldn't. Our leadership fell apart because of money pressures, criticism of each other by some of our singers; we lacked the encouragement, the mutual trust, and the central responsible decisions that people could accept. We got into disagreements, broke up, and everybody went in different directions. We still keep a small part of the group together, but some of our other former members are overdoing and bragging up their Porcupine Singers image. They've become know-it-all experts on Indian culture or ceremonies or traditional songs. They've overstepped their limits and now can't return to the rest of us at the drum.

I myself have tried not to overstep my limits as a singer. I understand a lot of ceremonies, but there's always a medicine man or master of ceremonies or announcer who is supposed to know or run that event properly, so I never interfere, or get out in the center, or take over somebody else's ceremony. Even at the drum, in singing as a head singer and drum keeper, when we sit down in that circle as Porcupine Singers or another group, I don't interfere with the lead singer starting that song. I think our singers need to have that understanding, to hold themselves back in the right way.

You have to earn your place at the drum. You don't just jump in and start singing with Porcupine Singers because your father is a singer. You have to earn the right. In the same way, I wouldn't barge in on another drum unless I'm invited, and then I remember I'm a guest at this drum.

I think this is why I was happy that my boys Junior and Melvin and Ted Means' boys, Ted, Jr., and Redboy, formed their own group, Brotherhood Singers, a few years ago. They formed this group to start to sing and learn about singing, and when they sing with us Porcupine Singers, I'm glad that they never take over songs or start beating on the drum real hard or play around with the drum. They respect the guys that are there, Irving, Ronnie, Calvin, Francis, and the rest. They understand we are the Porcupine Singers and they still haven't earned that place. As a father I was happy that they made the decision to start their own group and first learn about singing and to develop their voice and rhythm so that later on they can take their place at our drum. But we have other kids that come in and take over at the drum because their father is a Porcupine Singer or a singer with another group, so that they automatically feel they can just take over the drum. I think their parents need to talk to them carefully so the proper understanding is there.

One of the thoughts I've had as I thought about it all is that our singers who don't live in heavily populated urban areas, not in big cities but out here on the reservations or in smaller towns in the western South Dakota and Black Hills area, somehow are more levelheaded. I'm not trying to put anyone down, but somehow the guys in the big cities can't seem to cope with the fast city life and still maintain their traditional values. Maybe the pressures of being in the public eye and being surrounded by another culture demands too much from them; they forget the right ways.

Songs to Pray and Honor

To understand Lakota songs, which mean so much to us, I think we should identify songs as those before reservation days and those after reservation days. I call 1880 the dividing line because the whole social structure of Lakota life changed by 1880. In 1862 the U.S. government just started rounding up our Sioux people and moving them to different areas. Many of our sacred ceremonies and customs changed because people were now forced to move often during that treaty period of around 1860 to 1871. Other tribes too, like the Cheyennes, were moved south; the Nez Perce were moved, and the Utes. Their former hunting grounds and battle grounds were all of a sudden different for them. With Carlisle Indian School in Pennsylvania in 1879, the federal boarding school system came in for Sioux people and the various Christian churches increased their work among our people. Our ceremonies were outlawed, our traditions were considered pagan, and the government, with the help of the churches and schools, tried to stamp out our old way of life. When we look at the history of our songs and dances, it documents our changing way of life after 1880. I'll share some of our songs with you so that you can appreciate what we feel and why.

Before the reservation days, respect and honor existed and there was always an order in life no matter what. After the reservation policy came in, the whole social system changed and Lakota people—especially the warriors—started losing their identity. The warrior songs from those earlier days used to tell stories. Even when we sing those old songs that only repeat a few words or phrases over and over, they are high-spirited songs because they tell a story. For example, we like to sing a song that just repeats the words *"Wasose mani pelo"* (The warriors are walking). People who listen to and understand the words realize it tells a story that was often told in the old warrior days. In this brief meaning these words make us remember or imagine a longer story of a warrior who is so brave and fearless that when there's a big battle going on in an enemy tribe's territory or our own, he's walking with purpose in the midst of the battle. There are arrows and bullets flying, smoke and dust blowing, but he is walking with a warrior's purpose on that battlefield. In this song we are telling the story of the way of life of the old Lakota warrior in a very few words. We can break down the meaning of those few words because they explain the life of the warrior, why he became a warrior, the danger of his way of life, the worried affection of his relatives, the encouragement of his comrade warriors, the pain, sadness, and honor when he gives his life for his people.

Let me talk a bit about the role of the warrior in our Lakota tradition. During the prereservation days before 1880, a Lakota man identified with two distinct and two highly honored traditions. He had half his mind on spiritualism and the other half on being a fighter, a warrior. He had to live both of these lives to be a fearless and effective warrior. He needed to have the spiritual side so that he could walk at night, see things at night as well as in the daytime. In order to outthink and outmaneuver the enemy he was going to face, the most courageous thing a warrior can do is to walk hand in hand with death. We call that *nagi gluha mani,* walking with the spirit. The Lakota man had to prepare himself to be a *nagiksapa,* wise in spirit. He had to get the power visions and dreams so that he was an effective, a fearless warrior but also one who walked with the spirit, a spiritual warrior. Before he goes to war, he'll go through ceremonies like the sweat lodge to cleanse himself so that if he is killed by the enemy, then he will have a direct line for going into the spirit world and be accepted. If he is going into enemy territory, he will put on his sacred paint, use the sacred symbols he received in his visions, and call on all the spiritual assistance he has earned over his life as a man.

One of the things about the warrior life I heard from both my grandma and my dad is that a very few of the *wicoti* (camps) were honored with twin children, a great blessing. So before a warrior went to face the enemy, he would go to those twins and have them touch or breathe on his weapons or even on his horse so that these would be given that twin power, so that his horse would respond to the rider on its back, to his body movements and the pressure of his knees, to dodge and run faster than the enemy's horse. Then, when the warrior came back from a victorious war party, he would honor and give gifts to the twins because they gave him a double spirit to come back alive.

Some of the warrior honor songs we sing have long stories behind them. One of them is the Plenty Wolf song I told you about earlier. Another song that needs to be understood is what is known today as the Sneak Up Song but started out as as a *hunka bloka olowan*, or honored warrior song. *Hunka bloka* refers to a very outstanding warrior, perhaps of the Brave Heart society of warriors, and *olowan* is the word for song. When the singers sang this special song for this *hunka bloka*, they would put him out in the center of the dance arena, representing a wounded and fallen warrior either because the enemy knocked his horse down or he fell to the ground wounded. His comrades backed off and when the cloud of dust and shooting cleared up and he was still lying there, they charged the enemy who were surrounding their fallen friend. They came so far, fired at them, then advanced again until they killed the enemy or drove them away. Then they would pick up their wounded friend and bring him back. In the song and dance, that's why they advance partway four times, and stop each time and advance again until after the fourth time when they move through the center. So this dance really reenacts the rescue of a fallen warrior by his friends. Later on the name was changed to Sneak Up Song, maybe as part of a show dance or for a Wild West show. Today this song is often misused as part of a dancing contest or for show. Only warriors were supposed to dance to it, but now you go to a powwow and little girls in shawls dance to it or all the dancers.

Around 1978 at Rosebud Fair they asked us singers to dance to the Sneak Up Song, so we put Francis Menard, one of our singers, half lying out in the center. We then charged him four times, a little further each time, and then picked him up and took him around the arena. That's the way it's supposed to be done. So at a gathering, if there are any wounded veterans, then you put them out in the center, advance charging four times towards them, and then rescue them and bring them around. That's the right way of using that song. The words to the song are: *"Heyuha manipe* (eight times) *Lakota hoksila wasoseape. Heyuha manipe* (four times)." These words should be interpreted as "They are walking with him, the couragous Lakota, they are walking with him." The words stress the rescue part of the scene.

There's another song you won't hear anymore today which goes way back in history. It also deals with the spiritual side of the warrior's dance outfit. Back before the reservation days, when warrior societies would get together to dance and honor each other, some would wear a special kind of back bustle called *kangiha mignaka,* or crow bustle. They would put the feathers of birds hanging down and put two spikes of wing feathers sticking up with plumes at the end like arrows. Some might be crow, or magpie, owl feather, or hawk feather, stripped and mixed. As part of the warrior society ceremonies, they would lay these bustles down, smoke their bustles with sweet grass to purify or bless them because they were part of the symbol of battlefields, of birds that show up first after a battle or how a warrior doesn't care if the birds would fight over his body once he's dead. This song just says, *"Kangiha ki le wakan yelo* (3 times). *Waci wicasa kangiha ki le wakan yelo* (2 times)." (The crow bustle is sacred. Men dancers, the crow bustle is sacred.) If you don't know all the history behind these simple words, you have a hard time appreciating what we Lakota understand as we listen.

Just before the reservation days there was a real turnover for that Lakota warrior. His whole life changed from the up-close bow-and-arrow days to those of the rifle, the Winchester rifle or whatever he got from an enemy or a trader. With bullets he now didn't have to get close to kill his enemy. Now he could be at a greater distance and, using the power and the effectiveness of that rifle, he could put his enemy down at the same time, if he wanted to. There is an old warrior song that tells of this change. *Itazipaca wecun yelo.* This says, "I'm still a bow-and-arrow warrior." The warrior who is speaking is saying, "I'm still that fearless warrior. I can go close to the enemy and still shoot him with my bow and arrow. I don't now have to depend on the rifle." That tells a story about the whole transition of the image of the warrior during that period when non-Indian goods came in.

Still, even though technology changed the way our warriors fought in battle, the basic idea stayed much the same into the twentieth century and even up to today. In the old days, from the day a male was born, he was supposed to become a brave warrior who could die anytime. This is why in his tipi the man had a *catkuta,* a place of honor, along the wall furthest away from the door. Even in the First World War and Second World War, men went to war ready to give up their lives fighting. So they were given an honored place. Veterans are still honored at public gatherings because they are defending their people.

This is the feeling behind a song I once again heard an old man sing last night. *"Tukta kesa munkin kta ca le waun."* (I'm willing to lay down my life anywhere.) This song doesn't have the words "in enemy country" in it, but the way we understand it is that it is honorable for the warrior to die in enemy country. A lot of these old songs to honor the warrior way of life have these ideas in them. Let me sing you another one: *"Tokala kunmiye ca ya ohitika waun kun wanna hena mala eya."* (I was a fearless Kit Fox Society warrior and here I am now vanishing.) The warrior is saying to us that he was once the fearless warrior but can now no longer ride a galloping horse or hang from its side to shoot an enemy, or if his horse is knocked down, he can no longer get up and run. At his age he is not that effective warrior any longer. He regrets the passing of that life but is still honoring his part in it. Whenever there is a public gathering, they will sing a song for him.

We have another song connected to the Battle of the Greasy Grass, or the Little Bighorn, against Custer that is also a good example of what we understand about the words of songs. *"Kola tokile* (eight times) *kola ceya pelo. Waziyata ki ciza pe. Kola tokile, kola tokile, kola ceya pelo."* When you only translate the actual meaning of the words, it says: "My friend where are you? (eight times) We made the enemy cry. There was a battle up north, my friend. Where were you? We made the enemy cry." When you know the meaning beneath the song, the code of the warrior, the history of the Custer battle up north, you can feel the vibrations of the words. When they sing this song for someone, it's like the warrior who was actually there is pointing a finger at a young man or young boy who didn't join in and is saying, "Where were you?" Here this warrior who risked his life to fight Custer and came back victoriously is singing a victory song and is saying: "Where were you? We made the enemy cry!"

The warrior societies, the *akicita okolakiciye,* like the *tokala* (Kit Fox) or the *Cante Tinza* (Strong Hearts), all had their own group songs with a set pattern. In their warrior society gatherings, everyone sat in a certain place according to their rank in that society, and when they would sing certain songs, individual warriors would get up and act out a story as they dance. We call that *waktoglaka waci* (telling a story dance). The Plenty Wolf song is a good example of this. They would reenact what they did on a war party; some danced with scalps, or with guns, or with horse tails.

Everything was sung and done in order so that you maintained the order of life for yourself. Then, anytime you are called to the spirit road and the hereafter, you are ready. Your life is in order so that you have no problem going. You know what you're committed to; you know what your responsibilities are. There is a center to the circle of your life.

You also have to remember that as these songs are sung through the years they become emotional and patriotic favorites, like "From the Halls of Montezuma"—I served in the Marine Corps—or "O, Shenandoah," or "God Bless America" are for white Americans. Our people thrill to these words; they feel great pride to celebrate their finest moments. Songs are a way of sharing in the pain and the glory.

After 1880 those old victory songs over other tribes or against Custer and his cavalry survived and were used as World War I victory songs. During the years 1918 or so, they used to bring the soldier boys back as veterans to Gordon and Rushville, Nebraska, by train and the victory dances at both depots played a very important part in keeping these warrior songs alive. The wording changed, like the Germans became the enemy instead of the Pawnees or Crows or the cavalry, but the meanings of the songs were kept alive. The Indian families of the returning veterans and relatives used to follow each others' wagons and camp, and when the soldiers came back and crossed to the open area on the south side of the tracks or the area on the east side of the depot, they had victory dances. Some of the town merchants supported them because those big families would go and buy things—horse harnesses, wagon repairs, saddles, and plows. So it was also often a business trip at the same time as going after their son as a soldier coming back from the war.

In World War II the Gordon depot and the Rushville depot still played a big part because they were departure and arrival points for soldiers in World

War II. During those early 1940s and right after, the social system really changed. So many Lakota people were involved in World War II that lots of veterans' honor songs were sung and composed. The Germans and the Japanese were now the enemy. On both sides of us, the Pacific and the Atlantic oceans, there was war going on. This encouraged families to sing for their sons or their brothers, their uncles or their fathers, that were or had been in the Second World War. It gave them a chance to honor their servicemen by singing for them in public places. Since then, many public dances have been held for our modern warriors. The Korean conflict also involved our Lakota boys, though not as many, and even the Vietnam and Persian Gulf conflicts led to the honoring of our warriors, although new songs weren't composed for the last two as much. We started using some of the earlier songs and changing them just a little to fit.

Another type of song that represents our warrior tradition is what might be called a death song, where a warrior prepares for his death or the giving of one's life. In this death song, when he's ready to give that final charge, he'll go to a molehill, brush the dirt on top of the molehill aside and get that fine dust below, throw it on himself, and sing his death song. As a warrior his life is like that fine dust, soon gone. I think this is where the word Oglala comes from. It's often translated as "to scatter one's own," but I think it's based on "to scatter on oneself," as the fine dust shows us that we can give our lives as warriors. The warrior throws it on himself and sings a death song for himself. That song belongs to that warrior alone. No one else can sing his song; that's his. Other warriors have their own. They all stress that they are willing to lay down their life in enemy country.

Then you sing another death song the day the warrior dies. The grandfather's and grandmother's role, or even the father's or the mother's role, is that the day they hear the news that their son was killed in enemy territory, they face west—insted of east like they would for a new baby—and sing an *ic'ilowan,* a death song for the one who died, the son they gave up that day. When they bring his body back or when they hold the final funeral ceremony, they sing a similar song called *wicat olowan* (mourning song). This song would often be sung by an older warrior or an older woman on request. Then a year later, as part of the memorial ceremonies, a *wicat olowan* would be sung again to end the year of mourning. They might have a sacred Releasing of the Spirit ceremony with special songs to let the soul of the beloved travel to the spirit road or, if the deceased liked a particular song, a parent might also say, "My son liked this song and he used to like to dance to it, so I want the singers now to sing this song." In these ways, songs were used to dry the tears of the relatives one last time.

It's important to realize that some of these sacred songs we sing are personal or private, like the warrior's own death song or the songs we receive from the spirit world when we go through a vision quest. For example, some sacred fasting songs can only be sung by the individual going on the hill to find his vision. Nobody else can sing them, but he has to be in the sacred altar that he sets up for himself or a medicine man set up for him. He will sing these songs because they are dreamer songs which come to you in a dream or while fasting and you can hear the words and the tones inside yourself. They will stay with you like you've been singing these songs all your life and they are yours alone. Other sacred songs, like the mourning songs or Sun Dance songs, are also sacred but can be sung in public.

There are also a lot of spiritual songs for children. On the day the baby is born they sing a song for him, and the day he learns to sit up they sing another. When he learns to stand on his own feet, they sing a song for that. As he grows up and proves that he is becoming a man, there are different songs we sing in public for him.

Those songs that are private and personal should only be used in that way, in a closed gathering with only certain people there. Personal healing songs like elk medicine or eagle or buffalo medicine songs are part of what I would consider closed ceremonies. Today, however, they're bringing some of those sacred symbols and ceremonies into a general powwow or public gathering. Some of our dancers or ceremonial leaders seem to want to let the public know that they are some kind of spiritual men, so they put those sacred symbols and items that are parts of private and closed ceremonies on their powwow costumes. I've even seen guys out there dancing at powwows with the special ropes used when a dancer pierces during the sacred Sun Dance tied around their shoulders. But, again, those belong to a sacred ceremony and shouldn't be brought out for general public display. The same is true for those personal, private sacred songs. Even those sacred songs that are public, like Sun Dance songs or sweat lodge songs, should be used only in the right way, at the proper time.

In a healing ceremony, for example, the *itancan,* the leader that runs that healing ceremony, sings those necessary sacred songs. He has to put his ceremonial altar in order; he'll sing a sacred pipe song and load his pipe. He'll sing a song to put the colors black, white, red, yellow in four directions; he'll sing a song to put his tobacco ties out, and so on. There are sacred songs that go with each part, but he doesn't have to sing real loud and let everyone hear them. To himself and God he will sing softly. These sacred songs are so sacred that even you as the leader sing them softly and you pray softly. These songs are given those ceremonial leaders by the spirits. Usually in these private ceremonies only certain people and relatives are invited. If too many are involved, maybe your power as the *itancan* will not go fully to help or heal the person the ceremony is held for.

Our chiefs also had songs identifying each one so whenever he went in public, he was recognized as a leader and people respected him for that by singing the first song for him, the leader. Then everything fell in order after that. In this way before the reservation days each warrior, woman, or child identified with special songs; they knew and respected sacred songs, individual and public songs. I talked mostly about the spiritual warrior because it's that *tokala* (Kit Fox) side of my family that I identify with the most. And all those songs had to be in order. No one before 1880 would go out in public without knowing the proper order for ceremonial songs in sequence. Ceremonial events were *wakangliotake,* the gathering of sacred things, and involved respect and order. Those are all traditions we need to put back in order.

Dancing behind Drawn Curtains: Social Dance Songs

From the early 1880s, when the U.S. government started to forbid our sacred ceremonies, to the 1920s, when they still tried to force us to become good modern white citizens no matter what we wanted, we reacted in different ways. Our public Sun Dances sort of went underground and were held way back in the grass-roots communities someplace. Our warrior society parades and ceremonies were adapted to fit white American patriotic holidays like George Washington's or Abraham Lincoln's birthday, or Memorial Day, or Flag Day in June, or July Fourth so the BIA agent would allow us to dance. But the new result of these assimilation policies was the social dances that developed just around and after the First World War. Since ceremonial and warrior dances were being forbidden, the social types of dances, where men and women dance together as partners or in a large circle, grew. The Indian police that the government had put in place to break the power of the chiefs and their *akicita,* or warrior societies, would come around to any ceremonial and warrior gatherings to break them up. If they found a sweat lodge set up, they would throw ropes and pull it down. Also if any dances were held with people in costume, they would show up and break them up and harrass the participants. As a result, our people started to have dances at night at someone's home, with the curtains drawn. If any car lights showed up in the distance, the young guys who were on lookout knew this had to be the BIA police or the boss farmer, since they were the only ones with cars at the time. People would put their hand drums away, and since no one was in costume for these social dances—you didn't wear headdresses, feathers and bells—the police had nothing to go by. What was happening was the start of the social dance tradition.

In our Lakota tradition we didn't have social courtship kinds of dances like white people had. The only dance even close was the night dance, where under strict chaperoning by relatives, young men and women under the watchful eye of elder relatives who were in attendance exchanged gifts and danced together in public. There was no other dance where courtship was involved. Men and women observed their separate place in our society at all times. In this way, we tried to preserve the honor of our young girls and women. When we saw some of the dances at the forts and the white towns, we realized that we could have dances in private homes without being disrupted by the Indian police. We could dance in our street clothes at someone's house behind drawn curtains, and if any car lights showed up at the main roads, we could pretend we were having a family gathering, playing cards or some other kind of meeting. During this period, then, social dances like the rabbit dance became very popular.

Rabbit dance consisted of men and women in pairs, behind each other, all dancing in a clockwise direction, the man on the left, dancing together to songs that dealt with courtship and romance. There are stories that rabbit dance got its name because the steps, two forward with the left foot and then one back, are like rabbit tracks, or that the first time the people started to see rabbit dancing, the people who brought the dance drove off in a wagon up on a hill in the distance and then jumped out and turned into rabbits. In any case, when rabbit dance songs first got started, just before World War I, the song texts started with the word *cepansi,* older sister, or cousin in the white way. Rabbit songs always spoke from the woman's point of view. Even though men sang the songs, they were expressing the woman's perspective. They always told a little story. It was like the woman speaker was confiding some romantic thought about a man to her older sister or cousin. It was like she was looking to her for advice, "Is he all right? Should I get his name? Where is he from? Should I talk to him? Would you?" These thoughts of the modest Lakota woman in those early days were then replaced by the English word "dearie," which showed that the woman was now talking directly to the man instead of just confiding in her sister. Over time, these rabbit songs showed the impact of modern white values, of alcohol, and of family breakups which came with modern times.

The words in these songs started getting really strong after a while and they were making people jealous. I remember two or three times when some women got hit and some men even got knocked down by their wives. So this rabbit dancing died off a little in the 1960s because of family problems but it kept going as a social dance, and even today, although in a limited way, we still do rabbit songs and other social dance songs at certain times.

I think that at the same time these rabbit dances started to hit our culture we had *wioiste*, or love songs, become more popular. People didn't dance to love songs; they would just be sung and often would also be played on the flute. I think one of the most widely used love songs that all the flute players used to play is this one: "*Ho o'kawinh waku welo, ho o'kawinh waku weha. Tiwahe tanka ca omicele na ho o'kawinh waku welo. Cante waste win el waglihuni we. Ho o'kawinh waku weha. Cante waste win el waglihuni we.*" This says, "He went all around the circle of the camp to look for other women (two times). A number of times he went around that circle looking for other women but always comes back to his woman saying, 'I always come back to her.' He went all around the camp looking for other women, but 'I always come back to her.'" He walked the circle of the camp but couldn't find the equal of his sweetheart.

There are quite a few of these love songs since almost everybody at one time fell in love, or got their heart broken, or found an old love, or remembers the flame of an old love; so they all sing love songs for different purposes.

These kinds of love songs and the rabbit dance songs are the specialty of my *tahansi,* cousin, Irving Tail, who is sitting here with us as we talk. These kinds of songs are Irving's specialty. When you head down the road on a long drive, he can sit there and sing these songs one after the other.

IRVING TAIL: This song was made by a guy by the name of Roy Looks Twice. He was incarcerated at the time at Leavenworth, and while he was there with all that time, hah, he made up some songs. One of these songs goes like this: "*Iyotan cila kun, iyotan wokiye. Iyotan cila kun, iyotan wokiye. Iyotan cila kun, iyotan kiye mayaye.*"

SEVERT: That says, "I think the most of you and yet you are giving me a hard time." The texts to these songs are often really simple, but that allows people to put in their own feelings or memories for someone. Next I will ask my *tahansi* Irving to sing some rabbit songs. We'll start in from the early days of rabbit songs around 1920 or just before.

IRVING TAIL: This is one of the first rabbit dance songs that really became popular in the 1920s and it survived this long. *"Cepansi, kici wayaciki he tuwe so. Takeciyapi na tokiyatan hi so okiyakaye. Imacuka ca kici wowaglaka wacin ye."* This says, "My older sister, the man that you are dancing with, what is his name? Where did he come from? He sure attracts me, so I want to talk to him."

SEVERT: This song has a really nice tune and the words are very demanding. *Cepansi* is the older sister or cousin, which is the first word in these early rabbit songs, and the younger sister is asking her for advice and support to, in a way, talk to him, to let him know that she wants to talk to him and get to know him. But at that time to just come out and talk directly to a man was not proper for a young girl. Later on, in the late 1930s and 1940s, this first word *cepansi* is replaced by the word "dearie" in English, which now has the newer woman talking directly to the man. Maybe this English word was used at first as a sign that addressing a strange man directly was not the traditional way for a young Lakota woman to act. Most rabbit songs since then have used this word to start the text even when the rest of the words were all still in our Lakota language.

Irving also made a rabbit song when he spent time in jail in Lincoln, Nebraska. We call it the Hole Song. Irving made and sang this song while he was on bread and water down in the hole, solitary confinement, or whatever you call it. He served 120 days on bread and water because he had a disagreement with one of the inmate truck drivers. After that guy kept pushing Irving around—it's traditional for a Lakota man—at the end of the fourth time, Irving, who is not a big guy, got up and beat the hell out of the white inmate he had trouble with. At the time, the Indian population in the Lincoln facility was so small that the white prison system didn't listen to minorities. They didn't listen to Irving's side of how that other inmate was pushing him around and how as a traditional-minded Lakota person he finally defended himself. He ended up with 120 days in the hole. There's no light; you sleep on a cement floor with a bucket for a toilet and another for water, and with bread and water.

Singing kept him going. Singing to himself softly inside this tiny dark cell, he made this song. He composed it to remember something back a few years behind him. The traditional Lakota singer, when he's having a hard time, will come up with a song, *alowan,* a song about somebody that he remembers. It will make him feel good inside and he will endure through his singing. Even after this incident Irving kept singing while he was in Lincoln, and when he came out to sing with us, he was a good singer. While in jail he had kept up his family singing tradition and it helped him keep his mind together. This is very encouraging for those of our youth or other relatives who are behind bars. By singing to yourself and thinking about songs, your father's or grandfather's, no matter how difficult a time you're going through, it will give you added strength and serenity of mind.

If Irving can remember that song now, I want to ask him to sing what, in a humorous way, we call *Ohoka Olowan,* Hole Song.

IRVING TAIL: Let me remember it for a minute. Here it is: *"Dearie, tokiya tehan yaun esa ohinniya ciksuya. Tohan cante masice can iciye wiksuya."*

SEVERT: This song that Irving just got done singing and I gave a little history about says: "Dearie, no matter how far away you are, I have always remembered you. Whenever I feel lonesome or brokenhearted, I will always remember some of the things that you have said." I think my *tanhansi*'s song gives that encouraging message that when someone is living through difficulty and darkness, the words to good songs come to him as a singer and give him courage.

Another rabbit song from the 1940s was made by Pete Good Lance, who was gifted in making Omaha songs plus a lot of these rabbit songs. *"Dearie, waemaya kiyaska maweh'unwe wanna hena la kte. Itowapi kin micuna usniye."* This one says: "Dearie, I have heard that you have said some things about me, so now this is the end. Give my picture back and don't come to see me anymore." Again, we have a woman singing to a man. She has heard back through relatives or friends that he has gone someplace and said something unkind or negative about her. So this is a short, traditional song that tells a long story. If you have a lover or a boyfriend, he shouldn't talk about you or reveal things about you if he is going to be your lover. In this song she wants her picture back because her feelings are hurt. Oh, by the way, this happenend to me many times. I know a lot of women have asked for their pictures back from me! I was at some powwow and I was with a different girl and they found out, or I was at some rodeo with someone else, and the one who hears about it wants her picture back. So over time I spent a lot of money on stamps sending pictures back, sending them back UPS or special delivery. I'd never keep pictures if they were wanted back. Look at all these spots all over my walls. There were at least fifty to sixty pictures hanging there but they all wanted them back. It's hard to be a great lover.

I'll ask Irving to sing another rabbit song that talks about the difficult times lovers have.

IRVING TAIL: *"Dearie, wicoiye otaye, wicoiye otaye, itokasniye. Wancala wiconiye toksa iyecetu kte."*

SEVERT: This song says: "Dearie, there's a lot of talk about us, there's a lot of talk about us, but don't worry about it. There is only one lifetime and everything will work out for us." This song points out the difficult times lovers will have. I know how that goes too! I've had to mail back not only pictures but also support hose, and one woman asked for her orthopedic shoes that she left behind in my house. Ha! Other complications with families and living a great distance apart are involved in these songs too.

This other rabbit song was composed by Herman Arapahoe in the 1950s. It says, *"Dearie, mastincala waunci yunkan ehanni waweksuye na iha wau canna otakuyeko ai unyape."* This means "Dearie, as I was dancing a rabbit dance with you, I remembered some things about us a long time ago and I smiled as we danced. Now even our relatives are talking about us." Here it's understood that maybe the woman is married again but she danced with her former lover and, remembering a long time ago, she has a happy smile on her face so that relatives start to talk about the two of them. A long time ago there was respect among all the blood relatives and there was no time for gossip or spreading rumors. By the 1950s, when Herman Arapahoe made this song, maybe the whole social system had changed and now relatives were gossiping about each other instead of praising each other by their relationship, uncle, auntie, mom, or dad, as before.

Besides all these rabbit songs, where men and women dance as partners behind each other in a big circle, we also developed round dance songs at this time, although these weren't as much of a fad. In round dance, *naslohan wacipi*, or shuffling feet dance, the beat was a little faster than in rabbit dance and men and women danced in a large circle next to each other to the left. The songs often didn't have any words at all. Sometimes they were honor songs for warriors or soldiers, and sometimes they had words about romance. This song goes back to the thirties because then families were still picking husbands and wives for their daughters and sons. Families agreed that they wanted their children to marry each other and gave gifts to each other to seal the deal. The parents would then talk to their son or their daughter and inform them of their wishes. Often things worked out well, but as this song shows, in modern times young people thought they knew better.

IRVING TAIL: This is a song about a woman who is married but isn't happy: *"Miye cinkala higna wayesni ye sa. Iyotiye kiya mayuha ye. Inawakina niye unkun kte."* This song states, "Even though my family picked this man for me, I'm having a difficult time with our marriage. I'm willing to quit him and stay with you."

SEVERT: Still another rabbit song, from the late 1950s, goes like this: *"Dearie, tawicuya tunna nicinca ota yesa waste cilaka waun we. Wacin ki tiwahe najuju cinyin kte."* This song has the woman saying, "You are married and have a lot of children, but if I want to, I can break up your home and be with you." This one tells about how respect and honor of marriage no longer matter. If a younger woman is attracted to a man, she is willing to take him away from his wife to be with him. She is now the aggressor. It's like throwing a bomb into the middle of a family and breaking them up. I don't know how many times I've been married and I have lots of kids, but all these young girls are still after me and they always threaten to blow up my family, so they sing this song about me quite a bit. So you can call this the Severt Young Bear theme song.

Sometime in the early 1970s they started to put these rabbit songs into English. Two of these that our Porcupine Singers use a lot are: "Dearie, every time I see you, I can still remember the time when I was with you. I don't care what they say about us, honey, I still love you." I believe we heard that one first from Fort Kipp Singers from Montana. Another one with English words is kind of our group special: "Dearie, take me home, take me back to Porcupine. If you don't take me home, I will tell Momma on you!" Here this young woman, knowing how desirable our singers were, was asking to go home with one or she would raise a fuss. Maybe this is meant in fun, but of course it's true too.

These social dance songs—and there are many more than just these few—are a way of showing how, when the religious beliefs and ceremonies were outlawed after 1880 and the warrior societies and their dances were outlawed, the new social system brought in new social dances where you didn't need a traditional costume to dance; you could just dance in white street clothes. The words to these songs then also reflect these changes. In the early 1920s, rabbit dance songs have kind of innocent words like a young woman asking to meet a man, or a young woman remembering a bittersweet love affair. Then gradually in the thirties, the woman becomes bolder and more aggressive towards men. By the Second World War, women are talking about leaving their husbands to be with a lover. Alcohol and the problems it brings are also starting to show up in the fifties, and by the early seventies some songs are being composed in English. Irving Tail and his father before him, and other guys like Pete Good Lance, Herman Arapahoe, and Reuben Looks Twice were making these rabbit songs and identifying these social changes along the way.

In the old ways, a husband and wife could not dance together—I think it was a way of making them immune to jealousy—but by the 1960s things had changed so that husbands and wives were dancing together, and if a woman now found her husband dancing with another woman, he might get kicked or hit with a purse or even beat up. More jealousy was coming in over words in songs that never really happened; people didn't trust each other any more, and they forgot they were there to have a good time. That's why in the 1960s social dancing really lost its popularity.

I went through that myself. Some of us are so overly possessive that we don't allow our wives or girlfriends or our husbands and boyfriends to have a good time. If we're going to bring back understanding and identity, then we need to teach our children that the social dance songs with those strong words in them are saying at the same time that there is no room for being jealous or being overly possessive. The songs should be toughening us against jealousy rather than giving in to it.

Dancing for Money: Contests

When I became a traditional Lakota singer, my life took a new direction. That lifestyle brought me many gifts, friends, and honors; but most of all, it helped me find meaning in things. As part of all that, I began more and more to do research about our songs and our dances, our ceremonies and the right way songs should be sung for these. I often talked to our elders like Dawson No Horse, Royal Bull Bear, my dad and Uncle Henry, and many others. They shared many things with me to help me understand, and I try to share them in a humble way. Nobody knows everything, but we can try to gather different people's ways of understanding something and put ourselves in relationship to it all.

The way Irving Tail and I went through some of the ceremonial songs, the spiritual warrior songs, and social dance songs so far helps to show how our culture changed since the 1880s. The history of our Lakota dancing since that time can also help us put things in order. Dancing is such an important part of our tradition that we need to understand it better.

Before reservation days there was only one large, annual gathering of people. They would pick a site someplace, kind of central so that all could go there to camp two or three weeks or more. They would do all their sacred ceremonies—the annual Sun Dancing, naming ceremonies—our warrior societies would hold their dinners and parades; there was lots of visiting and even courting for the young people. There was also lots of dancing in the smaller gatherings of bands throughout the spring, summer, and fall and maybe a little less in the small winter camps.

Once we were put on the reservation, all that was restricted. We were told to be farmers and ranchers, so they restricted our traveling. In order for us to leave the reservation, we had to get a special permit signed by the superintendent. You could go visit your relatives at Cheyenne River or Standing Rock agencies but you could only stay for three days, and since it was the horse-and-wagon and horseback days, traveling was very limited. The songs that were sung at the time would only spread so far because as oral tradition, if you heard them, you had to catch them by ear and mind, memorize them, and with little traveling, songs didn't get spread very far. Although the travel restrictions got better in the 1940s, tape recorders weren't around until the 1950s and not popular till the middle '60s. After that, though, with recorders, and people getting better cars and pickups, songs spread far and wide across Indian country very quickly. Tribes were recording each other's songs and singing them in different places right away even if they hadn't caught them in person. The tape now was their memory.

Like I explained earlier, the reservation agents and superintendents also discouraged our *wacipis,* our dances, so we now danced on white American holidays or we sort of went underground by developing the social dance tradition secretly at people's houses. In the 1920s the commissioner of Indian affairs even sent out two orders to all reservation agents to stop our people from dancing and having our traditional giveaways. I've seen copies of these.

Let me talk a little now about some of our traditional dances that need to be understood. In the old days when you built a powwow shade or arbor—

we build them in a circle with the opening to the east and cover the frame with pine branches so spectators and dancers can get some shade under them—you first had an elder bless the ground. Then you would put up the uprights and cover the frame with the pine. The first day of the powwow, before you start to dance, you have a special victory dance called *owanko-nasto,* or grass-flattening song. The warriors would dance in a special way in the same direction so they would put down the grass for dancing. In this way, when the powwow was over, the grass could eventually stand back up. After World War I it was an honor for veterans and, later, American Legion members to get out there with their honors and flatten the grass in one direction. They would fire blanks in their rifles and reenact some battle dance with a Japanese or German flag. It wasn't really a grand entry type of thing like they have today where all the dancers dance into the arena behind each other at the beginning of the dancing. But later on, I think in the 1960s at the Pine Ridge Sun Dance Powwow—they held the Sun Dance in the mornings and the powwows in the afternoon and evenings at the same time—they did snake dancing in the arena. What that meant at the time was that they wanted to count all the dancers, so they had them dance in a follow-the-leader way in one long line.

That plus the influence of the grand entry they have at rodeos, where all the riders and queens and princesses with fancy shirts and colorful chaps and different flags ride in, led to the grand entries they started to have for many powwows since the 1960s. When dancing contests for more and bigger prize money came in, in the 1960s, the grand entry was also a way to get all the dancers out on time for every dance session or they would lose the grand entry points. To see all the dancers come in and fill the whole dance arena gives you a special feeling of being part of a big contest and powwow.

In the old days along with *owankonasto* they had a traditional way of people coming into the dancing circle or arena called *Omaha gli otake,* Omaha dancers coming and sitting. In those days when there was a celebration, they camped by bands. Each little band camped together in its own area around the dance shade. When they were ready, their chiefs, their Omaha dancers, their warriors, and other dancers would bring their own singers with them. They would stop four times before they came to the entrance of the arena or dance circle. Then they would dance into the arena under their band identity. They might have their singers get out in the middle and do four or five different songs and then sit down under the shade.

A long time ago there was also a woman's society made up of those who had brothers, sons, husbands, or fathers in the Brave Heart or the Kit Fox warrior societies. They would have special victory dances of their own. Sometimes they even used women singers to sing or they would ask men singers to get out in the center to sing for them. The women would get out into the arena and form a circle and dance in the *ipsila waci,* up-and-down fashion of dance. They carried sticks with scalps attached or other articles taken from the enemy their men had killed. While they danced they showed these trophies so the people could see that their brothers or husbands, their sons or their fathers had won these scalps. Later on they called this type of dancing where you jump with both feet leaving the ground *kat'ela waci,* which means they-really-dance-up-and-down dance.

This woman's society also had their own victory songs where they expressed their pride in their men and encouraged them to be brave against the enemy. One of them went like this: *"Koskalaka ki han ena wioyuspa hanpo. Miyestuka zuya omawani kte."* This means, "Young men, those of you who don't want to be warriors, stay here and chase women. I'm going on a war party to defend my people." Another goes like this: *"Kangi ki han wakta po! Sunkmanon sa he miye ca wa u yelo."* This says, "Crows, be careful! I'm the one who steals horses. Here I come again." It was a special society for women only and the drumming was like a fast round dance beat. Some of these songs are still around, but it will take some time to identify these songs and maybe bring that society back.

Another special society related to dancing were the men called those-who-carry-a-forked-stick. They had a special role in the ceremonial kettle dance. When the ceremonial kettle was put out in the arena and after several songs were sung for a group of eight dancers who danced around the kettle, then these two dancers would dance and charge the kettle four times. In the beginning it was a kind of short, choppy song and toward the end of each rendition there would be four heavy beats on the drum and they would get down. Then with the start of the next song, they would use a fluid toe-and-heel dance rhythm to approach and charge the kettle. Each time it gets a little faster until at the end of the fourth time, one of the two dancers—they both carry forked sticks but only one is picked to stick the forked end into the kettle—finishes it by putting his stick into the kettle. It's like a *tokakte,* killing the enemy. Charging and striking a dropped eagle feather is also *tokakte* and so is the striking of the kettle with the forked stick. It's now considered free of any evil spirits, and in this kettle dance the ceremonial offering of the dog in the kettle can now be completed.

The dancers who used those forked sticks were part of a sacred society and in modern times there was only one man who was recognized for that, a real good dancer, the late John Attack Him, Sr. Before that, Kenneth Short Bear and Alphonso Good Shield from Porcupine were fork dancers too. John Attack Him would dance at powwows with a forked stick with feathers and stuff on it identifying himself as a fork dancer. I don't know of him ever passing that right to another, but at powwows you often see dancers out there with that forked stick, maybe because they saw John win first place at some contest with that stick so they start to carry one too. Only the ones who are real kettle dance forked-stick dancers should carry one. That's the respectful way.

Another part of our old-time dance history is the *oskate,* or show tradition. From the 1890s to the First World War, a lot of Indian families were taken along on Wild West shows like the Buffalo Bill Cody Wild West show or the Ranch 101 Wild West show. They traveled around the world showing the Indian people attacking stage wagons or people whose wagons were upside down. Our people also danced in the parades advertising the shows and during the shows. They also had chuck wagon races, bronc riding and Indian dancing and singing. Some even chased buffalo across the arena.

They would sing special *oskate* songs for those who were show people. Here's one from the early 1890s: *"Pte San Wicasa blihic'iyayo. Oskate wayinkta waciniyanpelo. Mni wanca watakihotun hi najin ki cante iyani pa kte lo."* (White Buffalo Man—his name was Sam Stabber—be brave! There's a big Wild West show coming for you. When you hear the sound of the boat, your heart will beat faster.) This next one is one that my cousin Irving Tail often sings: *"Oskate wan iyayinkte ca iyapi wapaha iwekcuna winyeya he wa u."* Then they name that person, like *Pte San Wicasa,* and then it goes on, *"heina oskate ekta iya."* This says, "There will be a Wild West show that will start soon, so I got my war bonnet ready and I'm ready to go. This is what White Buffalo Man said, and then he went to the Wild West show."

Back in the 1920s and 1930s the *Omaha wacipi,* Omaha dance, came on strong. That's probably why the BIA tried to stop it. The *tokala,* or Kit Fox warriors, had used small bustles of mostly hawk and owl feathers mixed and only two eagle feathers in their roach headdresses. The Omaha dancers wore *u*-shaped or butterfly-shaped bustles of eagle feathers with plumes on them that were more attractive. They wore louder bells and colored shirts and sang different dance songs, even some about how a young man wants to get a woman. So they weren't just singing about warrior themes.

Earlier on we had the Lakota grass dancing, *peji mignaka*. Dancers would go out and get that tall grass, tie it together, and wear it like a back bustle or like a sash across the chest. They do a lot of fancy footwork, cross their legs over and go sideways, make circles, and like that. Omaha dancers and Fox Society dancers, who were straight dancers by comparison, might go down low but nothing fancy like the grass dancers. There were also Buffalo Society dancers who wore orange-color buffalo grass as a small bustle. Up north it's different; they have ribbons and shaggy yarn wool on their legs. Each tribe is different.

Originally this grass dance and the Omaha dance were two different ways of dancing, but later on their songs and costuming came together. The dancing started to change, too. You started to dance around the arena in a circle instead of every which way. The warrior dances, the Omaha dance, and the grass dance merged together to form what we call traditional dancing today. Now everybody dances, even little girls, to all kinds of songs.

During all these changes, the government kept trying to take the warrior image away from our young men. Starting in the early 1880s we were harrassed to stop doing sacred ceremonies, to stop doing fasting and the sweat lodge. The Sun Dance was outlawed and the warrior society dances as well as the Omaha and grass dances were discouraged and even forbidden. You kill the spirit in the Lakota man once you take all that away from him. Once you do that, you'll have an empty man who easily gives in to anything that pressures him from the outside, an empty man who can be manipulated. They used public laws and congressional acts to get at him at the same time they used the Bible. He was pushed to be a farmer or rancher, he had to be baptized and be a Christian. So that was the Lakota man's fight, that was his constant fight from 1880 to 1973. In 1973, with Wounded Knee II, when the American Indian Movement took over Wounded Knee, we finally overturned that system of almost one hundred years of going after the spirit of our Lakota people.

During that hundred years of persecution, it was the few traditional people way out in the Badlands and way out here in the grass-roots districts who continued to sing those songs and continued to talk about the ceremonies and who lived that traditional, simple way of life. No matter the hardships and the hard times, they survived and their songs and dances and their ceremonies survived. So it's not the leadership at the agency that saved our tradition. It's the humble traditional people way out here in the hills who in the evenings, when nobody was around, would sing and talk about these ceremonies and talk to their kids about it. With Wounded Knee II in 1973 there was no attempt to return to the traditions of before 1880, but an attempt of reviving without fully understanding what they were reviving. So that hundred years of choking off our culture might have come to an end in 1973 at Wounded Knee II, but we have to work hard to put it all together again without going overboard because we don't fully understand some things anymore.

I think the main way to bring some kind of special order into our communities and *tiyospayes*, our extended families, is to start putting the different societies back together. I think we need to recover those that could have meaning today like the Elk Society, the Buffalo Society, and the Brave Heart Society. We have a lot of World War II, Korea, and Vietnam veterans. The warrior society rituals need to be put back in order again so that members can practice the society rituals when they go to public gatherings. These kinds of societies would help members to identify; they could put on their uniforms and dance and represent themselves in an orderly and honored way. One of my uncles, Oscar Bear Runner, when he was younger, used to have a German flag he captured and a German helmet, and on any Flag Day, or Memorial Day, or Fourth of July, or Veterans Day he would have those and get out and dance. It was a source of pride and identity for him. Somehow all these customs are dying off. But I think we can save a lot of these practices if we can bring back the system of societies. The songs are still here.

We can also still do research to find things. One of the best research sources that I know of is the Walker Collection, you know, that doctor who came here to Pine Ridge about a hundred years ago and actually interviewed the old medicine men, the warriors, the society guys (we put his works in our bibliography at the end of this book). If you interpret and read between the lines, you can almost put that stuff in order. We have lots of other writers, many writing for their own reasons and with questionable ideas, who have written about us Lakotas, but they are not in-depth like Walker was. In a way he was trying to do for his time what we are trying to do with this book. Only by putting things in order can you get respect and honor.

With the 1960s and the new interest in our traditions that peaked during the Wounded Knee II takeover time, our dance traditions produced the dance contests that now take place all over the country where Indian communities, dance clubs, or university Indian students' clubs are located. In 1960 an American Association of Indian Activities (AAIA) started in Eagle Butte. They started the first dancing contest that I know of. I think first place was fifty dollars. Since then we have seen these contests grow and grow almost as fast as all the new gambling casinos on many of our reservations. Today the dancing contests are big business. Now they often have twenty-five hundred dollars for first place and one thousand dollars and five hundred dollars for second and third. This prize money has replaced what used to be at the heart of the traditional powwow, the honoring, giveaways, and name giving. Now they put you on a contest committee but you don't prepare yourself the way the traditional powwow, with its balance of honor and responsibility, made you do. Now you're part of a committee which gives out big prize money. The committee members now have excuses like "We're giving out big prize money, so I don't have to feed and I don't have to have a give away." Or "I'm contest chairman, so I don't have to have a giveaway, with that thirty-five thousand dollar total prize money." The mentality of honor and responsibility has changed. We don't prepare ourselves or plan like we used to. Now when the singers sing you a special song, you give away ten dollars or twenty dollars and that's it. The obligation has been forgotten.

But yet, that's what our youth needs to understand. They should understand why you sew all fall, why you bead, you collect things; every time you go shopping, when you have a hundred-dollar bill, you buy eighty dollars' worth for your family and twenty dollars' worth you buy for your giveaway. That's the heart of our Indian tradition. Contests have diluted all that and made it less meaningful.

Today we have two kinds of dance celebrations. We have some traditional-minded people that live that traditional way of life and mainly go to the small, traditional powwows and dance there for the enjoyment of dancing. But then we also have a new class of dancers. I call them powwow politicians. They only go to the big dancing contests; their name alone often helps them to win. The people look up to them as a star dancer, some kind of superstar. Often this way if you know the committee or the head judge, if you have a celebrity name, then you win. From my experience, some points in tabulating contest judges' scores are even changed after the scorecards are handed in. Favoritism and bad feelings get involved because money is at stake.

What makes you a championship dancer in this new contest situation? Your name and reputation, who your father or uncle is, your costume and its coloring, your actions as you dance. Are you friendly with the master of ceremonies? Do you joke with him and he with you? Do you shake hands with the committee and do you get along with everybody? Do you dance to every song and show good sportsmanship? All these things make a champion. Clear into about 1977, we had champion dancers whose whole body danced to the song. Good songs have a special feeling about them, in their melody, their pitch, to make the dancers move to that song. But now most of the dancers dance alike. It's like we have an aerobics instructor out in the center who tells us to swing our legs twice this way and three times that way and everybody is making the same moves. Too many dancers at contests are making the same moves. They no longer dance to the songs in a personal interpretive way. One time I said, "Why don't we just hit the drum without singing because they're just dancing to the drum, not the song." Some of the outstanding dancers who moved their bodies to respond to the song used to be Timothy Hale from Cherry Creek, Tyrone Head from Saint Francis, Acorn Tyon from Pine Ridge. They danced to the nature of the song. Even in traditional dancing, Amos Lone Hill, Ellis Chips, Ellis Head, and Dawson No Horse and some of the other traditional dancers used to dance to each particular song. They would interpret its special nature.

Traditionally everything the Lakota did in sacred ceremonies goes to the left. In ceremonial and social dances you also lead to the left. Only in Omaha and intertribal dancing do the men dancers go in a counterclockwise manner while women dance in a clockwise way. You also always step on the louder beat so that all dancers are moving to the same beat. Women's traditional dancers, when they dance in place, go up on the loud beat and down on the soft. Although in all of these songs the rhythm makes dancers move in time as they echo the beat, it is the motivation of the song that makes the best dancers show their stuff.

What seems to happen in the contests is that showmanship and competition take over from the sharing and honoring of the traditional celebrations. I think that contests are bringing young people out to the center and getting them involved, but often without understanding or knowing their family traditions. They might put on a costume because they saw someone from Oklahoma win first place with a special kind of face paint or a special kind of bustle; or they saw somebody from North Dakota take first place dressed in a certain way, so they put similar things on their dance costume just to impress the judges and the crowd. The authentic expression of family and personal pride is not involved. Something is missing.

The use of whistles today is a good example of the confusion that results from not understanding the specific reasons of an act or way of dressing. Now, there are two kinds of whistles. The eagle-bone whistle is a sacred instrument used for sacred ceremonies. It doesn't belong in the powwow arena or public social gatherings. The other one is the whistle carried by some dancers at powwows. Sometimes you might have three hundred dancers and most of them act like whistle carriers. But to understand the appropriate use of whistles at powwows, we need to go back to the old prereservation community structure.

In those *tiyospaye*, the extended families, they shared the authority, the recognition, the respect, and the honors within the bands. There was usually one drum keeper and one head singer, one whip man, one Eagle Society, one *tokala* warrior society dance leader. And there was only one whistle carrier in that village or camp. The reason he carried that whistle was that if some singers were singing a song, he might say: "Hey, this is a good song; people are enjoying this song. Towards the end of this song I will blow this whistle four times and make them repeat this song that many times to give additional pleasure and a good time to the people." So he had been given the authority to blow that whistle four times and that community knew him as their whistle man. That was once a highly respected position. If an elderly dancer who was the whistle carrier could no longer dance, he would put on a feast and giveaway. Then he would blow his whistle to the four directions and give words of advice and encouragement to the young man chosen to replace him. They wouldn't just hand it down and say, "Well, I was a whistle carrier, so I want my ten sons to be." It has to be someone who he felt would carry on the honored tradition in the right way.

I'll give you an example. If our Brotherhood Community was having a powwow, then the whistle carrier in our community has the right to carry the whistle here. If any other whistle carrier comes from another district or other tribe, he should come to our dance in respect and go to the head of the committee, give him tobacco or gifts, and say, "I'm a whistle carrier, so I'd like to be recognized for having the authority from my own people, and if there's a good song here, if it's a good time, if you let me, I'll blow my whistle and give a gift to the singers." He might also give a gift to our whistle carrier here and say, "I'm a whistle carrier and I might blow my whistle, so I want to shake hands and give you these gifts." In English you call it protocol or etiquette. The committee might then tell him to sit in a special chair and when that song comes that people like, he has been given the right to act as a whistle carrier here. When he does that, then he explains why and how he was chosen as whistle carrier back home and had been granted the right to be that here too. Then he would donate to somebody for having used his whistle.

Now remember, it's different from one tribe to the next. It's who you represent and who gave you the authority to carry that instrument. But at least dancers shouldn't carry and blow whistles because they suddenly feel like it. It should be done in the handed-down way and with thoughtful respect.

At dancing contests today it's too bad but all that is changed. Now lots of people blow the whistle when they feel like it, even little boys. I feel dancers are abusing the right way because they want to show off publicly or get attention, and so they go beyond the proper limit. Then, too, sometimes the attitude is "Well, this is a big contest with prize money, not a traditional dance, so anybody can blow the whistle."

The contest has affected things because competition for money is the reason why many dancers dance, and everybody expects a good show with lots of color and excitement, so the time-honored practices are changed, or ignored, or compromised on. Then, too, what happens at most contests is that different tribes get together and compete with their singing and dancing against each other. The set culture of one community or tribe is then set aside to be open to other tribes' ways, but the heart of that host tribe's ways is lost. Dancers and singers become careless and forget their tribal restrictions and guidelines.

So it's important to realize that even out in the center of the arena there is temptation to go beyond the proper limit, to go too far. I used to think about this often. I tried just about everything. I got involved in many things that went on in my district and tribe. One of my grandfathers, his name was Eagle Heart, said that everybody has a hill to climb and needs to meet that challenge, and in this way identify with the hill. Then my dad too said, "When you do something, if you're gonna do it halfway, don't do it at all. Give one hundred percent." He used to make us run and chase baseballs and ride horseback and run some more. So everything that I got involved in, I gave it my best. I also tried to think of other people first, their feelings, their needs, and their rights. I was never ashamed of anything that I did, because I remembered to maintain the limit.

One of these days after I'm gone to the happy hunting ground I will start another singing group or start another dancing club. I'll put on the biggest traditional powwow that was ever held, because all the traditional dancers and singers that are all gone to the beyond will be there. I think they will remember me because I tried to do the right thing and because I cared.

PART FOUR

*Running on
the Edge*

❧ The Search for Modern Lakota Identity

WHAT IS your place in this world? What is your history? Why are things done this way? What is your family tree? What do you believe in? These are some of the things that are troubling our Lakota young people. If we are going to offer them a way to center themselves, a road of their own choice, or a star to lead them in the dark night, we need to show them that after countless years of pain and joy, we have something to offer. We need to provide them a plan, a map that comes from centuries of living. What have we learned? Even though our Lakota ways have been bombarded by an alien culture from the outside, we have saved up some insights and some small bits of wisdom. The pains have left us with some outcomes.

Identity: Knowing All of Yourself

Our Lakota people understand some things. Identity is based on the idea of *slolic'iya*, knowing who you are. In connection with that is the notion that there are limits, of only going so far, of having a limit. Around us there's an aura, a barrier that goes around us, a limit of our being. To get beyond that to the universe and the Great Spirit, we use our voice, we throw our voice loud and clear, we get on top of a hill and throw our voice in prayer. In this way we hope to find ourselves. It used to work, but now it takes a special effort to succeed.

I think in today's world we're lacking those elders who would go to a family and give words of encouragement and advice. Our kids have too much meaningless time on their hands. One of the damaging things that lots of parents say is "I never had those things I want my child to have." That means a motorcycle, color tv, stereo, and other material desires that child has. And I think that brings us to that identity again. Identity requires knowing that there is a limit. In our traditional teaching the child or youth has to learn that he or she has to learn to deal with hard times. This is why the traditional Lakota system can't be applied to today's world, because that goes by too fast and we think in order for us to be good, loving parents, we just have to buy our children's love. Traditional parents deny certain things to their children till they think they have deserved them. Then they would buy things.

Back in the 1940s and 1950s some families would give their boy a real ugly plug to ride who was almost a dead horse so that boy could whip and kick it to keep it going. But that was teaching the boy to be in balance with that animal. When he balked and didn't want to go, that boy had to learn to have patience and be able to coax that horse to get into a little trot or gallop. Once you were not in rhythm with that horse, you fell off. So you cried a bit and got back on. And after the parents felt that you'd mastered the technique of balance on a horse, they'd give you a little better one. Then pretty soon, as you'd grow up, you'd get a real active, lively one that you'd be proud to ride in any gathering and show off a little bit in front of girls.

That was the traditional way of slowly teaching a child to make the commitment and accept the responsibility of how to be in balance with that animal. Giving a child the finest horse when he wasn't ready for it kept him from working his way through his own limits.

The whole system changed now in today's world because we have to buy our children's love. We feel that we have to prove to our children that we're loving parents even though we neglect them. We buy them the best from the start, so they have a hard time mastering that machine and equipment a step at a time. Eventually they get hurt by it. We push them to go beyond the limit right for them at that particular time. As soon as they turn thirteen, we say, "Hey, you're thirteen. You should have a girlfriend, so go ahead and take the car and go driving." Then when they get into an accident or hit a cow on the highway, we're the ones that cry, that shed tears. But instead of seeing our role in it, we blame somebody else. We blame the teachers or the police or some other car who went around him real fast and made him tip over. But if we thought about it, we're the ones who pushed him, we're the ones who gave him the keys that evening to go for a drive in a highly charged vehicle.

In the traditional way of teaching our youth, they have to master something in stages. If it's running, your elders might make you run up a hill for two or three years till you mastered that hill and were able to maintain the same speed till you got to the top. Then they might let you run longer and run a couple of hills till you mastered the breathing ability you'd need if the enemy shot your horse out from under you. Then you'd run even longer distances to improve yourself.

The traditional Lakota identity was developed by knowing the different limits of things. It's slow and you have to have patience to learn responsibility and commitment. You learn to master that horse, or your running ability, or the herding of one hundred head of horses by yourself. But the parents and other family members also have to show their responsibility and commitment to pay for that respect and honor in the eyes of the people. When something important happens to the young, you don't just celebrate in your small family circle, but you make it a public event and you put on a feast and giveaway for the whole community. All these traditional events were done publicly. They call that *oyate ki wayankapi kte* (in the eyes of the people). That is a bond or seal that you cannot break. The things you do inside the home only your mother or brothers might see. But in front of a crowd, in the eyes of people, you bond and seal something that you cannot break.

That's when you show your love for your child in the eyes of the people. On that special day you put on his best beaded moccasins and prepare him in his best clothing. You also prepare many other things. It's not an overnight thing. It takes a while to get ready for such an event. I explained preparing for a feast and giveaway earlier, so I won't go through it all here again. When it's done right, you as a parent and as a family are honoring the child or young person for mastering certain parts of his life. It's done in public so that the people honor and respect these children. When they go in a crowd, people remember their Indian names and what their families did for them. In turn, these children, in public, have to conduct themselves in a respectable manner so it doesn't shame themselves or their family. In this way the family used to provide a system of support but also of control and limits.

I think that system isn't working anymore because we let ourselves be isolated into one small family. We say, "I'll do what's good for me and what's good for my child. The heck with Grandma. Let's put her in a nursing home." Our old people have too often become a burden today and we don't listen to them anymore. The respect for the elderly is fading along with the parents' commitment and interest not only for their own children but the network of the larger family, that *tiyospaye*. The family history and family songs are also forgotten and the social system is out of order.

Courtship and picking a husband or wife used to have certain limits also. No *tahansi*, or cousin, could marry another. It had to be somebody from another band before the families would agree to a marriage. Marriage could be arranged in several ways. There's one system in our traditional Lakota system that was called *wi'inahma*, bringing a woman home secretly. They said "secretly" because even though the parents might agree, they didn't have the material things to make it public. Another reason is that one of the two young people might be considered *hlete,* or a wild and crazy one who came to the other's tipi after dark and stayed till early morning or even for a couple of days. If this *wi'inahma* worked and became more stable, they might stay together secretly till one of the parents stepped forward to give them gifts or to clothe their new in-law. That was a show of acceptance into the family. If that family didn't have the material things right then and there, they might go to the council of elders and ask permission for them to stay together but that a year from now or in two years they would get ready and marry in the traditional Lakota marriage ceremony where the two families agreed that their son and daughter would marry.

This formal way of marriage was called *wokiciyuze.* The families agreed and set a date, prepared, and asked an influential leader or a man and woman who have stayed married for a long time to marry them, to tie the bond of marriage. They would usually tie a piece of buffalo hide and wrap it around their arms held together. They would sing and pray; have them smoke a sacred pipe; tie a plume in their hair; eat *wasna,* a dried-meat snack; and drink *canpahanpi,* chokecherry juice, which are both ceremonial foods. Horses were exchanged as gifts from one family to the other.

Some leaders might have more than one wife; a few even had four or five. From the stories I've heard in our family, a couple of my great-grandfathers had multiple wives. There would usually be an agreement made between the man and the woman and also the other woman he was going to marry. She would often be a cousin or sister of the first wife. The reason they would keep it in the bloodline of the wife's family was so there would be no jealousy. The reason for taking a second or third wife might be due to the first wife's health, or some reason why she couldn't have a child or have a second one. The men who did this were high-ranking warriors who had earned many honors and horses in war. To keep their status and maintain their status they had to give many feasts and give gifts to their people and visitors. One wife just couldn't keep up with the work.

The women in a family prepared their daughters to marry a chief or leader. Sometimes that made it hard on the young men who couldn't go to war or become warriors. A warrior with many honors often had his pick of the best of the women in the village because he was a desirable provider and had great status his wife would share. It was also to the benefit of the wife's family to have such a respected man in their family now. Such men could also bring back women from other villages or even other tribes. I've seen a list from 1881 of Porcupine District which included quite a few Ree and Crow women who had been brought back and became wives but often had to do the heavy daily chores.

We also had traditional ways of divorcing. A wife could divorce her husband by putting his things outside the tipi door and in this way sending him back to his family, or she might just leave and return to her own family. Men had a couple of formal ways of divorcing their wives. This was called *wi'ihpeya*, to throw away the woman. This happened at times. Again, you would do this publicly. You would put the woman and her best on a horse, you ask the people to form a circle, go to the center, and announce the reason why you're throwing her away. Usually the reason was that she had done something against the social system or the family. A man would *waktoglake*, tell of his exploits, strike the drum four times, and tell why he was throwing her away. It was a disgrace for the woman. Often, before this divorce, the council of elders would debate the problem or invite a couple of well-known elderly women to debate this issue with them. If the wife to be divorced had committed a serious enough crime, they might cut her braid on one side, clear behind the ear. This meant that she couldn't go out in public until that braid grew to the same length as the other one. Or they might cut one ear lobe off, or for a very serious punishment, they might cut the tip of her nose off for being unfaithful to her man. This didn't happen a great deal. The old Lakota social system was very strict and there were very few women who broke its rules.

I'll tell you a story related to me by Nellie Red Owl, one of our respected elderly ladies here at Pine Ridge. A long time ago, she said, her mother and other people would see a woman dancing with a feather fan and waving the fan at certain times. So the mother and three other ladies, who were all young girls at the time, asked her father, "We are dancers too, so why don't you make us fans we can use when we dance?" He brought an elderly respected man and asked him to explain why that one woman was the only one dancing with a fan. After they fed this man, the father put these girls in a circle and the man talked to them. "You know, the reason why that woman is dancing whith that feather fan is that she was unfaithful to a man and she was thrown away by that man. She publicly has to hide her face and shame, even though she wants to dance." The he pointed to those four girls and said, "Were you unfaithful to your man?" They all said no. "Then you don't deserve a fan!" In this way the girls learned that such a woman was thrown away and was up for grabs or not worth marrying. This kind of *hlete winyan*, loose woman, was ready to sleep with any young man. Today many of our young women dancers carry feathers fans without knowing the real meaning of why a few women in the old days carried them.

I've spent many hours thinking about the identity search of our people. Starting with the 1880s the government attacked our traditional Lakota identity to make us into modern American citizens. The first step in this forced identity change was to kill our spirit. They cut our men's hair real short way above the ears, almost like an army or marine recruit type of hair-cut. So we lost the identity of long hair, the look of a traditional man and the spiritual meaning of hair. They went after our women, too, cut their hair almost above the ear and put waves in there. They also lost the Lakota look of their long, shiny hair. Men had to wear uniforms or white clothes and women had to wear cloth dresses. I have pictures of my father wearing a uniform when he was in boarding school. They marched every morning; they stood and saluted every morning. They shipped them away to school all over, to Carlisle, Pennsylvania, to Oklahoma or Santa Fe. They made every effort to wipe out Indian culture and language. They would deny you bread and food and raisins and apricots.

They spent a lot of time chasing the young guys who ran away. They whipped them and punished them in the boiler rooms. They put them on bread and water and locked them in their dorm rooms, but the first chance they got, these boys still ran. So they had our own Indian police chasing these guys. One of my uncles, George Gap, was known for that. The first chance he'd get, he'd be back here. He was a good, fast runner, so they had a hard time catching him. From the way my mom talked, they used to have three horses staked out so he could run in any direction, jump on one, and disappear. The tactic of the officials was to come early in the morning, walk in the house, and take the child, put handcuffs or a rope on him and take him. So a lot of these young guys knew that, so they stayed home all day and half the night and at midnight they'd go somewhere else, or they'd sleep out in the fields someplace, or in little sweat-lodge-type huts built all over. When their homes got raided early in the morning, they weren't there. They came back later in the day and sat around and ate and before morning they were gone again. These were the types of guys who survived and kept our Indian tradition.

Once the students from the schools returned home, they often didn't come back to the Indian side of it. My own generation came back to Lakota tradition even less. They were often embarrassed and ashamed of their traditions and didn't want to keep up their language and the *Lakol wicoh'an,* the Lakota ways. Without their own culture to hold onto, our young people started to imitate others, to copy somebody else. We now go the movies and they show somebody shooting drugs in their veins and dancing around snapping their fingers, playing a big ghetto blaster with rock music. So we buy one and put on some hip clothes. We do the different drugs and act cool, strutting around. It's like we always want to be something else. When Chubby Checker came out with the twist, it caught on here. Even the break dancing that became popular here in the early 1980s was popular because of the loudness of the music, the clothes, and the body movements. It said, "I'm a cool guy."

My younger brother and his crowd used to get into that. They would wear a real thin necktie, white shirt, and sportcoat and get into that twist. They would find Chubby Checker, James Brown, or some black guy that's doing break dancing. They'd have to get the right tennis shoes, black pants, the black shiny jackets, to become someone else. But they found a false identity to identify with, the main problem we have. Lakota youth have to identify with Lakota leaders in order to remain Lakota.

I once went to a workshop about unemployment in Rapid City. All the old questions and concerns came up. Why do Indian people not work steady? Why don't they leave the reservation to get jobs in the city? On the way back we got to talking. I asked a mother riding with us, "Why is it that your family has three sons living with you that never took the time or made the effort to go find a job and apartment in Rapid City?" The mother said, "You know, I hate to send my kids out. I would rather have my kids be part of the statistics here on the reservation, the eighty percent unemployment. I like to have them stay here with me so at least they will be safe. The only thing waiting for them in Rapid City is for them to get drunk, commit a crime, and be thrown in jail. The only thing waiting for them in Rapid City is to write a bad check and be sent to prison."

I think what this story shows is that our young people haven't taken on the identity that was pressed on them so hard in school, in church, and on television. Once they go out from the reservation, not only have they lost the support of their own culture but aren't at home in the outside white culture either. They don't know the limits of their own ways and break the limits of white society too. I think if they were more at home with their Lakota identity, they could adjust better to a strange one.

I think we need to express or put forth our Lakota identity to our youth.

We need tribal programs that deal with youth in order to in some way create identity for Lakota young people. We need teachers and elderly resource people to model identity. The curriculum from the state needs to be improved to enforce courses that have identity value for youth. Once you give a youth a chance to find himself and have some kind of identity, then he'll be more receptive to you and he won't have as many angry or negative feelings about everything. He'll be more receptive because he knows who he is; you can't deny his identity any longer.

Slow Thinkers and Silent Eaters: Lakota Leadership

One of the ingredients that kept our traditional social system in balance was the leadership that provided a model of behavior for the rest of the people. Leadership is very important because if you're going to be a leader and keep any group together, that takes half of your body. You can't just take care of yourself and your family; you have to take care of your whole *wicoti*, or camp, your whole community. How many persons can do that, can maintain that for a lifetime? This is why leadership in our tribe and the districts today often falls apart—because the modern elected leadership serves only a one-year or two-year term. You give part of yourself to the people, but in return you get paid for it while you're in office for a limited time. The old leadership is a different leadership.

I'll give you a story my dad told me. One of our relatives was a chief who had a younger wife. He also had a *tahansi*, a cousin, who kept messing around with his wife. So this chief said to his wife, *"Hecun sni yo."* (Don't do that.) He said to her, "I'm chief here in this village. Don't do that. You'll make it look bad for yourself." In this way he warned her three times. The third time he said, *"Hecun sni yo ogna ksuye nici yin kte."* (Don't do that; you'll only hurt yourself, so remember.) Then his wife and his cousin ran off; they both left their village. Then the people watched him to see what he would do. He was supposed to be a brave warrior, a great leader, so he might go after them, might shoot both of them. So the people watched him, but he went about his business normally, maintained his home, his horses, and his village, just went about his business. Then, all of a sudden, one day his woman—at that time they didn't say wife—came back. She went back to his tipi. He said, "Come in," so she went in. The people were watching, just wondering. They thought there would be a real big fight in that tipi, that the tipi would be bulging here and there, things would get thrown around, but nothing happened. It was quiet. So the next day they still watched him but he went about his business normally. The only thing he said to his wife was, "Are you happy now? You did all this and now you're back." She said, "Yes." He said, *"Iyo nicipe he?"* (Are you happy?) She said, "Yes." So he went about his business.

Then one day, his *tahansi,* his cousin, came back to the village to his parents' tipi. Again the people watched the chief. They figured that he might get jealous or get mad and go over there and do something violent. He was the leader, so he might even kick the whole family out. But he didn't do anything unusual. Then one day he caught two of his best horses, the one he went to war on and the one he caught buffalo with, his best, and he put his wife on the best and piled everything that belonged to his wife and even his own things on. He got ready and he sang a song for himself, went all around camp, and came up to his *tahansi's* tent. Right away everybody came out saying, "Oh-oh, big trouble!" He went up to that tipi, he sang that song, and he *waktoglake,* told his exploits, what he had done, what his life had been like. He called his aunt and uncle out, and his *tahansi* out too. Then he said, *"Tahansi,* I thought you were my relative, and I thought you were a man that could go out and earn those honors so that you could go pick any available woman in the village, and pick yourself a wife. But you couldn't do it, so I'll give my honor to you. I'll give you the horse I kill the enemy with; I'll give you my other horse I kill buffalo with. I'll honor you because you can't earn those honors yourself. You've been after my woman, so I'll give her to you. From this day forth, she's your woman," he said. "That tipi over there, with everything that's in it, that's your new home. You cannot do it yourself; you cannot go and kill buffalo and get enough hides and build that home for your woman, so you have to take mine. I'm a man, so I'll start a new home. I have enough honor so I can find myself a new woman." Then he gave his wife and everything away. That was a leader.

This shows how a man accepted by the people as leader because of his honor maintains it. If he had gotten really jealous and beat up his wife or beat up his cousin or kicked the whole family out of that village, or if he had any other thing on his mind about getting even, he would have never been the right kind of leader. Instead, to prove himself in the eyes of the people, he *waktoglake* to tell who he was, and then he even honored the man who had taken his woman.

In this way, the identity of our leaders was to maintain a normal, balanced life even though he was going through a family crisis. For the good of his people he kept the normal order of things. He showed that to be a lifetime leader, which our chiefs were, there's no room for greed or jealousy or petty personal things. If you're going to be that leader, you have to watch yourself and maintain self-control. That's very hard, and I think this is one of the real hard teachings of Lakota life that we don't see anymore.

In those old days, once a chief started a band and formed his own kinship group in that camp, then in marriages there couldn't be any inbreeding of families. You had to marry outside of the band. This is why a long time ago they didn't have any mind problems or any kind of deformity, because they watched the bloodlines of their families closely. So if the camps would camp close together and young boys and girls would eye each other, someone would say, "No, that's our relative, my cousin or my uncle!"

In those times we also had a council of elders that made decisions concerning warfare, accepting war pipes from other bands who wanted us to join them against an enemy, or decided which *toka*, enemy, we would go against, how many warriors would go, and what horses they would ride. We also had another council of elders that would make a ruling on the buffalo hunt. They understood that you cannot overdo anything, so they'd okay only killing those who were not females bearing calves, or only the older ones on the edge of the herd. So in some movies where they show Indians running three thousand buffalo over a bank, butchering some, and leaving the rest, it just wasn't that way. Maybe some other tribes did this, but the Lakota were very strict. You couldn't overkill anything, whether it was buffalo or deer. These decisions, when to hunt and what, were made by this council of elders. This council of elders also had different societies within it, such as a smaller group to deal with the movement of camp or another which decided which way to face camp. One of these was the Silent Eaters, a group that would meet for feasts and eat in silence to stress how important thoughtful silence was in their role as elders. The overall group was called the *naca*, the councilors.

In the old chief-and-council-of-elders system, the chief was often the poorest member of that band because he always shared what he had. Yet he was the wealthiest man in the way he took care of his people and the status the prayers of his people gave him.

The chief—the Lakota words for chief are *wicasa itancan*—was more or less there to provide executive leadership. In the old days, when they picked a chief as leader, four symbols were used to install him. In the earlier days it was a bow and arrow made for him and a *taniga*, animal tripe or paunch container—or after traders got here, a metal pot or coffeepot—then a sacred pipe, and a horse. They would explain the bow and arrow and horse symbols. Since he now was a leader, if the enemy came and circled the camp, he'd be the first to put on his weapons, get his bow, and charge the enemy so the fighting would not be in the camp where women and children would be hurt. He was to draw the enemy away from the camp and have the fight. You must also be ready to share your horses with the needy, the *unsika*. If a warrior had his pony killed or had a hard time keeping a herd of horses, then as a leader you were to give him your best one. The cooking pot was a reminder to always have food cooking so if somebody were hungry in the camp that day, they could come to your camp. There would always be food cooking. Finally, the sacred pipe was a sign that you were a leader. It was a sacred object to remind you that through family problems, sorrow, pain, or whatever, you were to take that pipe and smoke it. There was no room in you for hatred and revenge. You have to look at your people first. You smoke the pipe slowly and calm yourself. Later you go to the council of elders and ask for the right way to handle things.

These symbols of the traditional picking of chiefs are different from band to band. It all depends. Some chiefs in different bands were also medicine men. Or if a man was a war leader, his symbols of being a war chief were altogether different, like he might be awarded a special shirtwearer's shirt colored half red and half green or half blue and half yellow that showed that his band has picked him as a war leader.

Overall, then, the chiefs and the council of elders were wise and slow-thinking. Sometimes it would take days before they could make a decision. I think even after the reservation days came in, we had chiefs here in Porcupine who were slow-thinking as they made decisions for the people. They looked out for people and the land first. So at that time everybody who wanted to start a home or start raising chickens, horses, or cattle went to see this chief, who made sure everybody was taken care of, and they protected our tribal lands. Anytime roads were built out here or telephone companies came in, the leaders out here protected the interests of their own communities. The government through the Pine Ridge Agency officials had an especially hard time controlling those chiefs out here in the districts, so they picked certain chiefs who were easier to manipulate to be spokesmen for all the people, not just their own bands. These chiefs were treated better; they got more rations when these were passed out, they got education and became Christians and farmers. They got all this special help because they were spokesmen who favored the government policies instead of representing their districts. But the chiefs out here in the districts said, "Hey, we're not in support of this. You're not speaking for us."

Somewhere along the line, John Collier, who became commissioner of Indian affairs during the New Deal period, and Howard and Wheeler, who sponsored this act, came up with the idea of the Indian Reorganization Act of 1934, a new kind of home rule like the U.S. federal government. Before 1934, chiefs were appointed and served for life. Some handed down their chief office into their family, their next of kin, a son, a nephew, grandson, or whoever they thought was fit to carry on that role. Now the Indian Reorganization Act (IRA) was forced on them and they called it "democracy," a new word. You now would vote for your leaders and they would only be there for two years. Therefore, in our troubled history on the Pine Ridge Reservation, every tribal chairman gets all he can for himself and his family because he's only in there for two years.

Now he finally is controlled by the government because whatever decision he or the tribal council makes can be vetoed by the agency superintendent or the secretary of the interior. So it's not really the true voice of the people anymore. Those old-time chiefs that we had before, whenever anything came down, used to walk from house to house or ride on horseback to talk to people about what was happening. When you sat in public gatherings, they were the first ones to get up, the first to pray and give words of encouragement and words of advice. They encouraged the people to live on their land, till gardens, raise cattle and horses. Now under IRA government we don't have that kind of encouragement and social involvement from our leaders. Because of that two-year term in office, you're scared to go out into the public because you know that half the people voted against you. But how do you know at a gathering of five hundred people which ones are politically for you and which ones against you? It's hard for an elected leader to go out and be active in the community today.

In the traditional chief leadership way, that leader knew which community or *tiyospaye* he represented and which families belonged to his *tiyospaye*. So his role was easier and he wasn't embarrassed or had to be forced into making home visits. If some families were having problems, he would go and get his sacred pipe and *wahokunkiya*, give words of advice, and give words of encouragement. "Don't do that; you have kids, you have a home and are part of this *tiyospaye*." Those leaders were also elderly men, so you could be sure they knew what they were talking about; they had been through many things in life. Today, though, we have some councilmen or -women who are barely thirty years old, and tribal chairmen who are young. Overall, IRA democray didn't work for us.

One other problem for our tribe is that it places between fifteen and twenty thousand people under one leadership. This is why there is a break-down in the political system and in the social system. Even here in Porcu-pine District we have a district council that's trying to control twenty-four hundred members; that's too many. One of the Lakota principles of the tra-ditional political system was that when any camp or *tiyospaye* got very big, it would break up into new, smaller bands. Another leadership would then have a smaller community to control.

Under the present tribal government system, the tribal leaders have to deal with fifty-two groups that make up the Oglala Sioux Tribe. These smaller groups like Brotherhood Community here in Porcupine are strong culture bases with clear bloodlines and family ties. Yet we get into politi-cal fights every year. The government forces us to fight over one job or one check coming in, or it gets us to fight each other over one open position, and this is what breaks up family ties. "I wanted that position but they hired my sister's husband." This leads to anger and family tensions. Also, there is no way any government can be successful for our people if it's top-heavy and the directors and managers get paid three times as much as the people who live out here and are doing the actual work.

I remember one time I witnessed two guys being appointed to be tradi-tional chiefs here in Porcupine. Maybe my Lakota mind was different than theirs, but as they were taken out to the middle, smoked the sacred pipe, had war bonnets put on their heads, and were installed from that day as tra-ditional chiefs, I thought that the next morning they should have resigned their BIA jobs and let some other needy men have them. But under the sys-tem today, they couldn't provide for their people then. To maintain their high-paying BIA jobs and be traditional chiefs at the same time doesn't work. So after this, the poor people didn't respond to them as chiefs.

In my own life I experienced some of the difficulties of leadership. I wanted to stay within the proper limits. When I played basketball in my youth, I played hard but I shared the chances to score and be successful. When I played baseball, I did the same thing. In my many years of singing I cared, so I always shared the money, the honors, and respect with other singers, whether there were only three of us singing or eight or ten. I even hauled singers to powwows at my expense; I gave them that chance. Some of them were my family, my brothers, my cousins, or my friends, so I shared whatever I had with them. By caring, I think, I had to set the example of leadership; I had to live a simple life.

Even whenever people come to my home, or when we meet someplace, I never try to be different or unfriendly to anybody. Anyone who ever came to my house was welcomed with whatever I had. I think it's very difficult to be in that leadership role because it demands that commitment and responsibility of selflessness. But even in this role there's a limit so you don't go beyond what is proper and you overdo leadership. It's very easy for a guy to go beyond that limit and do all kinds of crazy things in front of people. He can put on a war bonnet for every event and dance around pompously in front of people, or take a sacred pipe and start holy ceremonies even though he is not a respected medicine man and doesn't understand these ceremonies fully. Being made a leader can make you greedy for power and do foolish things if you let it.

On that day when I knew my own identity, really knew who I am, it was because I found that I wanted people to remember how I cared. I think that's why when I take on any responsibility, I give my whole mind, heart, and body to it. Sometimes I abuse myself in this way, even on the health side. Maybe I overdo that leadership, maybe take on too much, try to get things done too fast. After a while you even neglect your own family besides your health. There's a very thin line between real leadership and over-doing it. Sometimes I've caught myself and tried to remember to ease up, to slow down.

A long time ago leaders seemed slow and poky, but once they're given a task or they're asked a question or have to make a decision, they're slow thinkers. They really reflect on all the issues. As a leader you plan, you think about it two or three times before you really decide. There is danger in making instant decisions, or, like we do today, in following cut-and-dried rules and regulations or bylaws that might actually hurt people. It took me a while to really understand this. Sometimes things would come along and slap me in the face and make me rush or decide on the spot. I realized "Hey, I made a mistake here" or "Hey, I didn't say this the right way; I hurt somebody's feelings." Maybe I got mad, edgy, or crabby at somebody at the wrong time. These are some of the personal challenges of leadership I've faced.

I managed basketball, baseball, and softball teams; singing groups and dance clubs; powwows and ceremonies. Leadership makes you almost have to take on the responsibility of a father image. When your members have problems, you talk and soothe their problems. There's an old traditional Lakota way of saying *wicakasto,* that's a soothing kind of soft rub on your skin or over your hair, a soft pat on the hand. Leadership does that and gives a word of encouragement. This can be hard and you have to commit half of your personal life to that group. You have to maintain a level of serenity within yourself so that you can live with yourself while, at the same time, you share half of yourself with those who see you as their leader. Once you take that leadership on, those people are the most important thing. If you want to be a chief or headman, then people are always more important. But it's very difficult for a leader, because if you're not clearheaded, if you're not a reasonable man, you don't have things in their right places, your group can become more important than your own family. You have to find the right balance.

I experienced that. I stayed with a lot of women and I broke up with a lot of women because of that. They couldn't understand why I spent half of my check for a basketball tournament or spent half my check going to a pow-wow with five guys in my car, just singers, while my woman stayed home at the house. It's very hard to keep a group together. I think part of the reason why the old leadership is being lost in today's world is because your wife and children become very important. Then your business is next—you're a director or teacher or whatever—then your car and home. You can't consider people first anymore. Traditional Lakota leaders considered the people first. Then if you were a leader and a warrior, your white horse is second on your mind; he's the one who always takes you to war and back and to the hunt and back so you can defend and provide for the people; then your bow and arrows, your weapons; then your firstborn child. Then your wife and family comes after that. Things were in that order. But today you can't consider people first anymore. I think that's why today our people start to divide up and become individual-minded, why we have many factions and divisions even within communities and families.

In the old days, when the chiefs talked and the council of elders talked in the *tipi okihe,* the council lodge, they were voicing the people's thoughts and grievances. I think this is where today we need to balance the political system and the social system. You cannot carry on a political system and forget about the Lakota social system. Then you have idleness and have sadness, you have grievances and mind problems with the people in that social system. If you don't balance the two, then you have problems in your own *tiyospaye* or your district or your tribe, whether with alcoholism and drugs, suicides, and whatever social problems we have today. In the traditional system the youth knew the balance of both. The chiefs and the elders, the grandfathers and grandmothers, the parents, the adopted *hunka* relatives all gave advice and encouragement, and they watched that the social system provided respect for relatives. The social system and the political leadership system were intertwined.

To be an effective leader today, you would have to be able to be a silent eater and slow thinker, to be serene and give advice and encouragement, to give half of your body to your group or your people, to have a very understanding wife and family who are behind you and support you. We need people today who can take on that responsibility.

Growing Up Lakota: Child Rearing, Health, and Education

Our leaders, our chiefs, our respected elders achieved those honors as they went along in life. They were exposed to the ideals of our Lakota tradition from the time they were born and even before, in the mother's body. Their older relations rarely missed a chance to remind them of the behavior that was most admired in a Lakota boy or girl, man or woman.

In the understanding and learning growth of small children, they learned how to deal with daily problems, how to gather chokecherries or dig prairie turnips, to shoot a bow and strengthen themselves in running or riding a horse, learned how to keep their balance with the rhythm of the horse so they could stay glued to the back of the horse no matter which way it turned. Boys tamed and trained their horses so that in the heat of battle or the chase that horse and they could almost talk to each other by the movement of the rider's body, to be in harmony and balance with that animal. While the boys were racing their horses back and forth, trying out their skills as future hunters and warriors, at the same time women were teaching their young girls how to tan hides, how to do porcupine quillwork, how to do all the women's chores, because these were different from the man's. They both had a respected role for what they contributed to the life of the community. They both also began to take part in the socializing and camaraderie that was enjoyed among the women at their activities and among the men. Telling stories and jokes, laughing and gossiping were enjoyed by both sexes in their own ways.

Both were also given tests to challenge them in their proper roles. Generally, for boys it had to do with courage and physical abilities they would need as warriors. For girls it had to do with their virtue and their artistic abilities as keepers of the home. Both were also expected to show respect and generosity in their own little lives. Older relatives were always happy when one of their young ones showed they could demonstrate the Lakota values. I'll give you an example of one of these tests. This one young boy about twelve or thirteen years old thought he wasn't scared of anything. He was ready to be a man. He kept bugging the different war party leaders to take him along. "Granddad, ask him if I can go with them" was one of his favorite requests of his grandfathers. One day, from the *tipi okihe,* the council lodge, the *tokala,* Kit Fox Society, elders called for him about one o'clock in the morning. They got him out of bed. It was pitch dark and the wind was really blowing. So he got up half asleep and walked over there. They handed him a little buffalo-horn cup. The old man sitting next to him said, "We're having a long meeting, so get us some water." The spring was pretty far away from that camp, so as he came out, he thought about the enemy, how dark it was, the snakes, and everything he could think of. He was scared of the dark. All of a sudden, he just closed his eyes and ran in the direction of the spring, just ran, lifted the cup, and turned around and ran back.

That elderly man looked in the horn and noticed a little fish swimming around in there but there wasn't enough water. So the old man said, "You didn't dip it right. When you go to the water, you swish it back and forth to swish away the fish and everything else that's there and then you dip it so there's water up to the rim of the cup." So they sent him back. This time he ran a little slower and took his time dipping and ran back slow, but again he had some little green weeds in the horn. The old man poured the water out and told him to go out again and get clear water to the rim of the horn. The boy finally realized that when he got water for his parents during the day, he would swish it back and forth, then dip his container, then swish it again and get more until he filled the water bag. He now did it this way even in the dark and walked back. The old man took a small sip and then spilled the rest and said, "I was really thirsty." He had to go back nine more times that night since there were ten elderly men sitting in a circle. Each one took a little drink, spilled the rest, and sent him back for more.

At the end they talked to him and said, "You can say things when it's daylight, but in the darkness your whole thinking changes. *Takoja,* Grandson, you're not ready yet. Once you're on a war party looking for the enemy, you cannot hesitate at any time. Whatever the decision, it has to be quick, a fast decision. You're not ready yet, *Takoja,* so go back and prepare yourself.

Then come back and we'll see if you're ready. Right now, *ni cante ki lel he.* Your heart is here, at the tip of your tongue. In the heat of battle, when the guns start firing or you've been encircled by the enemy and your horse is shot, then your heartbeat will come up and feel like it's here at the tip of your tongue. You might lose control of yourself or wet your pants, or you might be frozen. You'll think you're shooting your bow and arrow, but you're actually just sitting there. Getting water at night is nothing. *Takoja,* we'll take you along when you're ready."

I think our people knew there was a stage when you're ready for acting in a different way, for taking on a new role in life as a man or a woman. It was necessary to experience each one in turn as you were ready. People would often get impatient and try to rush through some of them or even skip one, but their older relations would watch out for them and make sure they didn't overdo things in their eagerness or ambition. There is a pace that's necessary.

Growing up can be seen in seven stages and we have different terms for babies, boys and girls, and men and women as they pass through them. The first is the term *hoksi onpapi,* which refers to a new baby that's wrapped. We believe wrapping babies is good for them physically and psychologically. The second stage is *wakanyan najin,* standing sacred, when a child can stand on its own, maybe wobbly and taking its first steps but standing sacred in creation, both boys and girls. Then when kids start to understand, we call them *hoksila* and *wicincala,* young boy and girl, when their identities separate and the boys are raised by their male relations and the girls by their woman relatives. This lasts until maybe twelve or fourteen, when they become *koska-laka* and *wikoskalaka,* young man and young woman, young adults. As *wicasa* and *winyan,* man and woman, they are now considered adults and mature. In the sixth stage they are now that *wicahcala* and *winuhcala,* the elderly, re-spected older man and woman. Finally, the seventh stage of the life circle, the road through this world, is being the best, the authority, the patriarch and matriarch of your community. As a man you might now be a *naca,* elderly councilor, or a *wicasa wakan,* a medicine man, or a *hoka wicasa,* that master-singer. As a woman you might be a *winyan wakan mani,* a woman who walks in a sacred way, or a respected *wicaglata,* woman singer, or a widely known artist with special designs.

I talked with my father, with Gerald One Feather, one of our tribal leaders from Oglala, and with Johnson Holy Rock, another elder, about their versions of early Lakota education. After thinking over what they said and what I know for some time, I've come up with the seven steps of how the

Lakota educate their children. First is teaching; the day your son is born you start teaching him to be physically active, your daughter, too. You exercise their legs and arms and talk to them about their future. "You're going to be a *tokala*, a Kit Fox warrior, or you're going to be a *hoka wicasa*, a great singer, or you're going to be a good woman, a great artist." You sing to them— teaching. Then, second, the child understands, begins to comprehend your teachings. Third is the step is when they start to stand up by themselves and start to experience what you've taught them. He might get a tiny bow and arrow and shoot at a butterfly or pound on something and sing, or she might put up a little tipi or try to paint a design on some rawhide.

The fourth step is knowledge. Both from the teachings of their elders and from experience, these kids are starting to gain knowledge now. That's a bow and arrow and that's how it's made, and that's a horse that a warrior rides, that's how you dry meat, and that's the month you go to dig *tinpsila*, the prairie turnip. On the fifth you can now actually perform things; you can sit down at a drum and sing, or go out and kill a deer, or tan a hide, ap- plying what you've learned. This is the very beginning of wisdom, the very first step. You're putting your knowledge together and putting it in your own mind and heart. The sixth step is intellectual in the sense that you can express yourself about the things you've learned. You can explain them, you can get up and pray and talk to people at gatherings, you are considered a gifted or knowledgeable person in the community. The last, seventh, level is when you're the elite, the best, the *wayupika*. You've reached that top level; you belong to the council of elders, you've killed so many enemies, you have ten wounds, you've stolen so many horses, you've become the best singer, the most respected medicine man. You are an authority; you've become the best and that standard will carry you the rest of your life till the day you die.

These seven steps—teaching, understanding, experience, knowledge, ap- plication, intellect, and being the best at it—each takes years, three years or five or ten. It depends on how you apply and dedicate yourself. Everybody goes through this series of steps in the Lakota way of life. Some never reach step seven, some only step four or five. This is where we have problems today, because some of our leaders, our medicine men, our Sun Dance leaders for- get that it takes years to get the knowledge, that power and medicine. It takes time. You can't fast one year and Sun Dance one year and become the most powerful medicine man around. In this Lakota way of life it takes time to acquire all that and rise to the top.

In my case, I don't know just what step I'm on these days. But around 1979, when I'd go to different events and gatherings on different reservations, people began to talk to me about a song and what it meant, or they would say, "I want you to come and explain to our people why they sing this song when they drop an eagle feather," or "We want Porcupine Singers to come to our powwow and we want you to come with them and sing this song because you know how to sing it right." I think you get the feeling as you go that you'll be asked to explain things to the people, to know how to do this old dance the right way, to know which song is right for this ceremony. At the right time the people themselves will advance you to the next stage in your life. Your achievements and experience will be recognized by them. I would never say that I'm the best singer or the one who knows all the songs. My Uncle Henry, for example, knew lots more than I did. Maybe I'm at the fifth step, leaning towards the sixth, because people are asking me to help out in their naming or other sacred ceremony; they're asking me to talk about certain things. When I travel today I try to remember things I've heard so I can be ready, because many places I go today someone may all of a sudden ask me something and I need to be able to talk about it. I think I'm still moving up—I hope.

Another way of thinking of these stages in your life is this. As we walk along the Red Road, we walk through seven steps of developing the four parts of ourselves: the mind, tongue, body, and spirit. The first I call the slippery step because it describes the first step the infant tries to take with his own feet. The second I think of as walking knee deep in mud when a child is walking on his own but with difficulty. The next stage then is the step of coldness when the early teenager is searching for an identity on his own with difficulty. The fourth step is when the young man or woman walks on thorns; they're restless, sometimes out of control, doing crazy things. The fifth I call walking among swarming bees because now as an adult you often have people picking on you, forcing you to do things, making demands on you. The sixth step of getting older is walking over the bodies of your relatives. If you have a strong mind and body, you will outlive many of your relatives. Finally, the last step before you go on the *wanagi canku,* the spirit road, is the step of loneliness. As you get older and experience this life and its pain and the losses we all have to go through, you accumulate wisdom and understanding and the respect of your people, but that wisdom and respect you've earned have their cost.

The Hard Things in Life: Limits and Commitment

As you get to the end of your own red road, you'll have understood that in our way there are four hard things in life. One is the death of your mother, especially when you're young. The second is to see your firstborn killed, brought back, and laid in front of you. The third is for your band to go hungry and freeze during the winter. The fourth is to be surrounded by the enemy. These are four of the hardest things in life. It's interesting to think about which might be the common hard things today.

I think in today's world you could say it's a baby not knowing who her father is and being the rest of her life on welfare. Another in today's life is unemployment, not being able to find a job and bring money home. Also, I think the death of your oldest child is often due to alcohol or drugs and is maybe still the hardest. Death doesn't care how you lose your life. It is still instant and not prejudiced. Whether it's through alcohol, drugs, car accidents, suicide, or even your relative flipping out and killing you, or you all of a sudden dying of a heart attack, death is not prejudiced. It will take you in any way. Maybe today death has less meaning; the spirit of living properly in an orderly way is often gone, so death has less meaning too.

As people reach different steps in life, the people look at you physically. Appearance is very important, not just the way you dress, but your physical nature. It's hard to be a leader if you're short and stubby because traditionally they looked at the ideal of the Lakota man as tall and slim. In the traditional way that we've been talking about, the day a baby was born, you start stretching and exercising his legs. You hold him up a lot so his muscle forms around the bone. So, a long time ago, Lakota men were kind of slim but very powerful. They didn't have bulging muscles or wide, bulky shoulders. Instead their muscles were built around the bone so that they could hang onto the sides of horses, they could run great distances, they could do anything. They formed their bodies so that they were evenly slim.

Babies were wrapped tight when they were in their cradles so that there was no loose shape of bones. Even tiny babies' feet, when the babies were wrapped up, had a little, tiny cloth ball put between their heels so that when they were wrapped up, their toes pointed in just a little bit. But now everybody wears big bulky diapers or Pampers and some kids are kind of deformed maybe in their hip joints or their legs are spread too far. It's because they don't wrap babies anymore and the babies lie flat in a crib all day and all night so that their feet are pointed out. If you try to get a boy whose feet are pointed out to run a hundred yards, he'll run it in about sixteen seconds. But if you run someone who as a baby was wrapped the traditional way, toes pointed in, he'll run it in about nine seconds. The pointing of the feet, the way you raise the baby, how you wrap that baby, and how you give him stretching exercises, all these things become very important.

Since physical appearance was so important to the Lakota and his lifestyle kept him very active, he stayed fit into old age. In those late wisdom years, however, the elders often liked to eat and weren't as active anymore and lost their muscle tone and their stomachs started getting big. In some of of our Lakota songs they would refer to them in a joking way as *tezi tanka,* big bellies, the old-timers who had potbellies.

I once talked for a while with this old lady, I can't remember her first name, the late Joe Rock Boy's wife, who said it's getting so that nowadays the mothers don't care for their kids by holding them against their breasts the Indian way, the Lakota way. They don't nurse them but instead put a bottle in them and throw them in the crib or playpen or on the floor and let them do as they please. So all the babies today are called *h'coka,* no shape. She said, "A long time ago my brothers and cousins were raised in the traditional way and were tall and slim, nice looking. But now I get after my granddaughters because they let their kids lie any way they want to. Those kids don't have any physical strength and won't survive if things ever get bad." I thought she was right.

I also talked with my aunt one time about it and she said that her grandmother's teaching was that you put caps snugly on the baby's head and wrap him tight in the cradle with his arms in and his knees up so he wouldn't get a stomach. Then they were well formed and kept themselves under control. If you notice my *tahansis,* my cousins, as young men I remember they were all slim and tall. Now they've all put on a little weight, but their own sons at eight or nine years old already weigh practically more than their fathers.

Traditional child-rearing practices and the active lifestyles of that traditional Lakota man and the demanding daily demands on the woman made them healthy and lean. Of course, their diet was important too. Before the reservation days the main source of the meat in Lakota diet was the buffalo. They used every part of the buffalo—tongue, meat, brain, the intestines, everything. They used the stomach to cook in like a pot. Most of the meat would be dried, seasoned in thin strips in the sun as *papa,* jerked meat, and they carried that with them. They also ate lots of deer and elk and a lot of bone marrow—deer, elk and buffalo. They would dig it out and when they boiled that *papa*, they would use the marrow or liver or the fat around the kidney to mix in. They preferred animals in the fall when they said that grease would come out on the top when cooked and formed a fat outside the fiber of the meat so that meat had a purely meaty taste to it. If you kill an animal in the spring or early part of the summer, that's when the grease and fat was in the meat fiber and it had a greasy smell and taste to it. In the Lakota way, wild meat killed before March or April is not as good because, I don't know what it would be, some fluid, maybe sperm, maybe hormones, the sex fluid—whatever it is—is absorbed into the fibers of the meat. They said that the meat during the mating season was mushy or spongy. Later in the year, when it comes out and they sweat it out, the fat and the meat is pure. That's why they preferred to hunt and dry the meat later in the season.

While we're on this, the same is true on the human side. If you have a newborn baby and you start having sex right away, that fluid gets into your system and also gets into the system of the baby. Then after a while it's no longer baby fat, it's spongy. Some of the old people can feel it when they touch a baby. When you show a baby to the old people, right away they touch the chest and the arms. It's a natural law that a certain time after the birth of the baby, a man and woman can't have sex because of the fluids in the system. When a baby is nursing, your fluids and your wife's fluids are in your systems and that will get into the baby's milk. So no sex during nursing was a strict rule of Lakota life. Some mothers and grandmothers would sit up all night to make sure the baby was raised right. There would be no sex so they wouldn't harm the baby until its body started forming meaty muscle fibers or the fluid had come out. The Lakota elders talked about how animal beings and human beings have things that blend together.

Their diet also included *tinpsila*, prairie turnip. The Lakota would depend quite a bit on the stars and the moon to pick and store fruits such as choke-cherries, plums, juneberries, even the little rose hips they made tea from. Water, tea, and soup was all they drank. It was all very natural and healthy. Even the buffalo meat the Oglala ate—I don't know how many of the rest of the Lakotas were the same—was especially healthy and even sacred because when those buffalo went into the Black Hills, they ate all the sacred herbs and medicines that are found there. Through the buffalo the Oglala then ate those same medicines. Sure, there were times when food was scarce and our people had to do without or eat some mules they came across by accident, but we were a healthy people.

Originally the diet played an important role in Lakota health and their well-being and survival. In addition, at that time traditional medicine men were powerful and they knew how to take care of their people. Most of the warriors were very religious people and so learned how to take care of themselves, what medicine was good for them in certain seasons, what they could do in wintertime, spring, summer, and fall.

People in each region of the world have their own special diet because of plants and fruits and meats and things that are available for them in that region. Once your body adjusts to that diet over time and absorbs that diet, when you're all of a sudden put on a different diet, it's a shock. Times changed for us in the 1870s and 1880s when the buffalo were wiped out; times were hard. Not only did we have to change our diet to what the government gave out, but many times it was such bad stuff and so little of it that we suffered and our health began to suffer. Cancer, heart disease, sugar diabetes, and even arthritis were not known among the Lakota people while they ate their traditional diet and lived that traditional life.

Maybe the nutrition they got from the animals and the plants, the fruit they ate, helped them resist those kinds of diseases. All of that changed as we came down into the reservation days. The government people were now issuing beef—beef made us sick at first—and it was often bad beef, bad bacon, bad rations to the people after the defeat of Custer in 1876. Some had nervous system problems and some got deformed from that poison food. Some of that government-issue food was even poison food. Some of the rations and the commodity government-surplus food we are issued is stored in warehouses for ten years. It's not fresh, it's not natural, it's not nutritious. It brought us heart disease, cancer, tuberculosis, and sugar diabetes. It started us on a path of slow death.

I've gone through the process of it all myself. Up until 1981 I was very healthy. Then, after an appendix burst, they found sugar in my blood, yet they never gave me insulin or a diabetic pill or anything. After I went through my second surgery, they found more sugar in my blood. This time I wanted to make sure and had a physical checkup in Gordon, Nebraska, hospital. I didn't trust the people in Pine Ridge hospital. In Gordon they found sugar again and put me on a diet of six grapes and a two-inch cube of meat and so many ounces of lettuce and so many leafy plants I was to eat. I couldn't eat sugar and all kinds of other things anymore. That was a hell of an adjustment for someone from a warrior tradition! After that I had a separate grocery list when we went to the store. When we ate at home, they would fix my dish separately from their own. I went on that way for about a month but somehow I was losing the muscle in my arms and my legs. In the morning I'd get up dizzy. I was weak. I didn't feel like it was a good day to get up and I spent much time sleeping. It was wintertime, too, so I kept the heat on low in order to stay awake. Everybody else was cold but if they turned the stove on so it would warm up, boy, I was out. Then, finally, one day I went to the bathroom and as I stood up, I blanked out and I fell. After I came to, I got up and staggered in. So right away I realized it must be that diet I had been on for about five weeks. I threw the diet away and started eating my normal diet, meat, very little salad. It's been a slow process getting back back but my sugar's not that high, about 170.

I thought of my grandfather and how he would eat lots of rabbit and pheasant. He'd rather eat that than go to the grocery store and buy meat. It was wild, natural game. I think, too, that after 1960 the nutrition value of meat changed. Until then, the cows the ranchers around here ran were wild. They ate wild hay and there was little vaccination of cattle. They didn't give them any kind of feed cake, any oil or anything. They were out here eating natural grass and they were half wild. It took you two or three days to run them in and take them to sale. You could also buy one directly from the rancher. You butchered yourself and you dressed it and ate it, almost a pure chemical-free cow. But today, the USDA requires ranchers and farmers to vaccinate cows with this in the spring and with that in the summer, and you have to do this with calves. You put so much chemical into the meat and those packing plants are also treating the meat. It may be an accident, but I can almost use the hospital records back to the 1960s and show there was very little heart disease and cancer or even diabetes. Maybe it just caught up to us at the same time.

My personal experience with diabetes makes me call it a lazy man's sickness. In my youth I was very active in sports, I ran and walked a lot, I traveled lots, I even built this house myself, tore it apart and rebuilt it. I was always doing things. After the surgery on my burst appendix, because of the big incision I couldn't lift anything over ten pounds. I had two other surgeries and had to be real careful because I might get a rupture. The doctor gave me six years to recover. "With this poison in your system and this big an incision don't expect that you're going to be a well man and start doing work that is real heavy or try to work or you'll be back in the hospital. It'll take you six years before you can really start feeling good and maybe at that time you might start doing things again." So I started sitting around, I relaxed a lot, watched tv, I sat all day in the office where I worked, and I let the active life go. Even you guys that are here today should notice that. Before, when you would come here in the summer there was always a new pine shade next to the house. The grass was always cut all around and even difficult improvements were made here and there before you came. But since then, when I got into that easy chair and stayed there more and more, I had problems with my sugar level, up and down, up and down.

But I didn't blame anybody for this sickness I had inside me. I tried to learn how to deal with it. I think I did pretty well these past few years. I even thought about just going strictly on traditional Lakota food—liver, kidney, and tongue—to see what would happen, see if my sickness would improve. Lakota people are born with a body that can absorb meat. If you, Ronnie, ate as much meat as I do, you might get sick from it or get some reaction because your system is different.

The thing I didn't understand was that I didn't eat candy and I didn't drink pop that much; I didn't use sugar much. Still I had diabetes in my system. Was it all the chemicals from eating today's beef, or not being active enough, or the different diet with all the modern foods? Maybe today's clock also has to do with it. Once you let the clock control you, then you again lose control of the natural side of being a human being. You have to be at a certain place at a certain time. In order to get there, you can only find time for a pop and some chips, or some frozen pizza and a bologna sandwich, or a fast fried hamburger. Nobody's home, so you have a quick tv dinner and some more pop. A long time ago our Lakota women used to take time to boil meat, whatever time it took to be done. Today we're in so much of a hurry that time controls us. We even lose sleep. In preparing food, if it took two hours to boil the meat, then it took two hours. If some ceremony went on for hours, that was all right. Things took time to be done right. I experienced that when I got so involved in politics and other things such as powwows, basketball, meetings, and more. I'd come back home and eat something fast and go to bed. The next morning I'd jump up, get cleaned up, and have to take off for somewhere by eight o'clock. The family might not see me again until two or three in the morning. So even though diet plays a big part in our health problems, the clock is also a controlling factor.

Since I've been out of a job these last two years, I've had plenty of slow, free time; time hasn't rushed me. My diet got better and somehow even my vision got better. Before that I used to depend on my glasses. Now I can watch tv or I can see clearly to read well without glasses. My diet has gotten better and my skin feels different. If you noticed, this summer my tan has gotten darker because of my diet and my slower pace. I didn't even spend that much time out in the sun. Now I eat meat, a lot of meat. Maybe once or twice a day I eat salad and I drink lots of cod liver oil. How I was convinced that cod liver oil is beneficial was when I went to the Yakima, Washington, powwow and I saw an elderly man who had jet-black hair two inches thick and about four feet long. Here I was gray-haired and my hair was straggly and short and some of it was missing. They took us to a dinner in some kind of prayer house. Their traditional food was a big red salmon. They gave us great thick slices because in their tradition that's what they eat. Before I went to Yakima, they gave me green-and-gray-colored capsules at the hospital to take every morning. When I combed my hair, bunches of hair fell out and my hair was getting pretty thin. So after I came back from Yakima, I cut down taking those pills to twice a week. Then I went to the Martin drugstore and bought two jars of that cod liver oil, vitamin A and D. For a while it gave me a stomachache but once I got used to it, it was all right. At first I took a little teaspoonful, but then I started to take sips of it. Since then my hair grew back and got thicker, still gray but thicker. The fish oil, my more careful diet, and my slower pace has made a big difference in my health.

Tiole: Looking for a Home

Besides the diet, pace of life, and change in lifestyles, our Lakota way of life involved a practice that kept our social system intact. At one time a very identifying practice within a *tiyospaye,* band, or even with a neighboring *tiyospaye* was the practice of Lakota people visiting each other, called *tiole,* looking for a home. Wherever you went you would visit a relative and they would take you in and share their food with you. You stay overnight, you visit, you talk, you share your stories. In this way they'd exchange family stories and family humor, jokes about their brother-in-laws and sister-in-laws; they would also keep that kinship identity by calling each other by the proper respect names of Uncle, Auntie, Grandma, Grandfather, Older Brother, Cousin, and so on. They would identify their relationships by calling each other by the family relations' names.

I grew up between the wagon and car days. I know we used to get ready to *tiole* when my grandma would say, "Get ready; on this day we're going to see our Grandma Young Dog." That was like fifteen miles cross-country, so we'd get up early in the morning, take some of the beef and dried meat she'd prepared ahead of time, get some of the goods and things she wanted to take over, and load up the wagon and take an extra horse to give to them. We'd take off early in the morning and drove off cross-country in that wagon. The rest of us used to ride horseback and kind of follow the wagon and looked like we knew where we were going. At that time there was no telephone, so once we came up to the ridge west of their house and they spotted us, you could see activity going on right away down by that house. Everybody was running back and forth; somebody jumped on a horse and rode to the nearby houses. Once we arrived at the house, everybody would gather around and they would hug and cry even though there was no sorrow or death in the family; it was a cry of happiness. They'd cry and hug each other and talk, and womenfolks would go in the house and start cooking right away and the menfolks would unhitch the team and give them water and tie them up for a while till they cooled off and then took them to the corral and fed them hay. Then my grandma would get her gifts out and pass them out to all the relatives. At that time they would all come out of the house to meet you when you went to somebody's house. Your relative's home was another home for you. This was the Lakota way of visiting, *tiole*.

In the traditional way, whether it was a relative or somebody from another band who was visiting in a community, one of our respected leaders would go up to them and welcome them to their home if they had no place to go. As a visitor you were given the honored place in the home. In the old days it was the place opposite the tipi door or the log cabin door. The visitor would also follow a certain set of polite manners. One of my grandfathers used to say, "Once you're fed and your stomach is full and you have a warm feeling all over your body, you drink hot coffee, you feel good." The wife will be gathering the dishes or washing the dishes, and the husband is sitting there visiting with you; they are waiting for you to belch and wipe the grease off your chin, or if your hands are greasy, you rub them on your braids. They'd expect a belch from you saying that now you are full and feel good.

But today even that is different. One of the table manners is that you have a napkin on the side and you wipe your mouth and hands and you throw it away without touching your braids or hair with the grease. Also according to white table manners, it's offensive to belch at the table.

According to the traditional Lakota manners, men were always fed first. This shows how the women of the family respect their brothers or their husbands. As my father explained that, warriors were always walking in the shadow of death. When they are fed first, they are honored in that way. Then, once they get done eating, the kids and the women sit down and eat. Today, of course, that's changed. Also, in the traditional way of eating, once you're done with your plate, you always leave a piece or corner of a slice of bread and take that last piece of bread and wipe the plate clockwise and that's the last piece of bread that goes into your mouth. It's like saying, "I've enjoyed this meal; now I'm full and my plate is clean. I enjoyed it." Then you praise that man or that woman sitting there with you, *"Ho tahansi, pila mayaca ho waksica ki le ikikcuwo."* That means "Thank you very much, my cousin; I'm done, so take your plate back." That's the honorable way to thank a cousin who has fed you. Those were respected ways when you *tiole*.

In the 1880s the government and the churches campaigned against this *tiole* because when you stayed at a relative's house for over three days, you were supposedly infringing on their time for gardening and time for taking care of their cows and their horses, for feeding their chickens, and you were neglecting your own farm back home. Also, we were giving too many things away to each other. So the agency superintendents and ministers wrote letters to the commissioner of Indian affairs and he wrote letters to the superintendents and boss farmers and ministers at the agencies, discouraging and even restricting our traditional ways of *tiole*, visiting, of *otuh'an*, giving away, and of dancing and singing in our traditional ways—like I mentioned earlier. There are documents to support this.

The reasons they gave were that we were supposed to become self-supporting farmers and individualists and no longer that community or *tiyospaye* of families and relatives. They made fun of the practice as if it were just a handout. I remember how it began to change young people so they would say, "Hey, the old man is coming *tiole* because he's hungry," and yet that was our grandfather coming. Or they'd say, "That guy is going over there to that house to *tiole* because he's hungry." They made it sound like you were infringing on the privacy of the home or you were going to a house to mooch. You had to get a special permit from the boss farmer to go visit your relatives, from Porcupine to Kyle, to Three Mile Creek, or to American Horse Creek. If you were going a little further, from one reservation to another reservation to visit relatives, they would restrict it, especially during farming season, since we were supposed to be farming hard and taking care of our gardens, not visiting and sharing food with our relatives.

Also, at the time, the different Christian denominations—Episcopal, Catholic, Presbyterians—were making a big push to baptize new members into their churches, so they would baptize people while they were in their buggies going to a store, stop them and baptize them in their buggies or wagons or on horseback. They would also go to homes, walk in, and start baptizing people. Some of the kids would hide under the bed or table and they would just sprinkle water under the bed and say, "Now you're a baptized Christian." Each of them considered their own religion better than the others, so if I were baptized an Episcopalian and my cousin was Catholic, the ministers would say that we couldn't visit each other because we belonged to different churches. We would be discouraged from visiting, because our relatives didn't belong to the "true faith." We would be sinners if we didn't follow church laws, or we were called backsliders or blanket Indians and other names.

In some cases, when our people couldn't visit each other, then they would move into one big log house or camp in tents outside their mother's or father's house, four or five families. Even after the 1930s and '40s they discouraged families from living together, for all kinds of health reasons.

In this way they killed *tiole*. This was the way they used to break the spirit of the Oglala person. They worked to break up the family ties in a community; they destroyed the traditional leadership. After a while the people became ashamed and embarrassed to visit each other. Once *tiole* was lost, we lost our identity as relatives. We don't know who our cousins are, we don't know who our uncles are, we don't know who our aunties are, our in-laws. And this was why, after a while, our young people began losing the respect between relatives. Today, if you visit a relative, they open up the curtain, peek out, and may not even come out; you have to knock three or four times before they say, "Come in." Maybe after you knock a while, somebody might open the door a little crack and say, "What do you want?" instead of saying, "Uncle, you're here. It's good to see you." Or they might talk to you through the screen door. The old *tiole* welcome isn't there many times. The order of the home and the family is disrupted.

What we need today is to talk to our children, to teach them the respectful way of welcoming people and our relations to our home, to share food with them and use the respectful kinship terms with them, not their English first names, but Uncle, Grandma, Cousin, Sister-in-Law, and so on. The whole family should be a welcoming committee. One day we should say something like, "Okay, today, my daughter, you stay close to the door. When visitors come, walk out with a smile and welcome them and talk to them if I'm not home. Ask them what they want and welcome them as relatives."

Another influence on us to change our health and identity of growing up Lakota was the plague put on us since the 1800s—alcohol. A lot of land was taken from the Oglalas, many families and communities have been destroyed under the stress of alcoholism. Some of the chiefs were drunk as they signed treaties. Now we are plagued with the kind of slow death we live under. We're having a great many problems today with all ages of our people because of alcoholism. I think it's really a problem of identity.

Even in the old days we had some individuals who couldn't quite achieve the identity of the honored warrior, hunter, or spiritual leader. We still have those people who don't know who they are or haven't found an identity they're comfortable with. Alcohol has made that problem become an epidemic. Today the guy who is unsure of himself becomes the best bronc rider when he's drunk. The guy who has little luck with women becomes a Romeo, a real stud, when he drinks. They get beyond the real, beyond the limit. The guy who is angry inside becomes the best boxer in the world, better than Joe Louis and Sugar Ray Leonard; nobody can beat him—when he's drunk. Some of the older guys were the best soldiers in World War II or Korea and the women over there just loved them—when they talk drunk. Alcohol gives them that exaggerated identity. They can say or do things they would normally never do in front of people when they are sober. Ninety-six percent or so of our Indian inmates in prison committed their crimes under the influence of alcohol. The rules of our social system are still so strong that when sober, our people are very law-abiding and restrained. When they're drinking, not only does their anger come out but their identity problems get magnified. The man who's unsure of himself with women, the more liquor he can get into a girl or woman, the more secure he feels. Of course, he needs to leave his own everyday identity behind, too. Alcohol lets him think he's more than he really is. Women also have an identity problem because when they're not satisfied with their boyfriends or their husbands or with themselves, alcohol makes the solutions so easy. Even though we are still Oglala Sioux with the bloodline of fearless warriors and virtuous women in our blood, and we have traditional values still in our blood, alcohol distorts all that to a grotesque shadow of what is real.

Today some of our kids are getting into drugs, marijuana, sniffing glue, coke, and LSD. These I think are a mind-altering thing. They can cause permanent damage. Alcoholism is a slow death, but there is hope because we have all kinds of sobriety movements going on, especially among our youth, but drugs alter your mind. Once you lose that mind, you're done, you're lost.

The final pressure that was put on us and broke up our system of bringing up our youth to be healthy and useful members of Lakota society was education. Starting in the late 1870s, federal and mission day schools and boarding schools, where kids stayed overnight in dormitories and often didn't come home until vacations, also started to break up the Lakota family, the closeness of family, the respect for and the honoring of relatives. Once you break up the inner circle of the family, then you kill the spirit of that family. Once you kill the spirit of the family, then you control the individual.

So at these schools they'd put three hundred children with different family values and beliefs and traditions in one big dormitory with no privacy or respect, and pretty soon they had cousins fighting each other, or they had sisters fighting each other at the girls' dorm. After a while the network of the family and how it teaches you and raises you and supports you was lost. After a while of this, you lose the respect of kinship because it's not around you.

They also cut the long hair which is the pride of Lakota people, made the women wear stockings and short dresses, and made the men wear uniforms. Once you went into the dormitories of the federal boarding schools or the Catholic mission schools, you lost kinship respect. You would often kind of isolate yourself to the boundaries of your locker and your bunk. I experienced that myself. I went to the Bishop Hare School over in Mission, South Dakota, on the Rosebud Reservation. I lived there for six years. I came from a very strict family. Grandmother was in overall control; my father and uncles were in control of the outside chores and activities. But once I went to the Bishop Hare Home, nine boys shared the shower, nine boys shared two basins, nine boys shared the dormitory in single beds, and once we sat down, we sat around the same table sharing meals. So no longer did I say, "*Ate,* Dad, pass me the salt," or "*Ate,* pass me the bread." There were no relatives to call by the right terms. Also, once you sat around that table, you kind of acted like a vulture. The first one to grab in got the biggest piece of bread or the biggest piece of meat. If you were grabby, you got more. If you were shy and at all backward, you only got small pieces or half of everything, or sometimes nothing at all.

So all these things broke up the health, the manners, and the closeness of the Lakota family. They've done a very good job to make us lose our identity. They set out to discourage our ways, to embarrass us and make us ashamed of our family ways, our culture, and who we were. Today, I've noticed that in some families younger children are ashamed of their mother or father.

I've seen the daughter turn and walk away from her parents, or the son have nothing to do with the parents when they went out in public. We don't have stable moral standards or any kind of stable social order in our families out here because of all this.

So now, a hundred years later, the same people that set out to destroy our traditions and family structure are coming in with alcohol abuse and drug abuse programs, with welfare programs and family violence programs to put our lives in order. A hundred years ago their goal was to disrupt and break up those families. Now they're spending millions of dollars trying to put it all back together again. They tell themselves, "I'm a good priest . . ." or "I'm a good BIA administrator . . . ," so they want to help put things in place again, to put a good social order in place here in Porcupine District. I think they finally somehow realized how much damage they did. They're upset that there's no respect here. A kid threatens a teacher or breaks windows at a school; they then want to see something done to improve things.

At one time, traditional Lakota beliefs, values, the respect for relatives and elders was there, the honoring of parents was there. The teaching started from when the baby was a day old throughout life. Now we want to correct the damage and bring it all back artificially, with federal, state, and tribal programs and in the classrooms. It's going to take more than that to walk the *canku luta,* the good red road.

Agony and Renewal: Wounded Knee I and II; AIM

I think that tearing down our cultural identity to replace it with that of white Americans went into effect in the 1880s when they made a mass drive of baptizing everybody here on the reservation and killing off all our sacred ceremonies. Other traditions were either suppressed or discouraged. We had to identify with something that was traditionally Indian. The Lakota heard about Ghost Dancing. We were desperate for something to hold onto, to give us some kind of hope. So we sent a delegation southwest to Paiute country to bring that Ghost Dance back. If we did the dances and the songs and used the symbols of that Ghost Dance properly, the good old days of the past would return and we could bring back the ghosts of our departed relatives that way. The way things were going among our people, we believed and Ghost Dancing became very strong among our people. When Ghost Dancing became real strong among many of the Lakota bands, the government and the military went after them. Several of the agents overreacted and demanded military action. The only way to teach all of us a lesson was to use the excuse that Big Foot's band, that was going south to Pine Ridge after Sitting Bull's assassination in the winter of 1890, was joining the Ghost Dance movement, and that this movement was getting dangerous. So the military surrounded them at Wounded Knee Creek and massacred them, men, women, and children.

I've read *Black Elk Speaks* and the way he talks about what Wounded Knee means to us and what it did to us as a people. We gave up! Black Elk said that "the nation's hoop was broken," that "the flowering tree" that was the Lakota people died off. I know that in my whole life, Wounded Knee always brings out some very strong feelings of sadness and anger.

I think the whole thing goes back to the defeat of Custer in 1876 at the Little Big Horn, or what we call the Greasy Grass. I have a tape recording of an elderly man called Eagle Dog from the Standing Rock Reservation. I recorded him in March of 1972 at McLaughlin, North Dakota. The American Indian Movement had a meeting at Billy Mills Hall here at Pine Ridge and appointed a delegation to go to all the reservations and hold hearings on the Bureau of Indian Affairs' abuses and try to document all other political abuses as well, and then go to Washington, D.C., and lay it in front of a White House aide and the secretary of the interior and other high officials to bring about some changes. They wanted to address these grievances because nobody had addressed them since the Indian Reorganization Act was put into effect in 1934. Anyway, while we were in McLaughlin, this elderly man talked about the reasons why Wounded Knee happened. I've read many accounts about it and I've heard many discussions about it, but this was a good story. He said the U.S. government and the military wanted revenge, to get at somebody. They wanted to make an example of somebody to pay for what happened to Custer's cavalry, some band or village who might make a mistake or get a little out of hand. Then the cavalry would gallop in and wipe them out. They didn't care if there were women or children or elderly people involved.

I think that Big Foot's band, which was fleeing from up north because they were afraid that what happened to Sitting Bull was going to happen to them, played that role when they were intercepted by the Seventh Cavalry between Porcupine and Wounded Knee. Big Foot himself was sick and there were few men with that band. They were going to Red Cloud's agency at Pine Ridge to talk to him about food rations and protection. But the military took them to Wounded Knee overnight and held them there. They were taking all their weapons away the next morning and somehow a rifle shot was fired. The troops used cannons, machine guns, and the infantry and cavalry just opened fire on them and massacred all those men, women, and children.

I think that any civilized nation, whether ten or four hundred people had died, would bury the dead in individual graves. But I think the government was ashamed of what happened at Wounded Knee, and because it would have to identify the women and children being buried, it had them put in a mass grave and it just mixed up the bodies so that the reports could just say that a village of hostile Indians were wiped out. That was to be the revenge on the Oglala and all the Sioux for what happened to Custer and the Seventh Cavalry. We can never forget Wounded Knee.

I had a grandmother that was marching with Big Foot towards the Red Cloud Agency that winter. My grandfather Young Bear at the time was in the warrior camp at the Stronghold in the Badlands where many Lakota fled to defend themselves. He wasn't with the family. My grandmother's name was Rachel Young Bear. She was carrying her oldest daughter, whose Indian name was Ta Anpetu Waste Win, Her Good Day Woman. This baby girl was my dad's older sister, my aunt. Grandma used to talk about it. That morning at Wounded Knee, all of a sudden—they were lined up and it was snowing a little bit; the wind was blowing. They were all lined up and the military was searching them. All of a sudden, a shot was fired and the military opened fire on them. She just ran northwest with her baby, my aunt, on her back in a blanket. She knew her husband was somewhere in that direction, so she just ran that way through the snow. Soldiers on horseback were chasing women and everybody here and there. She ran through a ravine for a while and ran on a flat and then ran through a creek for a while. She didn't even notice the cold water. Then she went on the side of a hill for a while and through some canyon. When she started running, she all of a sudden heard and felt a big, loud slap behind her and, she said, blood just started running down warm on the left side of her head and shoulder. As she looked back, blood was coming out of her baby daughter's nose and mouth.

She knew that the baby was hit, but she didn't know that bullet went through the baby into her shoulder blade. She didn't understand that her baby was dying, so she just ran on. Finally she knew that her baby was dead, so she just threw the blanket back and dropped her baby and kept on running. She didn't know how far she ran till she found herself lying on the ground from exhaustion. She didn't recognize the canyon where she was lying, only that there was timber on each side; she was face down, her mouth dry and her throat was burning like her lungs. She later figured out that on today's maps it would be one of those canyons straight west of Paul Iron Cloud's place or Tuttle's place, about four or five miles north of Porcupine in those canyons. After she found my grandfather and after they settled here in Porcupine, I guess, she recognized the place where she finally fell.

She told how she carried that bullet in her shoulder for a while. Finally they took it out—she didn't say who. It left a maroon color below her shoulder towards the middle of the shoulder blade. My grandfather Young Bear was a medicine man who had bear medicine, so he kept that wound from spreading. He used to have a little leather bandage, a patch, that he would put the salve, the medicine, on with. When the medicine dried, then he would put the salve over it and put that patch on it. He used a medicine called *pejuta haka*, medicine root. Later on, my dad talked about that root by describing it and how my grandpa used to look for it. The plant had a little orange fire when he found it, or a blue flame, and he knew by that flame that the medicine was good. My grandfather died in 1947 and almost exactly a year later my grandmother died because nobody took care of her shoulder. It got worse and after a while she couldn't raise her arm. She died from that.

So my grandfather was a *Wajaje*, one of the Oglala bands, and my grandmother Young Bear was a *Hohwoju*, or Miniconjou, a Cheyenne River Sioux. They wound up camping here at Porcupine Creek, and when the BIA came around taking the census and enrolling people, they were living here and got enrolled as Oglala Sioux tribal members. They were given an allotment about five miles north of Porcupine. Their group was called *Takini*, or survivors of Wounded Knee. Some other relatives of ours also stayed, such as Hollow Horn and High Hawk. They were also *Takinis* on my father's side. A lot of the *Takinis* later moved back up to the Cheyenne River area along Cherry Creek, Bridger, and Red Scaffold. So some moved back up north and some just stayed here. The mass grave at Wounded Knee just covered up the shameful deed of the Seventh Cavalry.

A little over eighty years later, after many years of federal government policies, Wounded Knee became the center of our efforts to say to the BIA and the U.S. government and the whole world, "Hey, things have become unbearable again." Let me explain how it developed, because I was a part of it.

One of the most widely known chiefs of the Pine Ridge Sioux bands has been Red Cloud, but that's always been a problem for many of us here. Sure, during the Bozeman Trail war that ended in 1868 with the Fort Laramie Treaty, he was one of the Oglala leaders, but after that he was a spokesman for the government and the people who lived around the agency at Pine Ridge, the *Ite Sica,* Bad Face band, of Red Cloud Community. But out here in the districts, in these valleys, we had other chiefs and their bands that had little to do with the government and who remained traditional Lakota people. At one time Lakota people out here would have nothing to do with the agency and agency people, and the agency people had nothing to do with the people out here. That mentality is still with us because even in tribal government today the Pine Ridge village councilmen and the councilmen out here in the districts often clash over issues or can't agree. They like to see high-pay officials sitting in the offices at the agency and the low-paying jobs out here for us. Very few jobs even trickle out here to the districts, so we always disagree over them. A tribal chairman who is campaigning out here will promise to decentralize all programs and put them out into the districts, but once we vote him in, his promises somehow never work out. So after a while, you can understand why traditional people out here don't have much faith in tribal government and don't expect much from it.

One time I interviewed ten people out here and only two voted in tribal elections. When I asked them why, they said, "Why should I vote? There's nothing there for me. I don't care who's in tribal government; we still eat cheese and beans." What those eight guys said was true, because nothing out here in Brotherhood Community has changed. The tribal government is supposed to be a legislative body to protect the natural resources, the human resources, and all the needs of our people. But so far none of that has been done. State Social Services is driving around out here trying to take Indian kids and put them in foster child placements somewhere in Massachusetts or California. Then the tribe also has become a big social-service agency. The Bureau of Indian Affairs is the third social-service body giving out grants and making home visits once in a while. Everybody works for our welfare, but things don't change for us.

We are landowners and supposedly the BIA is here to provide services for our people. I live on three hundred acres of land here, and I'm fifty-seven years old. Not once has a BIA employee from Land Operations or Realty or Vocational Training come out here to say to me, "Hey, you can plant alfalfa here, wheat here, or even plant grapes here so you can make your own wine. You don't have to drive to Scenic." Never once. All those high-paid employees are just there to change light bulbs and water the lawns at BIA buildings or just there to buy land for their relatives. They're not really here to provide services for our people.

I used to think it would be a challenging experience to campaign myself for a tribal council seat to start programs and different projects so people out here would have the opportunity to do things for themselves. I thought that would be the right process to bring change. But I soon found out that many council members are only interested in higher salaries for themselves, or for their own relatives, rather than thinking of the good of all our tribal members.

One example of this was the zeolite controversy a few years ago. Someone discovered zeolite in the northern Badlands portion of the reservation. They wanted to strip-mine for that zeolite and the uranium that's underneath it. At first a big thing was made out of it because the tribe could make quite a bit of money on it. But the aftereffects of that strip mining would also mean that we couldn't replace the natural cover of those harmful materials. Once you expose them, they become harmful. God's natural law put natural covers on them to protect the living beings. Still, many people wanted to profit from the zeolite discovery. I was part of the campaign against it. We finally stopped the plan. So even though here was a chance to improve the economics on the reservation, the tribal government finally understood that the profit wasn't worth the health of future generations. That they considered this strip-mining at all, I guess, is understandable in a way. The economic problems here are so severe that even a responsive tribal government and a responsible, competent BIA can't solve them all. I didn't bother to run for a tribal council seat a second time.

The tribal government and the BIA are acting as an outcome of the Indian Reorganization Act of 1934. In 1935 or 1936 our people voted on whether to adopt it or not. The main provision in it was that we would have a government like the United States federal government, with a tribal chairman, the tribal council, and the tribal court. We would also adopt a tribal constitution. Since it worked for the rest of America, it was also going to work for us. I had a copy of a document in the archives in Kansas City that showed that nine people voted here in Porcupine District. Four of them said no and five voted yes. We had a boss farmer here in Porcupine who represented the superintendent here. He made the report that sixty percent of the people voted for the Indian Reorganization Act, so the five district members became sixty percent once they put it in writing. A typewriter made a dreadful decision for the Indian people. Some of the old people said they thought that when there weren't enough votes, they even had nonmembers and members of other tribes voting. But at that time the government was still trying to disrupt the traditional chief leadership and wanted to do about anything to get their Indian Reorganization Act passed. The BIA officials were willing to move percentage signs and decimal points whenever they wanted it to fit their wishes.

Some of the old-timers also used to say that they were supposed to try that Indian Reorganization Act for ten years and if they didn't agree with it, then it could be changed. But when that ten years ended, the Second World War was still going on and everybody was emotional and patriotic about the war, so everybody kind of forgot about it. President Roosevelt came up with jobs and people forgot about IRA until we started getting college-educated people coming back and asking what happened with that act. So now the people are talking against it, that it doesn't fit our needs and that it was rushed on us. I think that around the 1973 Wounded Knee takeover, when everybody was highly emotional about tribal government, they said that if you could get one-third of the tribal voters over twenty-one to sign a petition, they could recall IRA. At that time they counted only fourteen hundred voters, so teams of ladies went house to house and got thirty-two hundred signatures. Then the government said no, the tribal enrollment was nineteen thousand, so we had to get two-thirds of that population. They just set up their own red tape and the recall effort died.

Since the 1960s they tried to hire more Indian employees at the BIA. I thought that maybe they would be more sympathetic and in support of our real needs. But when you go in and ask for services, they look at you like you committed a crime. You want to look at your own records but they won't give them to you unless you get a special card signed by the superintendent and the area director and the secretary of the interior because of the privacy act. Once these people are in the federal service and become permanent employees, they don't care. They're in; they're protected.

Public Law 93-638 was supposed to encourage self-determination and local control in Indian country. Yet, instead of supporting this movement, the government people are fighting local control. They don't want Indians to run their own programs, they don't want Porcupine District to contract for law and order, and they don't want Porcupine District to contract the schools. Even our tribal councilmen often vote against local control and the welfare of their own people.

I think we've come to a point in our tribal government where we need to divide as a people. We need a traditional type of government to address the needs of the full-blood people. But we also have some mixed-blood people here that need the IRA tribal government. They're still Oglala Sioux tribal members by degree of blood. So we need to come up with decisions someplace so there is an effective separation. There is nowhere else to go with the present system. In Brotherhood Community we have many traditional families. All they wait for is their pension checks and their ADC (Aid for Dependent Children) money and they have nothing else to look forward to. I think the old chief leadership government would be the right type to address these people's needs.

We also come to the point here where we need education and economic development on this land. I'm sitting here on three hundred acres of land and don't see any income coming off it other than some lease money. It's like back in old England or Germany or one of those old countries where they had the feudal system. A duke controls the whole area even though it's the small farmers that work the land. These small farmers raise grapes, wheat, they cut hay, they raise cows, but they pay taxes to that duke or baron. And he becomes richer, wears gold jewelry, has six black horses on his carriage. He gets richer and these small farmers still stay the same. If you look at us here today, that system is here. We have one rancher controlling the whole unit around us. He runs cattle the way he wants to, he grazes them, he uses the land the way he wants to. We're still the small landowners, and we're still the same. I still drive a beat-up car and he drives a brand-new four-wheel-drive every year, buys a fancy Trans-Am for his older son, a new motorcycle for his youngest boy, a new four-wheel-drive for his daughter, and so on. Our small landowners like Kills Backs here, and Westons, and Little Boys, and Brown Eyes, you go inside our homes, you look at our houses, and you look at our land; you look at our cars and the way we dress. Then you look at that rancher, go in his house, look at his cars, his tractors, look at his refrigerator! Things are no different here than when the local duke controlled many thousands of acres in Europe four hundred years ago and the small farmers were poor. That's where all the government policies have brought us since Wounded Knee back in 1890.

One of the arguments that the U.S. government has used against us from the beginning is that we're incompetent; we are the wards of the government. So the superintendent was sent here to maintain the federal trust responsibility and protect us. So here I am, a full-blood, so I'm still incompetent. BIA Realty and Land Operations controls my land. They do as they

feel is right for my land, not me. I can only run ten head here or thirty, whatever they say, because as an Indian operator I'm incompetent. But one white
rancher here next to me only has 160 acres, yet he runs two hundred or three
hundred head on that 160 acres. Nobody comes to him and says, "Hey, you
can't do that. You're running too many cows on that land!" At what time in
our lives will we be competent? The day I graduate from high school or have
a college degree? At what income level or degree of blood will they classify
me as competent? Who has that authority to give me a certificate and say
I'm no longer an incompetent child? From that day forward I could think
for myself, speak for myself, could do business for myself, could drive on the
interstate by myself, could go to Chicago and back by myself? Who could
do that for me? Is it Congress, the secretary of the interior, is it the BIA area
director?

We now have college-educated people among us, doctors, accountants,
lawyers, teachers. Why are we still incompetent? Then there are people who
qualify as Oglala Sioux who are way down to the three hundredth degree
of blood. One good nosebleed would disqualify them as Indian, yet they're
recognized. Somebody has to address these issues. Otherwise this BIA will
be looking out for us the rest of our lives. Those are some of the questions
that need to be answered and nobody wants to answer them.

Besides all these problems of health, identity, social system, and government, the Lakota have a special treaty relationship with the government. Even before 1776, the U.S. government through its Senate started
making treaties with Indian nations. As the white people migrated towards
the west—the expansion of civilization they called it—every time they met
any Indian people, they made peace-and-friendship treaties and gave certain guarantees, territory and conditions. This treaty-making process with
Indian people continued until 1871. Finally, Congress said that there would
be no new treaties made with Indians. Since then the U.S. government made
Indian policy under the administrations of different presidents. Even though
the United States Constitution said that treaties were "the highest law of
the land," somehow the Indian policies tended to override our treaties. We
Sioux have been known to make some treaties that were very strong. I think
probably the main one for the Lakota is the Fort Laramie Treaty of 1868,
which guaranteed us all of west-river South Dakota and parts of the surrounding five states forever or until three-fourths of Lakota men voted to
change it. That's never happened, so we consider the treaty to be in force.

Most of our chiefs and powerful medicine men who were part of that treaty couldn't speak one word of English, but the government, through its commissioners and interpreters, put everything into English words. I wonder how they were translated to our representatives. But now, after about 125 years, we are sticking by the treaty provisions even though the government looks like it's scared of its own English words. I think we need to find a court somewhere in this world that can address our treaty issues, because our federal judicial system cannot do it with our judges appointed and paid by the U.S. government. The only thing they can do is to make political decisions, not decisions on the merit of a treaty or of findings and facts. I think that our grandfathers, our fathers, and uncles died for three or four generations wishing that somebody could address the merits of our treaty claims and make a ruling according to the real facts of the treaties. This, too, has never happened.

All of these pressures and problems have also caused a problem of unity among our own people. Some think only of the money side of an issue, some think only of themselves or their close family members, some think mostly about what's in front of their eyes, and then some think of seven generations from now. The Black Hills issue, where the U.S. government took the Black Hills in 1877 in spite of the 1868 Fort Laramie Treaty, is a good example of our lack of unity. Some people want to take the money offered by the government for its illegal taking; some want some of the land back; some want all the land back or nothing; still others aren't interested either way and figure we'll never get anything back anyway. Then some back the Bradley Bill or the Stevens Bill. I remember seeing the paper announce the Bradley Bill to give us back part of the Black Hills, and that the bill was going in front of the Congress in 1987. The sponsors wanted a show of unity from the Sioux because once the bill went out the door, it might take another hundred years to find some sympathetic congressman or senator to place it on the floor again. Of course, they couldn't get any unity! We Lakota have always gone our own way, never a united nation with all the other Sioux bands. But after all the pressures put on us by the military, then the missionaries, the government officials, the educators, the mass media and their Indian portrayals, the small-minded rednecks, and even the "friends of the Indian" groups and the do-gooders, we're now often taking ourselves down. We're showing jealousy, envy, small-mindedness, lack of patience, family conflicts, violence, and other things that show our loss of respect for ourselves and our relatives. Under these conditions very few of our people are walking that red road.

Here at Pine Ridge Reservation conditions began to really escalate in the late 1960s. Tribal government was corrupt, the federal government and the BIA were not meeting or even considering our needs, the white population around us was revealing its racism without holding back—everything was like a volcano ready to blow up. Then in 1972 it began.

The American Indian Movement got started in 1968, I think, to monitor police brutality towards Indians in Minneapolis–Saint Paul. By 1972 they were forming a caravan to gather testimony about all the broken treaties that were making our lives so terrible. I was part of that caravan in 1972. I had a drum, and everyplace we went, they requested traditional warrior songs or the AIM Song, which I'll talk about later. We sang and provided the music. I traveled with the AIM leaders—Dennis Banks, Russell Means, and Clyde Bellecourt—to all the reservations, starting with Pine Ridge. They took down all the statements on grievances and other input and they had other people going to their own reservations to collect testimony and documents. Then they started the Trail of Broken Treaties. Three routes would start from different parts of the country, meeting in Chicago. From there they formed a single caravan into Washington, D.C.

Four of us were in that car as we traveled with the caravan from Pine Ridge: Dick Elk Boy, Cecil Spotted Elk, Calvin Jumping Bull, and myself. Everyplace it stopped, we sang. We traveled with it as far as Cleveland, Ohio. Then one of our singers, I think it was Calvin, got word of a death in the family, so we turned around and came back from there. We didn't make it to Washington. When the rest of the caravan got to Washington, it didn't turn out the way it was planned. They arranged for liaison people in Washington knocking on doors and arranging meetings and promising grievances and documents. When they got there, things were different, so they marched up to the Bureau of Indian Affairs building and demanded entrance. They went in and things got out of hand. They took over the whole building and held it for I don't know how many days. Finally, after much negotiating, they were told the government wasn't going to press charges and that they would give the caravan one hundred thousand dollars for expenses if they left Washington. So everybody in the caravan divided up the money and left for home.

Afterwards, while they were on their way home, the government sent its people out to the reservations saying, "Beware! Those guys are coming back and they are going to take over your agency and your building." So all of a sudden in Pine Ridge we had armed vigilante squads—we called them goon squads—fortified up on top of the BIA buildings and all around the agency.

They started harrassing people, which created an uprising here while those guys on the caravan were still on the way back.

During that whole process I went to Rapid City, and as I was coming to Sharps Corner, just north of the house, two cop cars stopped me and served a court injunction on me saying that since I was one of the national AIM leaders along with Russell Means, I couldn't go into any kind of meeting or gathering of people. Russell and I don't know why that was served on me, because I didn't do anything. Maybe singing stirring songs is dangerous to people in power. So that climate of tension and harrassment went on. Later on they started firing people who were AIM members or supporters. They fired four women who were Community Health Representative employees because they supported AIM. They tried to get reinstated, tried to get the tribal chairman, Dick Wilson, impeached, and later on formed the Oglala Civil Rights Commission. About the middle of February they started having eight days of meetings at Calico, north of Pine Ridge, to gather civil rights violations by the tribal government and the federal government.

One day they put out word: "We want all district chairmen and treaty people and chiefs and medicine men and all elders to be at this meeting." I didn't think of going right away because I had a court injunction on me, but one day about noon my uncle George Gap said, "You want to go to Calico? They asked me to be there, so I'm going." So I got ready and went with Uncle George that afternoon. There was a lot of shouting and talk going on; everybody was mad, but there was no leadership, nobody they could depend on. During that first meeting at Calico there was no American Indian Movement, but a few days after that they had a big demonstration and fight at Custer and a big fight in the streets of Rapid City. Everybody there was holding out at the Mother Butler Center. I went to Custer and I got arrested, and I almost got arrested in Rapid City when a busload of police came and chased everybody around.

I came back home and waited for a while, and then one day I went to Calico again. They were getting after everybody. It was mostly women and they were really mad. They told all the elderly men, medicine men, chiefs, and treaty people, "If you're not men enough to change things, take those pants off; we'll wear them if you can't stand up for us."

That evening, it must have been five or six, somewhere in there, I was standing against the edge of the door at the entrance of the Calico meeting hall just listening. I saw a few cars drive in and saw Dennis, Russ, and some other AIM guys walk in and stand in the crowd. Finally one of them made an announcement that they would have a private meeting at a church basement across the road in Calico. All of the old guys were putting on their jackets and caps. As they were all coming out, Chief Frank Fools Crow, one of our most respected elders, went by me, pointed at me, and motioned me to follow them. I thought they were going to ask me to escort them or something, so I just walked behind and moved with them to that church.

When we went in they had some guards at the door and around the outside. There were only a few elderly men inside and nobody from the American Indian Movement yet. They started talking about what they should do, and one man said to recall the tribal constitution and bylaws and not deal with the IRA tribal government but stand only on treaties, and they went on in this way for a while. Finally they asked Dennis Banks and Clyde Bellecourt and Russell Means and about four or five others to come in. They came in and Fools Crow got up and prayed. Then he said, "Are you willing to give up your lives?" Everybody said *hau*—that means yes. "The people need you; are you willing to give up your life?" They said *hau*. So I said, "You can go and take over the tribal building or the BIA building, but there's nothing there we want. That's the governments that are oppressing us. What's the point? There might be lease papers or welfare papers and maybe chairs and tables. It's no use going into those buildings and putting up a fight to take over those offices."

Fools Crow then said, "What we'll do is take over Wounded Knee store and church and challenge the government to reenact the Wounded Knee Massacre of 1890. Come in and kill us!" A lot of those old men got up and said, "Yes, let's do it. It should be done that way." Luke Weasel Bear and Tom Bad Cob and some of the others got up and said, "Yes, it would be better that way because right now, if you look at our tribal government and the BIA, they look out more for white people, not for us. If you go and slap Saniski and Gildersleeve and Reegert, the people who own Wounded Knee, and the Catholic Church in the back pocket where they keep their money by taking over the store and the church, then the government's going to do everything; they'll really react and put you in prison or kill you. They're going to do everything to try and get you out of that tiny little place." Fools Crow said, "*Waktapo, ogna wiconi ehpeya kiyapi kte lo.*" (Beware, you might have to give up your life.) They all agreed and they prayed again. Somebody had a sacred pipe, so they all smoked.

So after that we came out of the church and went back to Calico. By that time there was a big crowd there. I didn't have a car, so I was trying to find a ride and here I saw Louie Bad Wound standing in the doorway. Dennis and Russ got up and said, "We're willing to take a stand, but we're going to have a meeting and dancing and talk some more. This building is too small, so we're going down to Porcupine community hall. We'll decide there if we're going to unite; all of us have to stay together so we form a big caravan down to Porcupine." So we helped them line up the caravan and then Louie Bad Wound and I, according to plan, left ahead of the caravan.

We first came to Pine Ridge. There was a big force of police there, goons and BIA police and U.S. marshals. We drove through there and went on to Wounded Knee. There was only one policeman there, parked on a little hill on the north side of Matterson Reserve. We went by and drove down to Oscar Hollow Horn's place and asked him if he would open up the community hall. "*Ohan,* yes." he said. "What's going on?" "Well, we don't know, but just in case we need it," I said. "We're going on to Porcupine." We left and when we pulled into Porcupine, there were about fifteen police cars parked at the Porcupine store, and at the entrance of Our Lady of Lourdes School there was another bunch of police and all along the road there was more police.

Somebody in Calico must have radioed ahead that everybody was going to Porcupine, so the main force of police was already waiting in Porcupine. Of course, that was the plan we made at Calico, to make like we were all headed to Porcupine. Louie and I went into the community hall. Since I was district chairman, I had a key and opened the doors. That was the brown building that's right across and below Our Lady of Lourdes. We moved the benches around and swept and turned all the lights on, turned the outside lights on, and made as if we were getting ready. Pretty soon one of the police, he's a cousin of mine, Lee Weston, came in and said, 'What's going on?" Since he was acting as if he didn't know anything, I did the same. "A caravan's coming down; it's big, so we're going to have a meeting and dance." He said, "*Hau,* they told us to patrol this." I said okay. They hung around for a while and backed up and left. Then, all of a sudden, all the police turned their red lights on and followed each other towards Wounded Knee. About twenty to thirty cars took off for Wounded Knee. Then, about ten minutes later, they all came back towards Porcupine. They all parked in the old day school parking lot with their red lights going.

I guess they went to Wounded Knee. All the lights were out there. When the police cars got close to Wounded Knee from the bridge east of Wounded Knee, those inside Wounded Knee started firing at them, so they all turned around and went back. Our decoy plan worked. That's how Wounded Knee II got started.

It turned out to be really true what those old men had said. The government brought in marshals and Canadian Border Patrol, and FBI, the 82nd Airborne, and even special sharpshooters from some rifle association out of Georgia to kill the top elders inside Wounded Knee. It was almost like Korea or Vietnam. There were flares and machine guns going twenty-four hours a day, and all the military was behind this. What those old men predicted and prayed about was happening. The United States military went all out to get ready to kill everybody who was inside Wounded Knee. They accused us of having all kinds of weapons, even Russian-made ones. They said we had antitank weapons, but it was really those propane gas stovepipes, about two or three inches wide, and we carved handles and little wooden scopes and painted them black. We had enough service veterans among us who knew about military weapons. We also made imitation shells and carried them around in the open during daytime to make it look like we had bazookas and .50-caliber machine guns. Our armored cars were old vans with plywood on the insides. Even helicopters wouldn't get down low enough to fire inside Wounded Knee because we put up a fake big machine gun. It was carved out of lumber that somebody had found in the basement of the store.

This went on for a couple of months, and maybe all the newspaper coverage from all over the world kept it from being another massacre. Finally both sides started negotiating. I was the youngest to be a spokesman or negotiator. There were six elderly men, three of them medicine men and three chiefs, who were appointed, all of them treaty people. I was the seventh one. It was an honor, but I got thrown in jail over it because they had a picture of me with Jim Abouresk and George McGovern, who came in to help settle the takeover. All that time during the negotiations the FBI was letting me in and out. They let me in and I signed the time, and signed when I went out. Still they used that picture against me and arrested me and I spent ten days in jail.

But the price I paid was worth it to me. In 1890 they killed my aunt; my family blood was spilled there at Wounded Knee. Even my dad got involved in it because he was willing to spill his own blood and die to make a change because his sister had been part of the original massacre.

All the news going out was controlled from the agency, and only the news they wanted going out went out. By going in and out, I knew what the reality was inside. There was a lot of high spirits; there was an identity again, a warrior identity. A number of the young guys inside are today on alcohol and drugs because they gradually lost their identity again since. At that time, though, those guys were tough. There was very little food and maybe four or five .22 bullets for those who had a .22 rifle, a few .30-.30 shells, and maybe a handful of shotgun shells at any one time, but they took a stand and made a stand. I think the old revenge mentality for the defeat of Custer showed itself again, because they came out with all the top military weapons to kill us.

It was the first time in U.S. history, I believe, that the 82nd Airborne was assigned somewhere in civilian clothes. They must be part of the Seventh Cavalry. They probably would have forced their way in, but there was lots of media coverage from across the world all along the ridges and along the edge of the outside perimeter. We had media from France, Germany, Belgium, Africa, Japan, and elsewhere. The black leaders, Jesse Jackson and Abernathy, were there; everybody was here. If nobody would have cared about it getting on the news, then they probably would have gone in. At that time some reporters sneaked into Wounded Knee and we got lots of media exposure. We had some real good warrior-type runners out of Oglala, Manderson, and Porcupine that would take people in and out through the Badlands. I think this is where the spiritual power of the Lakota was very important, because some of these runners moved at night and went by trained police dogs.

But at the same time that government people and tribal officials showed that they didn't care about our people, we had a division in our communities. The people who believed in treaties or lived the traditional way of life supported Wounded Knee II. They decided to hold a mass meeting to express support for all activities and actions taken at Wounded Knee. When they got wind of it at the agency in Pine Ridge, they sent a delegation to take part. Two of the guys they sent were former Porcupine Dictrict members. They came and they pleaded and they talked with little shaky voices and tried to get the sympathy of the people. I think that was the biggest mass meeting ever held in Porcupine. I was in jail, serving my ten days, as I said, and Paul Iron Cloud, who was the vice chairman, ran the meeting. They passed a unanimous vote that they didn't want any government roadblocks on the Porcupine road to Wounded Knee, that there should be no criminal charges coming out against anybody who was in there, and that they would stand on the 1868 Fort Laramie Treaty and go to court to abolish the IRA tribal government.

Over five hundred people went to that meeting, all Porcupine people.

They had used that community hall as a kind of information center. They also had lots of people coming in who had no place to go and needed some place to eat and sleep. Then it was also a first aid station. We even had an attorney staying there twenty-four hours a day in case somebody needed a lawyer. But a couple of the local policemen said that people were using drugs inside, even though they had never gone inside, and that there were drugs and weapons in that hall, so on that verbal complaint, they went in with an APC (armored personnel carrier), escorted everybody out, and closed down the hall. That was a district building, given to the district. Even our own district members were on both sides of the conflict because some of them were getting paid as BIA police officers, deputies, or goons. It's an old colonial technique to use our own people as police against us. These goons were mostly mixed-bloods who got fifteen or twenty dollars an hour, and they went around beating up people and shooting at them. These guys did more shooting around Wounded Knee than the military. When the military and the people inside Wounded Knee agreed to a ceasefire one time, those goons, with about ten pickup loads of guys, went on the west side of the town of Wounded Knee and started shooting, and that started the shooting all over again. Those goons committed lots of violence and harrassment and even rapes, but nobody got prosecuted.

When negotiations finally got started, we wanted to talk only to top people. I think Henry Kissinger was in office then. The top people from Washington came to Rapid City and a delegation from Wounded Knee flew in a helicopter to go meet with them. Later they designated Fools Crow's place in Kyle as a negotiating camp. So they started a camp over there for government officials to meet with our people on their grievances. To get to Fools Crow's place, you had to go through four roadblocks to discourage people from going there to file their complaints. That's a tactic the government used to keep people away. They allowed two goon roadblocks, the Bureau of Indian Affairs had one, and the U.S. marshals had one. It was a tactic of intimidation and harrassment. In the middle of that I was going back and forth. I used to take everything out of my car that was sharp or looked like a weapon, the jack handle, screwdrivers, everything, and I went. But somehow by digging around in my car they found a hunting knife that was broken in half. My brother-in-law, George Squirrel Coat, who stayed with me at the time, used it to open cans of oil with. I think the blade only stuck out about two inches and the rest was broken off. But they found that and they arrested me for carrying a concealed weapon. How could they get me for a broken, rusty old knife? It was bad.

There were lots of negotiations going on and the government made some promises that were never kept. They were willing to sit down in Rapid City with attorneys present to negotiate and then hold some congressional hearings. But once we came out of Wounded Knee, nothing happened. Also, some guys inside were taking drugs and I think that disrupted the leadership inside. Finally they said, "Well, it's seventy-one days and we'll come out. The government had them pile their weapons and they couldn't believe they only had .22s and shotguns and .30-.30s. They spent about six months with those metal detectors going over every inch of that ground looking for the bazooka and that AK-47 machine gun, the Russian weapons that they knew were inside there, but they didn't find anything. But they did charge everybody. The tribe brought about 387 charges, and the U.S. government also had about 400 charges even after they dismissed some.

One of the things that elderly man at Calico talked about was proven. The material possessions of those white people meant more than Indian life. They spent millions of dollars on court costs and many man-hours during Wounded Knee II and after.

Some of the good things that happened after Wounded Knee II ended were that we achieved more local control of law and order and of our schools and their curriculum. They started teaching Sioux language and our old stories and bringing our elders into the classroom. I think, too, that the traditional community had been brought together. But the AIM leaders paid the price. The government continued to go after them to put them in prison or outright murder some. For years after that the leadership had a hard time staying out of jail. They would get out of one charge and other charges would be filed against them. They were always on the lookout for getting killed. They were afraid they would end up like Crazy Horse or Sitting Bull or even Spotted Tail—killed by our own people.

One of the most misunderstood or controversial songs during the AIM days was the AIM Song. The actual songmaker of that song is unknown; maybe it was Drury Cook. In 1968, down in the basement of the Holy Rosary dormitory, they had a powwow and our old Porcupine Singers— Drury Cook, Uncle Henry Young Bear, Irving Tail, and some others—sang that song. It was just a general powwow song with no words. Then a couple of years later, after the abuse and murder of Raymond Yellow Thunder in

Gordon, Nebraska, there was a march and takeover of Gordon. After all the negotiations that followed and everything got settled a bit and the chamber of commerce was happy, some police got fired and a special committee on human rights was formed to look into things; religious people in Gordon were saying that we've been friends and can live together again with a better understanding. Everybody agreed and at last in Gordon, Nebraska, there was a happy feeling and there was a celebration. The Gordon auditorium was full of white people there and Indians.

I had my drum there that time in Gordon. We took it out to the center of the dance floor and we stood around it. I think it was Tyrone Head, a singer and champion dancer from Rosebud, who took the flag down and put it around himself as a kind of cape. Someone took a picture of him and it made some of the national magazines. There was Tyrone and I forgot who else, Billy Black from Minneapolis and about six or seven other singers. The host committee requested a victory song. We thought about an appropriate song. We didn't know if AIM had a victory song or if Gordon had a victory song to commemorate the occasion. The only song that came to my mind was that song, so we pushed it up. We sang it in the auditorium and then out into the street back to the main street intersection. There were about seven hundred people following us out there celebrating, hollering, dancing, waving the U.S. flag and the Oglala tribal flag. We kept singing it; people danced and felt good.

A few months later, Dennis Banks wrote to me and said that there was going to be an AIM convention in Cass Lake, Minnesota. He said, "We want you to be there and sing that AIM song you sang in Gordon. The delegates from all the American Indian Movement groups want to hear it with the possibility of that song or another song or two being adopted as a national AIM song." He also sent me some money, so I left from here with my older son, Junior. We got up there, and all the white fisherman and hunters from that area were all angry and hostile. They were confronting each other over Indian treaty fishing and hunting rights. They had rifles and were patrolling the roads, so it got a little hairy sometimes. It was still a good convention. I think it was Saturday morning that I went in front of the delegations and I talked about that song and how it represented both the anger and the protest against the violation of human rights. Two other guys got up and sang their songs, but they adopted this one as the national AIM Song.

For some reason that song seems to make everybody a top singer; it motivates them even if they're drunk or on drugs. They put a red bandanna on their arm or head and they make a fist salute and they start singing the AIM Song. It is an emotional song of pain and of protest and of eventual victory over many years of oppression and racism. It also pulls alike-thinking people together to take a stand. There are no words but there is an emotional power to that song. It does something to people, even the law enforcement people who seem to be upset by that song. From their point of view it must say something against police or against law and order because they really get upset when we sing it. I'll give you an example. In 1975 Oglala Community had a fair and rodeo. That Saturday night they took the drum out in the center and someone requested the AIM Song, so the singers sang it. They got surrounded by the BIA police, who arrested all the singers, took their drum, and threw them in jail.

Somehow that song upsets people and gives others an emotional boost. It was connected with people getting beat up and stabbed and shot. It caused people to serve time in tribal jail or BIA jails, county jails, city jails, state prisons, and federal prisons. It pulls all the feeling of anger and protest together. Even today on the FM KILI radio station here in Porcupine, when the AIM Song is played, some tribal members don't like it because they think it represents something that's not traditional—they would prefer a chief's song or a veterans' song—but instead it is only militant and revolutionary. They would call the program director about keeping that song out as an opening or closing song for the programming of the day, but that's the way it was planned earlier when AIM sponsored that station and they are sticking by it. Whether people are against it or request it, that AIM Song sure gets people emotionally involved.

After Wounded Knee II in 1973, I saw lots of signs of a growing positive identity among our young people. I saw lots of young boys and young men growing their hair long again and identifying themselves as Indian. Even women started wearing their hair long again and were now fasting and Sun Dancing. They had many of those AIM leaders and those who took a stand with them to look up to as models. It was a time of real positive identity. Many of these young kids were now wearing beaded belt buckles and traditional costumes when they danced and they were proud that they were Lakotas.

I think one of the problems the AIM leadership had was that some of them themselves had problems with alcohol and drugs. After a while they couldn't keep up their leadership role and image, and after a while our youth started losing their direction again. In the early 1980s somehow they had lost much of that positive Indian identity they had gained after Wounded Knee II, and got into break dancing like they were doing in the city ghettos. I think some of that happened because they didn't have any kind of leadership they could look up to.

Right after the occupation there was identity expressed by wearing bead-work jewelry, and porcupine quillwork came back, and ribbon shirts became popular. At first after Wounded Knee II, young men's sisters or wives made nice-looking ribbon shirts and dance costumes for them. They also made beautiful buckles or leather belts with Indian designs on them and beaded key chains dangling from the side. They wore long braids or ponytails. Some-how with time that identity lost its appeal. Then after a while, the ribbon shirts, buckles, and key chains were sold to the pawn shops, trading posts, and to the guy who owned the liquor store. Those guys had more ribbon shirts and belt buckles than they could wear or sell. After a while the guy who had been proud of his Indian appearance ended up wearing a t-shirt with an Indian design on the front, and after another while, by drinking and abusing himself, he ended up wearing a ragged tank top or beat-up overall jacket. Not all went that way, but too many did.

So after 1973 a positive identity resulted, but I think the liquor, drugs, loss of identity and direction took its toll and got in the way of their iden-tity again. After 1973 Sun Dancing came back real strong, with many young people taking part. After that also at many powwows the arena was full of dancers, especially young men and women who were traditional dancers. They were getting out there for the enjoyment of dancing, to express their pride in themselves. Somehow since then that has given way to big-money contests with five-hundred-, a thousand-, two-thousand-dollar prizes. Our traditional dances are dying out. Many dancers and singers go where the big money is. If we put on a traditional powwow here in Porcupine, maybe half of our local singers and a few of the local men and women dancers might show up.

One person who was involved with many of these same events and issues of tribal government, the AIM demonstrations and takeovers, and the iden-tity question was my brother Ted Means. Since he was involved with some of that in a different way than I was, I'll ask him to tell his side of it.

TED MEANS: The American Indian Movement was first brought to the Pine Ridge Reservation on a request from Severt Young Bear and Birgil Kills Straight, who had gotten in contact with my brother Russell Means in Cleveland about the Raymond Yellow Thunder situation. Raymond had been tortured and killed in Gordon, Nebraska, and no one was doing anything to raise the issue or to bring any kind of prosecution against the people who were responsible for Raymond Yellow Thunder's death. So from that the American Indian Movement came in and, of course, there was a confrontation in the city of Gordon. I think a couple of positive things that came out of that particular confrontation was that a human relations commission was established there which gave people, especially Indian people, the opportunity to have their grievances in terms of police brutality and discrimination in the city of Gordon dealt with. It brought about an awareness in the community that Indian people would no longer just quietly sit by and allow our people to be abused and have their rights violated.

From these demonstrations also came a series of meetings and gatherings on the Pine Ridge Reservation, where a lot of documentation was gathered relating to our situation here at Pine Ridge Reservation and the issues affecting our people. We conducted civil rights hearings in each district and all that documentation was turned over to the Justice Department. This documentation revealed abuses in the areas of land issues, health issues, and civil rights issues. Since that time there's been a presence of the American Indian Movement here on Pine Ridge. This kind of mobilization continued through 1972, culminating with the Trail of Broken Treaties, which came through the Pine Ridge Reservation in the fall of 1972 and continued on into Saint Paul, where a twenty-point position paper was developed by the people and eventually presented to the U.S. government. Also the takeover of the Bureau of Indian Affairs building in Washington, D.C., took place.

After the Trail of Broken Treaties there was a group formed here on the Pine Ridge Reservation called the Oglala Sioux Civil Rights Organization, which began to highlight and expose the abuses of tribal government and to raise issues affecting the people here. That organization again contacted the American Indian Movement, which at that time was operating out of Rapid City. We had dealt with issues surrounding the death of Wesley Bad Heart Bull in Custer, culminating in demonstrations and some violence there. Some of the AIM leadership was invited down to a series of meetings in Calico Hall. After long discussions, the chiefs and headmen went into a private meeting and called some of the leadership of the American Indian Movement into that meeting to discuss not only ways of highlighting abuses that were taking place on Pine Ridge but, I think more importantly, to raise the issue of the 1868 Fort Laramie Treaty and how the violations of that treaty had resulted in our present situation.

So the decision was made there to go to Wounded Knee, and because of the spiritual significance of the mass grave and the massacre that took place there in 1890, it was decided that Wounded Knee would be the place where we made our stand as a people. Wounded Knee, of course, gained international attention, and I think the establishment media keyed in on the sensationalism of the event and didn't really deal with the legal and human issues that were being raised there at Wounded Knee. The media and the government, of course, just made it out to be a civil disturbance without ever really dealing with the issues.

I think the most important event that took place at Wounded Knee was that the people inside Wounded Knee, for seventy-one days, experienced a small taste of freedom, because even though they were surrounded by, you know, all the power and might of the federal government, they controlled their lives inside Wounded Knee. They were able to establish a health center of sorts inside Wounded Knee. They were able to establish a school for the kids that were inside. They had to make decisions, but decisions that affected them and which they controlled. Nobody else had any influence or control over those decisions. It also gave the people a sense of pride and a sense of realizing that for years we had all been brought up in an atmosphere of prejudice and an environment that just accepted Indian people as second-class citizens. And I think that standing up at Wounded Knee gave people an understanding that they were not second-class citizens and that we had a right to be treated as everyone else is treated. Also, you know, the issues themselves were important. It gave our old people, especially the old treaty people, a renewed sense of hope, because these were mostly old men that had been working all their lives to try to achieve some type of just treatment in terms of the treaty of 1868. The events at Wounded Knee II gave recognition to the 1868 treaty and some recognition to those individuals who for years had been voicing these concerns and were not being heard.

I think there were a lot of side effects—some bad, some good—that came out of the events at Wounded Knee II. I remember Elija Whirlwind Horse used to say publicly that the new Crazy Horse School that was built at Wanblee was the direct result of Wounded Knee and the actions of the American Indian Movement to raise people's consciousness. I think those are some of the positive effects that came out of the experience of Wounded Knee because the government realized, "Hey, we've got to do something to quiet these Indians down." So what they did was to pour lots of money into Indian reservations, and, you know, when in 1976 they came up with the old CETA (Comprehensive Education Training Act) program jobs, everybody had jobs.

We realized that we made some mistakes at Wounded Knee II and right after Wounded Knee. Of course, we were tied up in the massive prosecutions that were taking place, but we had no real strategy for the people who considered themselves to be AIM people, so it created a lot of confusion and a lot of negative things took place. But I think the positive effect on Indian people and Indian programs and the developing Indian colleges was an understanding by the government that now Indian people were going to make their own decisions. You know, as I look back at Wounded Knee II, I see it as a focal point in our history, an important time in our history when a change of direction took place for our people. People began to more realistically think in terms of the ability of Indian people making rational decisions for Indian people, and that we didn't have to accept the paternalistic approach of the federal government which had historically been used with Indian people.

I also think it was a time when there was a kind of cultural renaissance that had been taking place among Lakota and all Indian people without much notice. Wounded Knee II was able to bring a focus to that renaissance that was taking place. The Sun Dance was given back to our people before that, but it became part of a celebration, not a priority of its own, and it was operated more as a show than anything else. I can remember that in that old Sun Dance they had to quit early Saturday mornings because a parade was planned and then they would have to quit at noon so the dancing contests could get started. At the same time the Sun Dance was going on, they had a carnival, softball tournament or baseball tournament going, all kinds of distractions. There used to be only that one sideshow Sun Dance in the 1960s when they allowed the Sun Dance to start again. After Wounded Knee II, the Sun Dance became increasingly more traditional and more like it used to be done before it was outlawed in the 1880s. More and more people started going back and reidentifying with the traditional Lakota religion, realizing the importance of knowledge and wisdom of the old people. Now there's Sun Dances all over, even among other tribes. Before that time there was very little recognition of our elders, their knowledge and their wisdom. We didn't really realize the beauty that we had in our midst, and I think Wounded Knee II helped to bring about that kind of realization.

Today many things haven't really changed a lot. Conditions are the same on this reservation. Some of the same kinds of situations, the same kinds of abuses, are happening as before Wounded Knee II. It's just the government has become more sophisticated now. They're still attempting to rip off the land. They're still trying to exploit our resources, and they're still trying to basically call the shots. Tribal government, as well, is designed to do exactly what it is doing. I think my involvement in tribal goverment as a council-man has crystallized the understanding that tribal government will not work as it's been developed after IRA. There is very little desire to put forth any real kind of change. We have some individuals that have the understanding and would like to make much-needed changes, but the system itself doesn't allow for that kind of change, and it's very hard to bring people's minds to that kind of understanding. You know, being in tribal government has made me realize how dependent the system has made our people. It's a situation that's going to take a long time to turn around, to change. But I think there are individuals among our people who are interested in making those kinds of changes, to build again.

I think Wounded Knee II and a few years after was like a high point and the curve started heading downward again. Now we're in a situation with eighty-five to ninety percent unemployment and all of the conditions that go along with it, alcoholism and its effects on the people. I think we're sort of at the bottom again and beginning to look forward to another move. I'm not saying another Wounded Knee, you know, but another move to bring about some change here on this reservation. As long as we wait for the sys-tem itself to bring about this change, we're just going to continue to wait. As long as we wait for tribal government and the federal government to create these alternatives to what we have, it's just not going to happen; it'll just get worse and worse. It will have to come from ourselves, from within. The people are now in a situation where we're having to look for alternatives and realize that there are other ways of trying to accomplish meeting the needs of people other than waiting for the tribal government, the district government.

Poverty is a situation in which people who have no choices lower their standards and begin to give up in a lot of ways. But I think there are alter-natives and some possible solutions. I think that tribal government, for one thing, is too top-heavy and that more decisions need to be made locally. We have a tribal constitution and bylaws, we have a tribal code, but those things were developed back in 1934–35. I think that we need to sit down and develop a constitution and bylaws that are applicable today and will be applicable in the future, or at least include a process for revision in the future that is workable. Another thing that needs to happen is that we need to involve the minds that we have here on the reservation to develop the strategy that we need to follow. Part of the problem, you see, is that tribal government today functions on a crisis basis. There is very little planning that takes place.

With tribal elections every two years, the system works two years at a time and that's not really enough time to do the things that need to happen. It doesn't allow for creativity; it doesn't allow for any real kind of change or stability. Unfortunately, a lot of our people are comfortable in that kind of system rather than dealing with serious change. If you look at tribal government, the faces change—rarely does a tribal chair get reelected—but the conditions here don't change. I firmly believe that of course we need jobs, but jobs alone aren't going to do it for us, because we don't have to look very far to when there was a whole lot of employment on the reservation because of federal training programs in the 1970s. But in the long run conditions haven't changed. Maybe the jobs were low-level, artificial, and temporary; maybe we need a complex, integrated set of changes.

When you talk about complex solutions, you only have to go to the taking of the sacred Black Hills by Congress in 1877. Even though the U.S. Supreme Court has finally agreed that the taking of the Black Hills was illegal, the U.S. government will only offer us a bunch of money for them. Then in the 1980s Senator Bill Bradley from New Jersey proposed the Bradley Bill to give us back some of those Black Hills. The tribal council at first went on record as supporting the Bradley Bill. I think that action was followed by a great deal of confusion and lack of understanding of the issues in the Bradley Bill. I think people didn't appreciate the compromises that had to be made, but if we could achieve that return of land, even though it was a lot less than outlined in the original Fort Laramie Treaty, we could create a precedent and we've created a situation where we could now have some leverage. We could use it as a starting point again in dealing with the federal government on a government-to-government basis. There was, of course, some opposition from our people to the bill, but I think part of that is based on personalities and part of it stems from the compromises that had to be made. I think the people who were opposed to it were not opposed to the return of the land, but were opposed to some of the decisions that were made in terms of the bill itself.

Overall, I think there was general support among the Lakota for the Bradley Bill. Even though the bill seems to be stalled, I think one of the positive things about the bill and others like it that may come up to settle some of our claims is that it will make our Lakota people become more responsible in terms of the decisions they make, not only regarding the Black Hills, but of the decisions our leaders make for our people. And I think that is a result of the stand that we took at Wounded Knee. I believe it started there, because back then the people were talking about selling the Black Hills or taking the original $117 million the government offered after the Supreme Court decision about the Black Hills came down in our favor. Then we would have nothing. But due to a lot of hard work and a lot of sacrifice, we were able to convince the people that it would be spiritually wrong and morally wrong and politically wrong to allow the sale of the Black Hills to happen. So I think that another positive thing that came out of Wounded Knee, a result that the American Indian Movement is not solely responsible for but played a key role in bringing about, was that kind of broader and more thoughtful understanding. The people were ready for it. You know, it's been a long-standing joke to say to our relations and friends, "When we get our Black Hills money, I'll pay you back." This case has not been settled for so long that in a joking way that meant, of course, never. Now I think we understand that if we ever accept any money, the Black Hills will be lost forever, and so the people have changed their thinking because of what went on.

In terms of the AIM song and what it has become, and what Brother Severt said about it, let me add this much. Originally it was first sung at Gordon, Nebraska, and I'm not sure where the song came from, either, but it was used at that time as a memorial to Raymond Yellow Thunder, and then it was used again and again to cause us to identify as AIM people. After Gordon it was officially adopted as the song of the American Indian Movement. It's a song that has been used at funerals; it's a song that has been used to honor different individuals; it is something that represents a kind of spirit, something really positive, to the people. It's now actually recognized internationally as a song that identifies with struggle. It is a song that represents the sacrifice people had to make; it's a song that represents the beauty of the Indian people. There's a lot of positive feeling in that song because of all the things that AIM has been through. It represents some of the positive things that AIM has been able to accomplish; it's a song that represents pride in oneself and pride in the people.

The American Indian Movement, fifteen to twenty years ago, was a lot easier to move around than today. People had fewer individual responsibilities. What also happened over the years is that AIM, people who often became involved on a national scale, at different sites, have gotten involved in local issues and gotten active in their local areas. As a result, AIM as a national organization has come to a standstill. The identity still exists because there is a movement of AIM people in their local areas dealing with the local issues, but as a national organization, we've gotten into a situation where those who were recognized as national leaders now have other responsibilities in their own local areas. There's less communication on the national level. Because we've sort of moved away from confrontation politics, there is less exposure on a national level as well.

Of course, there are those who have succumbed to some of the pressures of being recognized as leaders; they began to act in self-seeking or selfish ways, to seek publicity, and to disappoint the expectations people had of them. Since that time there is no national strategy of rectifying the condition of our Indian people. I think that what Severt was saying is true. There was a time when the national leaders within AIM provided role models for our people, young and, to some degree, even the old. Now they have lost their influence and our young people are confused. They are less concerned about projecting themselves as Indians with the braids, chokers, and ribbon shirts. But I do think that maybe there's more of an understanding of who we really are. Before, I think, it was a situation where people wanted to let others know they were proud of their Indian identity, but now in a positive way it's a situation where people are now more comfortable as Indian people in terms of their own identity, that they feel less of a need to project a dramatic image than before. I think that as proof of this there's still more cultural activity and people participating in it than there were twenty years ago. There are more people taking part in Sun Dances and ceremonies, and spiritual runs, and in powwows as singers and dancers than before. That's a positive sign.

The international exposure during the Wounded Knee II and AIM activism days has given Indian people recognition in terms of their special treaty status with the U.S. government. It has not only given a broad recognition but it has also helped the federal government realize that it has to deal with these issues in terms of Indian people partly because of pressure that has been generated internationally through the United Nations process and the emergence of international groups that support Indian issues. There's more of an understanding, and, of course, the U.S. government has to be more careful in how it deals with Indian people.

As far as my local role is concerned, I think I'm less optimistic now than I was when I first ran for the tribal council seat. I believed at the start that as an individual my first role was to try to bring about some kind of change here locally in terms of the people of Porcupine District and then, of course, to create some kind of change within tribal government. I believe that in two years of being in office, if I can get people thinking in terms of alternatives and maybe moving a little bit in that direction, then I'll have accomplished what I set out to do. Then, after two years in office, I can reexamine my effectiveness in that role.

I think I've had to make some decisions that have not been easy. But I think having had to make those decisions has helped me realize more and more that all this has to change in order for us to survive. If I can maintain my sanity for the next year and a half, I'll accomplish my goal in a small way. That tribal office is swarmed every day with people that have emergency needs, whether it's a death in the family or the light bills that aren't getting paid. What I'm trying to do each of those days is to shift this dependency on the tribal government to the local districts to provide a vehicle for local districts to deal with these situations, because they're in a better position to realistically help the ones that need help. In a lot of cases the ones who really need help don't get it at the central Pine Ridge tribal office. There's the potential of a certain amount of abuse in this because there's a lot of people that are repeaters, so to speak, that have learned who to talk to and what tone of voice to use, how to approach certain people to get what will be perceived as emergency needs. I think that the districts themselves know who the people are and those who really need the help and also those who are only trying to use the system. In this way we can be more effective in helping the people in real need.

You know, I'm a firm believer in education. But if you look at education today, it's becoming harder and harder to compete. A person with a bachelor's degree ten to fifteen years ago was in a fairly good position. Nowadays it's getting to be where you need a master's or doctor's degree. If we're going to need more and more education to keep up, I support the idea of community education. Our Oglala Lakota College concept has the potential of becoming a quality institution and competing with other universities like, say, Black Hills State or the University of South Dakota. But we have to tighten up the education process internally. Local control is only part of it. Even when we offer classes in a dispersed way in small communities and local community buildings, the quality of these classes must be guaranteed. I think Oglala Lakota College, like Sinte Gleska University over at Rosebud and those of some of the other tribes, has done a credible job, but needs to struggle on to provide education with a Lakota flavor, and with a high degree of quality and success.

Below the college level, I think, local control of schools is also important, but the communities have to become more involved in the issues that are affecting us. Here in the district, you have community government and district government, yet there is very little participation in terms of young people. There is almost no opportunity for them to express themselves or to excel during the wintertime. They need youth programs, more alternatives, more opportunity. Of course it's a question of dollars, but the people who are making the decisions on where dollars are spent should pay more attention to the needs of our youth.

In terms of curriculum, I believe that cultural education, bilingual education, bicultural education, or whatever label you put on it, is as important to our young people as conventional education because if we lost the language, if we lost the songs and lost traditions like the *hunka,* the making of relatives, and lost our sacred ceremonies, then we would be lost as a people. If many of those kids aren't getting these in the home, they should at least get it in the school every day and be familiar with and respect these traditions. If they start in Headstart, kindergarten, and all the way through the twelve years of schooling, they're going to be in a better position to compete because, for one thing, they'll know who they are and they'll know where they're headed and they'll know why.

In my particular situation, for example, the Lakota language is not spoken in the home. My kids have gone through the local PCC (Parent-Child Center) Program and there's an old man who has worked there for years. His name is Jake High Hawk. He speaks to those kids in fluent Lakota and my kids come home and say things, talk in Lakota, you know. I can't reinforce what they've learned because I'm not fluent. This shows a responsibility lies with the parents, too—maybe coordination with adult education to create opportunities so that kids can be reinforced at home. If kids grow up with the language and understand the importance of our language, they'll pass it on to their kids. You know, my parents were a part of that old boarding school system where they spent the entire year at school and they were punished for speaking their Lakota language. It's not that far back that our people had to abide by these kinds of rules, and I believe it was part of a sophisticated and thoughtless effort to strip us of our identity and make it easier for our people to be exploited. Now it's going to be very difficult to counteract that and bring our language back in those families.

All in all, then, though the demonstrations, the meetings, the takeovers, the court cases, and all the activist, confrontational tactics of the American Indian Movement are no longer taking place, there was a time when that brought about some critical changes. Today, I believe, many of our AIM people are struggling on at their local levels, often working within the tribal systems or on their own to improve the living conditions of our people, to improve the health and the education services needed by our people, to guard our resources and our rights, and to maintain our rights, our pride, and our dignity as Indian people. Thank you, Brother Severt, for asking me to present my views on these things.

Lakota Humor

The summary my brother Ted Means gave of some of the American Indian Movement concerns and actions points out our frustrations and our struggle to keep our treaty rights, to keep our resources, to be proud of our Lakota ways in a very oppressive colonial situation. But all those serious issues shouldn't make us forget that a balanced life involves joking and laughing. Our Lakota peple have always used humor to keep that balance.

I think Indian humor plays a big part in the whole social structure of the Lakota, and here's my way of interpreting that. In Lakota family life there's a barrier across the generations that's often still so strong that certain in-laws don't talk to each other. For example, a son-in-law doesn't talk to his mother-in-law and a daughter-in-law doesn't talk to her father-in-law. They avoid each other out of respect. There's also a barrier between a brother and sister once they get older that's also a sign of that traditional respect. Where the humor comes in is that brothers-in-law and sisters-in-law make jokes about each other whenever possible, to crack those barriers a little bit. Lakota humor plays a part here by telling us that the jokes mean that the respect is still there, but that in certain family relationships certain kinds of humor are allowable. It's like in white society where a joke teller tells jokes to cross some barriers, too.

There's still respect between in-laws, but as a brother-in-law I can tell things on my sister-in-law and maintain the humor relationships. It's almost like it's my duty to make sure I play tricks and say funny and even nasty things about my sisters-in-law. I remember one time I was announcing at a celebration and I noticed several of my sisters-in-law were in the crowd. I know they don't trust me anymore because I've told some jokes about them in the past and played a few little tricks on them, so that day I was very serious and I called each of them out to the center of the dance arena and said that I would like to honor them. When they finally all got out there, I asked the audience to stand because they were going to see a really old ceremony.

Then I announced that my sisters-in-law were going to have a traditional stretch-mark contest!

Another time one of my sisters-in-law was dancing out in the arena, so I couldn't let the chance go by, so I announced to the audience that I had good news. "That wasn't an earthquake we felt before; it was only my sister-in-law dancing around the arena." Now before you feel sorry for them, remember they joke about me whenever they can, and my wife seems to really enjoy that.

Brothers-in-law tell jokes about each other all the time too. My *tahansi*, cousin, Calvin Jumping Bull, is really good at that. He tells one story about how one of his brothers-in-law had a friend whose battery died, so he needed a push to start his car. His friend told him to push him at about thirty-five miles per hour to get it started. So Calvin's brother-in-law backed way up and then sped up to thirty-five miles per hour and drove forward and smacked his friend in the rear bumper and dented both cars! These kinds of stories show how when you have a brother-in-law or sister-in-law, they better not find out when you do something wrong or say something silly. They'll make a joke out of it right away. Even if you didn't really do it, they'll make it up and pretend.

Since brothers and sisters in our tradition really look out for each other and take care of each other, this kind of humor keeps the tension with in-laws from building up, and we enjoy the public teasing that helps to release bad feelings.

Among the Lakota, no matter what hardship there is, whether it's a death in the family or a serious ceremony or a discussion of a problem we might be concerned about, there's always humor connected with it. I think that humor brings us back to reality and reminds us that we are not really that important, or that the issue on the floor is not really that bad, or that somebody who is a good speaker or a mature leader knows when to lighten things up by telling a funny story or making fun of himself or somebody in the audience. We all get a smile on our faces and nod agreement and feel better. When somebody can't laugh or enjoy a joke in the middle of something else, we take it as a sign that they're not comfortable with themselves, or aren't too sure of themselves and can't laugh at times. No matter how serious the situation, there's always humor which is told in such a way that it doesn't hurt people's feelings.

Let me tell you one little example of a situation back in the 1960s when some of my nieces were invited to an ethnic women's conference, somewhere in Michigan, I think. My nieces were modeling traditional dance clothing and I was introducing them and explaining what they were wearing and putting in a little humor here and there. Pretty soon there were some feminists in the audience who started kind of heckling me here and there for not allowing the women to do their own introductions; they didn't need a man to do that for them. After a while I finally explained to them that in our culture it's an honor for a niece to have her uncle introduce her. I think that's an example not only of cultural ignorance but also that those ladies took themselves too seriously. In our Lakota culture that's a sign of immaturity.

Another example of this kind of thing took place at one of our powwows several years ago. One of the national AIM leaders was dancing at a powwow where one of our clowns was going around making fun of people in the audience and some of the singers, and making fun of the dancers. Well, this clown started to dance in back of this guy and making fun of his steps and exaggerating everything. Now, it's expected among us that if a clown picks on you, you're secure enough that you either ignore it or you laugh along because you're sure of yourself. The people watch how you react. This AIM leader got upset when this clown started to make fun of him, and said something nasty to him. Afterwards people were talking about how this guy who was supposed to be a leader couldn't laugh at himself. He lost some of his reputation there.

Our old-time *eyapahas*, announcers, were really good at that. On the spur of the moment as they were announcing things, they could make fun of somebody in such a way that everybody laughed and didn't get angry, but felt good. Our modern powwow announcers who are good still know how to do that, to make people lighten up and become less serious and to stop criticizing each other all the time. One of the current powwow jokes that's making the rounds is the one about how two guys—the announcer will usually pick on two of the dancers or two of the singers around, like Irving and Calvin—got themselves into trouble. He'll say, "Irving and Calvin were drinking one night, and they really got hungry. They wanted some pork chops. Irving, who is the smarter of the two, said, 'I know a farmer who's got this prize hog. Let's go grab it and have some pork chops.' So they went to the farmer's place and grabbed this prize hog and ran off. The farmer called the BIA police and told them that these two guys had stolen his prize pig. When Irving and Calvin were driving along holding this hog down on the seat between them, they saw a BIA roadblock up ahead. It was getting dark, so Irving said, 'I have a plan.' They put some lipstick on the pig's mouth, some nail polish left in the car by one of their girlfriends on its toes, and put a red scarf over its head and put sunglasses on it, and drove up to the roadblock. The BIA cops shined their flashlights in the car and told them to go on. Irving and Calvin were really relieved to get away with it. As they drove away, one of those Indian BIA cops said to the other one, 'I wonder what that pretty white lady was doing with those two *ugly* Indians!'" That's how these announcers keep the audience relaxed and having fun.

Even at something as sacred as a Sun Dance, if they tell us that everything must be so sacred and holy that you can't laugh or tell a joke or start your car, then I feel that Sun Dance leader isn't very sure of himself as a leader. He is setting down rules because he's not a real leader, so he tries to force the people to keep a sober face and not say a word. I think that it's the special person who can get up publicly and tell a joke about himself. That's a sign that he's a happy person, happy with himself. He's honored to be there at that gathering and in front of people, so he's willing to tell a joke about himself.

I think this is where we have to really look at what is real Indian humor and what is only making nasty fun of people. Our tradition tells us you can make fun of a brother-in-law or a sister-in-law. Then again, at many of the ceremonies and powwows in the old days and up to the 1950s and 1960s we had *heyokas,* sacred clowns, who had special dreams about the thunder beings in some way, dancing out there to make people laugh. They would dance backward awkwardly or fall down or dance in all kinds of crazy ways. They wore costumes with big cotton noses and big bellies or rear ends, all to make people laugh. They did it so people would laugh, have a smile on their faces. I think the clown was there to take that nasty making fun of people or the criticizing mind away from that activity in the center of the arena. He was, in a way, the middleman between the center and the outer circles. Traditionally, nobody was to make nasty fun of each other or criticize each other till you could perform the same things as those that were being done in that circle.

That *heyoka* guy that danced out there might jump in the air on the last beat of the drum when the dancers were supposed to stop, and shake his leg up in the air, act real proud when he was doing something crazy, and do other things to take people's negative criticisms away. If you notice, today's big powwows or dancing contests don't have that *heyoka* out there performing that function. So people sit there very seriously because a thousand-dollar prize is very serious business. They sit there in a tense, businesslike manner, and if you bump into one of them, they give you a dirty look or curse you out. That humor is no longer there; the *heyoka* is missing. A person also doesn't have the chance to tell a joke about a brother-in-law or sister-in-law. That funny middleman isn't there to use humor to keep that respect and honor in balance. The fun side of it all is gone.

One of the few times where humor is still working the way it used to is the small New Year's dances that are held in some of the communities. The first New Year's dances I heard about were held was sometime after the First World War. Here in Porcupine they went to the superintendent and said, "You outlawed dancing and singing, but we want to honor the new year, so we want to put on a masquerade for good health and so the cattle will grow fat in the spring and our horses will be strong and all the garden produce will grow well for the next district fair. We want to honor the new year." So the superintendent said, "All right, that's very good of you Indian people." So they allowed us to dance and they had three or four nights of New Year's powwow. Lots of people made pledges to dance as masqueraders, almost like for a Sun Dance. They pledged for good health for the people for one year, or that nobody in the family would have anything bad happen to them. They would get ready for the New Year's masquerades and the honoring giveaways. These masqueraders didn't have to be the sacred *heyoka* dreamers, the sacred clowns.

They have masquerade dances during New Year's evening where men dress as women, with scarves, a woman's plastic face, with makeup and a dress, stockings, and high-heeled shoes. They put in a big bosom or really big rear end. Or some lady will dress up as a man with a suit or a cowboy with boots and a big hat and rope, or an old farmer with bib overalls and big work shoes. Then sometimes the old year with a big sign will dance in as an old man, and the next year will dance in as a baby with diapers and a bottle and chase the old year around during the night and then finally chase it out at midnight. I think the purpose is to have fun by doing something opposite to the normal way of dressing, acting, and dancing.

One time here at Porcupine New Year's powwow, they were passing out people's names and descriptions. Whichever one you drew, you were supposed to dress like that person and go to the masquerade dance and dance like they would. They talked me into doing it that time and I drew a name that said "Old traditional woman dancer." So here I came back and showed that to my family, so my Aunt Elizabeth, my mother's sister, sewed some old canvas together and cut big, ugly fringes onto this imitation dress and painted great big Indian designs all over it, and then I borrowed her woman's breastplate and other stuff. My aunt also made me some big black yarn braids to go with my mask and a scarf to go around it.

That New Year's I did the *ipsila waci*, the old woman's jumping dance, dressed like an old woman. As I danced I got a little carried away, and because I danced real fast to that song, my legs were getting wider and wider apart and I had a hard time pulling my legs together. Everybody really laughed at me. I also had a big pillow on me with *"ipsila waci"* sewed on it and that pillow was bouncing up and down behind me when I danced. I guess I was quite a sight. Most of my cousins really laughed; they didn't know that was me. When I sat down on the floor and when they started singing again, it took me about two or three minutes to start getting up real slow. I was stooped over trying to get up and I held up my canvas dress a little bit and showed part of my legs to get up and start dancing again. Many of my relatives really laughed, and when we got done, they put us out in the center and they took our masks off and the announcer asked why we had danced as masqueraders, as is customary. He announced everything and made it a little more comical, and all my cousins and all my relatives laughed at me. Then they got out and they donated to different people to honor me for dancing like that at New Year's. I danced for good health for all and my family and a good year coming up.

When they took our masks off and when the announcer had announced it all for the people, they made us dance again without the masks. I still had that canvas dress on, and when they sang another song, we were still supposed to clown around. But somehow with that mask off, I couldn't dance again like I did before.

That kind of humor takes the edge off the criticism and making fun of those out in the center by people who are sitting around the outside. It takes the edge off the criticism resulting from not understanding what was going on out there in the center. The *eyapaha*, announcer, then also played a part because he told funny stories about why the clowns were doing that. That humor pulled people from the outside in and made them a part of it all. Everybody laughed and couldn't stay apart and separate and critical. In this way they carried a big smile from the old year into the new one.

These masqueraders at New Year's dances and the real *heyokas* who were the sacred clown dreamers played a very important role in all these gatherings and *wacipi*, dances. We don't have these guys anymore and they're not playing that important role of keeping the circles in balance. We had *heyokas* like Kermit Bear Shield, Roy Jealous, and Chauncy White Wash who were *heyoka* dreamers and were there for a purpose in that inner circle of all festivities. They had their own specialty dances of turning everything around and showing the people a different side. For example, I remember there was a specialty dance at a powwow where they would put a ten-dollar bill folded real small on the ground and the dancers would have to dance up to it and pick it up with their mouth without their hands touching the ground. All the dancers would try it and usually couldn't pick up the money.

Then the *heyoka*s tried it, too, and some fell on their face or fell on their back. They couldn't get it either. So while the singers were still singing, the *heyoka*s had a little conference. They were talking and one was waving and shaking his head around, and another was making all kinds of dramatic motions, and they pointed fingers at each other, and another one said, "No!" real emphaticlike and pointed at the other guys. It was like a tribal council meeting. Finally they all raised their hands and they pointed at one. That guy kept shaking his head but he was outvoted. Everybody backed off and they put him on the ground on his stomach and one guy grabbed him by his leg and another on his other leg, and two other guys grabbed him by his arms, and they came dancing holding him close to the ground. His face was close to the ground, so as they came dancing up to that ten-dollar bill, he picked it up with his mouth and they just danced around in a big circle, like a victory round.

Using humor like that of these *heyoka*s broke the edge of making fun of someone and took people's minds off criticizing others. We use humor in general because it brings people together and reminds them that they are still only human beings. The laughter makes us feel better and keeps us from thinking too much of ourselves. But these days we're getting away from that. I have a lot of brothers-in-law and sisters-in-law and all these years I've joked a lot with them in a traditional way, but a respectful way. Only one time did one of my sisters-in-law get mad because of the humor I used. After that I never joked with her in the traditional way again, because I realized her life must be different from mine. She was the only one to take offense at the usual brother-in-law and sister-in-law humor.

Today we're also starting to lose the humor at our meetings. Partly, I think, we're stuck with time restrictions and Robert's Rules, bylaws, and regulations. I remember back in the 1950s and 1960s I used to listen to the old guys talking at the old Porcupine store. They might be talking about something serious like treaties, but in the middle of it all they would use humor and they'd joke and laugh and then still return to the treaty. At our council meetings, a councilman might still get up and tell a joke or use a little humor and then read his resolution and have a council vote. He could still use humor in a serious council meeting. I hope that we don't start hugging the agenda so much that because of rules and regulations, we lose that ability to have fun.

I also think that's what's been so unique about Porcupine Singers. Everyplace we've gone ever since we started back in 1963, somehow the master of ceremonies always tells jokes about our Porcupine Singers or they have funny stories about one of our singers, or we might have something funny to tell about them. I've told you a couple of these earlier. There's always humor going back and forth, and people, I think, enjoy that good humor. In public that adds recognition. Even at our drum we're always all sitting there laughing and joking and that plays a big part because it shows that we are happy. Then when we'd start a song, we'd sing it with joy and we'd sound happy. When you have a good feeling, you sound good and you sound happy. I think that's something that singers have to learn as they travel through years of singing. How you feel inside your heart will affect others. People notice things. They notice if you're mad; if you're sad, they know it; if you're happy, they know it. Your face or your eyes give it away. Your enjoyment will transfer to them.

The way things are going, in addition to all the other programs to help maintain our cultural ways for our young people, we might have to have humor education to preserve that side of Lakota life.

The Four Circles

Last spring I was visiting with an elderly man from Fort Thompson on the Crow Creek Reservation. He was saying that a long time ago there were some people who were called Standing-in-the-Dark. What he meant is that when our people gather, they always sit in a circle for ceremonies or for powwows or for any public gatherings. There are always some people who are respected and honored, who are out in the center, whether as dancers, singers, announcers, or committee members. Next, outside of them, there is a circle of people around at a little distance who are supportive of the activities going on out there in the center and who might understand what they mean but are not the real leaders and doers. In outdoor gatherings these are the people who sit under the pine shade and look on and occasionally take part. Outside of them lies the third kind of circle, mostly young people whose main interest in life is courtship and the opposite sex. Rather than sitting, these young people are always restless and on the move, circling the arena over and over, looking to do what we call "snagging," to make time, or whatever term is used. But then another fifty or a hundred or more feet away there is another ring of people way back from the center. This outermost circle includes those Lakotas who lost most of their Lakota values and family traditions and maybe even their language. They've lost their cultural center and so they wait out in the dark away from the center of activity and the center of light.

As we were visiting, I thought about how what he was saying was true as a way of thinking about Lakota identity in these modern times. Out in the center of public events some people are making a commitment and taking responsibility. This center circle—those who are literally standing in the light in the evenings under the bright lights—is the focus of everyone's attention. That center area is what we would call *hocoka*, which is made up of *ho* (voice) and *coka* (center). I see this as the center place from which a voice comes, the announcer's voice, the voice of the singer. Sacred and important mind- and heart-engaging sounds are sent out from there. You can't send your voice from the outside. Take our Sun Dance ceremonies, for example. Out in the middle are the Sun Dance leaders who go out there with their sacred pipes and all the sacred symbols and acts of the Sun Dance which they wear and use as they go through the dances, the songs, and the ceremonies out in the center.

This central circle has two thin circles as you move outward. The first of these is the *wawiyokpia* (spreading of humor), where the sacred clowns do their antics to take the edge off feelings with their humor. The second of these two rings is the *otakuye* (relatives) ring, where honorable relatives take part with their kids. They actively take part in the center doings, the ceremonies, the dances, the giving away of things to honor the children and their families.

Then the second circle sits under the shade, alongside the singers, watching and taking part when appropriate. This I would call *wawayanka* (looking at something clean). This ring is witnessing and observing what is being done in the center, but is often passive and lets those in the center do things.

Outside of them, sometimes standing around the outer edge of the shade or just beyond, are the young people looking to find a honey. That is the third, the courting circle. This is the *wiyapaya* (by choice you bump into each other) ring.

Then you have another row of people, back further in a camp or parking lot, the cars that form a ring around the outside of the Sun Dance bowery. They sit in a car or stand behind or lean against cars because they lost their ways or they don't want to be identified with what's being done out there. They don't understand what's going on in the center two circles, so they stay way back in the dark. This is the circle of the *onuniyata* (lost or disconnected).

This set of four circles is also true of our powwows, what we call *wacipi*, celebration, fair, powwow, dancing contest, whatever we call it. The four rings are still there. You have dancers that are out there having put on their costume, their best beadwork, best feather bustle, their best head roach. It often takes them two to three hours to prepare themselves to look a certain way, to dance and act a certain way. They go out there with awareness and a humble confidence. Again, they make up the circle of respected and honored people. Next we have the people who sit under the shade in their lawn chairs or metal folding chairs or are sitting in the bleachers to watch and pay attention and sometimes take part. Then, just outside the dance shade, there is a sort of walkway around the arbor. Here the young people walk, meet, talk, and tease each other about hickies on their necks. Further out we find the outer ring that has those who are in the dark. They might be drinking or just spending their time here because they have no interest in what's going on out in the center. They don't really care what's going on out there, or don't identify with it, or are too embarrassed to identify with it.

At our last Oglala Nation Fair, Rodeo, and *Wacipi*, I was standing up on the announcer's stand and thought of this idea of the four circles of identity. I watched the people active out in the center and then the people under the shade and how they acted. I then turned around, went to the back of the announcer's stand, and stood there looking out towards the back and watching the people who walked back and forth, all the way around the shade, all day and all night long and all the next afternoon. And then, too, there were those in yet another circle out there in the parking lot, the people who just lean against cars; some just visit, some just sit in their cars. Maybe their son was dancing but they didn't have any interest, so they sit out in their cars even in hundred-degree heat, but in their own personal darkness.

These four circles show a good deal about cultural understanding and identity. For example, some of the people sitting under the shade and the third ring outside of them don't fully understand what is going on out in the center, whether it's a dancing contest or giveaway or whatever, so they criticize. I think this is where the elderly have an important responsibility. They have the chance to sit back and watch what's going on, and if a dancing contest rule is not right, if the singers are not singing right, if the dancers are not dancing right to that song, that elderly man or elderly woman should get up and come up to the announcer's stand, and, using the right words, publicly encourage those singers or dancers or other people in the center that are making the mistake by saying, "That's not the right way. This is the way we've done that. This is the way to sing this song; this is the way to dance to this song; this is why you're having a giveaway; this is why they're having a naming ceremony; this is why you're out in the center."

In this way our elders can keep even the people active out there in the center from taking too many liberties or putting too many personal interpretations to our songs and dances, our ceremonies and other ways of doing things in the right, respectful, traditional manner. But instead, unfortunately, too many other people criticize in a negative way that creates hard feeling and controversy rather than agreement and mutual respect.

Those people in the center who conduct ceremonies, who are dancers, singers, announcers, or whatever, have learned by experience from their grandparents or parents, who are often the more knowledgeable people among the Lakota. They are confident people, sure of themselves. That's why they're out there. I think, in a way, people in a community help put them out there to run ceremonies, to perform naming ceremonies, to lead the songs and dances, to announce at gatherings, because they have trust in them to do it right. In spite of some of our cultural losses, as shown by that outer group standing in the dark, those individuals towards the center, with the encouragment of our respected and knowledgeable elders, can become our light-bringers and remain our truth-keepers.

After some careful thinking about it, I decided to begin our whole book with the story of my names and the names of some of my relatives because through the proper understanding of names, the giving of names, and the remembering of names, each of us is given a personal identity by becoming part of a social reality. We are then like a leaf on a cottonwood tree or a thread in a spider web—connected to every other part of the tree and of the web as a living being.

The idea of the four circles of our Lakota culture today is another way of trying to understand ourselves. That's why, looking at it all from a positive point of view, we picked the title for this book as we did. What is so disheartening is the amount of people in the outer ring, the circle of darkness where people live without direction. They need to be able to put things in order, to know their cultural and their family history, to recognize and to keep the limits in this life, to realize the time and preparation needed for the balanced, meaningful life—what we call *canku luta,* the red road.

On the pages above, we've tried to provide a special look at Lakota culture as we see it here at Porcupine Brotherhood Community, so that those people waiting in the dark—perhaps we have a little of them in all of us—can approach the light.

Severt in his favorite hat and jacket
(Courtesy of Rand's Studio)

SEVERT YOUNG BEAR SR. died on August 24, 1993, just as this book was going to press, an event he looked forward to with anticipation. He stated more than once that he wished to be remembered as one who tried to make a difference. The intense loss felt by all who knew him is perhaps softened a bit by the legacy this book represents.

Pronunciation Guide

T<small>HE</small> spelling of the Lakota words in this book is based on an evolving orthography developed primarily by Stephen Return Riggs and Eugene Buechel. The following is intended to provide a reasonable pronunciation guide.

In general, vowels are pronounced as follows:

    a as in far
    e as in let
    i as in bit
    o as in go
    u as in boot

Consonants are pronounced as in English except:

    c as ch in choose
    g as g or as the r in French *rue*
    h as h or as the ch in German *machen*
    j as the g in montage
    k as g, kch, or k
    n after a, i, or u is nasalized as in French *fin*
    p as b, pch, or p
    s as either s or sh
    t as d, tch, or t

Raised commas within Lakota words represent glottal stops.

Selected Bibliography

Sioux Life Stories

Black Elk Speaks: Being the Life Story of a Holy Man of the Oglala Sioux as Told through John G. Neihardt. 1932. Reprint. Lincoln: University of Nebraska Press, 1979.

Buechel, Eugene. *A Dictionary of the Teton Dakota Sioux Language.* Edited by Paul Manhart. Pine Ridge, S.Dak.: Red Cloud Indian School, 1970.

Crow Dog, Mary, and Richard Erdoes. *Lakota Woman.* New York: HarperCollins, 1991.

DeMallie, Raymond J., ed. *The Sixth Grandfather: Black Elk's Teachings Given to John G. Neihardt.* Lincoln: University of Nebraska Press, 1984.

Dudley, Joseph Iron Eye. *Choteau Creek: A Sioux Reminiscence.* Lincoln: University of Nebraska Press, 1992.

Eastman, Charles Alexander. *From the Deep Woods to Civilization: Chapters in the Autobiography of an Indian.* 1916. Reprint. Lincoln: University of Nebraska Press, 1977.

——— . *Indian Boyhood.* 1902. Reprint. Glorieta: Rio Grande Press, 1976. Lincoln: University of Nebraska Press, 1991.

Howard, James H. *The Warrior Who Killed Custer: The Personal Narrative of Chief Joseph White Bull.* Lincoln: University of Nebraska Press, 1968.

Lame Deer [John Fire], and Richard Erdoes. *Lame Deer, Seeker of Visions.* New York: Simon and Schuster, 1972.

Madonna Swan: A Lakota Woman's Story. As told through Mark St. Pierre. Norman: University of Oklahoma Press, 1991.

Mails, Thomas. *Fools Crow.* New York: Avon, 1979. Reprint. Lincoln: University of Nebraska Press, 1990.

Mallery, Garrick. *Picture Writing of the American Indians.* 2 vols. 1888–89. Reprint. New York: Dover, 1972.

Riggs, Stephen Return. *Dakota Grammar, Texts, and Ethnography.* Edited by James O. Dorsey. 1893. Reprint. Marvin, S.Dak.: Blue Cloud Abbey, 1977.

Standing Bear, Luther. *Land of the Spotted Eagle.* 1933. Reprint. Lincoln: University of Nebraska Press, 1978.

———. *My Indian Boyhood.* 1931. Reprint. Lincoln: University of Nebraska Press, 1988.

———. *My People the Sioux.* 1928. Reprint. Lincoln: University of Nebraska Press, 1975.

Zitkala Ša [Gertrude Bonnin]. *American Indian Stories.* 1921. Reprint. Lincoln: University of Nebraska Press, 1986.

Music

Black Bear, Ben Sr., and R. D. Theisz. *Songs and Dances of the Lakota.* Rosebud, S.Dak.: Sinte Gleska College, 1976.

Curtis, Natalie. *The Indians' Book: Songs and Legends of the American Indians.* 1907. Reprint. New York: Dover, 1968.

Densmore, Frances. *Teton Sioux Music.* 1918. Reprinted as *Teton Sioux Music and Culture.* Lincoln: University of Nebraska Press, 1992.

Herndon, Marcia. *Native American Music.* Norwood, Pa.: Norwood Editions, 1980.

Heth, Charlotte, ed. *Traditional Music of North American Indians.* Los Angeles: Department of Music, University of California, 1980.

Paige, Harry W. *Songs of the Teton Sioux.* Los Angeles: Westernlore Press, 1970.

Powers, William K. *War Dance. Plains Indian Musical Performance.* Tucson: University of Arizona Press, 1990.

White Hat, Albert, and John Around Him. *Lakota Ceremonial Songs.* Rosebud, S.Dak.: Sinte Gleska College, 1983.

Audio Recordings (Albums)

Porcupine Singers. *Porcupine Singers at Ring Thunder.* 2 vols. Phoenix: Canyon Records, 1976.

———. *Concert in Vermillion.* 2 vols. Phoenix: Canyon Records, 1980.

———. *Rabbit Songs of the Lakota.* 2 vols. Phoenix: Canyon Records: 1987.

General

Bad Heart Bull, Amos. Text by Helen Blish. *A Pictographic History of the Oglala Sioux.* Lincoln: University of Nebraska Press, 1967.

Deloria, Ella. *Dakota Texts.* 1932. Reprint. Vermillion, S.Dak.: State Publishing, 1978.

————. *Speaking of Indians*. 1944. Reprint. Vermillion, S.Dak.: State Publishing, 1983.

————, *Waterlily*. Lincoln: University of Nebraska Press, 1990. [Completed by 1944.]

Gagnon, Gregory, and Karen White Eyes. *Pine Ridge Reservation: Yesterday and Today*. Interior, S.Dak.: Badlands History Association, 1992.

Grobsmith, Elizabeth S. *Lakota of the Rosebud: A Contemporary Ethnography*. New York: Holt, Rinehart and Winston, 1981.

Hassrick, Royal B. *The Sioux*. Norman: University of Oklahoma Press, 1964.

Hyde, George. *A Sioux Chronicle*. 1956. Reprint. Norman: University of Oklahoma Press, 1980.

Marken, Jack, and Herbert Hoover. *Bibliography of the Sioux*. Metuchen, N.J.: Scarecrow Press, 1980.

McLaughlin, Marie. *Myths and Legends of the Sioux*. 1916. Reprint. Lincoln: University of Nebraska Press, 1990.

Meyer, Roy. *History of the Santee Sioux: United States Indian Policy on Trial*. Lincoln: University of Nebraska Press, 1967.

Olson, James. *Red Cloud and the Sioux Problem*. Lincoln: University of Nebraska Press, 1965.

Powers, Marla N. *Oglala Women in Myth, Ritual, and Reality*. Chicago: University of Chicago Press, 1986.

Powers, William K. *Oglala Religion*. Lincoln: University of Nebraska Press, 1975.

————. *Sacred Language: The Nature of Supernatural Discourse in Lakota*. Norman: University of Oklahoma Press, 1986.

————. *Yuwipi: Vision and Experience in Oglala Ritual*. Lincoln: University of Nebraska Press, 1975.

Rice, Julian. *Deer Women and Elk Men: The Lakota Narratives of Ella Deloria*. Albuquerque: University of New Mexico Press, 1992.

————. *Lakota Storytelling*. New York: Peter Lang, 1989.

Theisz, R. D., ed. *Buckskin Tokens: Contemporary Oral Narratives of the Lakota*. Rosebud, S.Dak.: Sinte Gleska College, 1975.

Walker, James R. *Lakota Belief and Ritual*. Edited by Raymond J. DeMallie and Elaine A. Jahner. Lincoln: University of Nebraska Press, 1980.

————. *Lakota Myth*. Edited by Elaine A. Jahner. Lincoln: University of Nebraska Press, 1983.

————. *Lakota Society*. Edited by Raymond J. DeMallie. Lincoln: University of Nebraska Press, 1982.

————. "The Sun Dance and Other Ceremonies of the Oglala Division of the Teton Dakota." *American Museum of Natural History Anthropological Papers* 16(2) (1917): 51–221.

Index

AIM Song: origin of, 155–57, 164
alcohol, 136
alowan (song): etymology, 41
American Association of Indian Activities (AAIA), 99
American Indian Movement, 148; AIM Song, 155–57; BIA building takeover, xii, 148; at Calico, 149; current role of, 164–65, 168; Custer demonstration, xii; intervention, xxxi; invited to Pine Ridge, 158; problems of leadership, 157, 165
announcer (*see also eyapaha*): as motivator, xxiv
Arapaho, Herman, 93; rabbit song, 91
Around Him, John, Jr., 42
Attack Him, John, Sr., 97

babies: wrapped, 126–27
Bad Cob, Tom, 150
Badger, Dave: Sio Paha story, 19
Bad Hand family: makers of songs, 51–52; Red Leaf Takoja Singers, 46; Willie song, 52
Banks, Dennis: AIM Song, 156; at Calico, 149–50; invitation for host drum, 74; invited to Pine Ridge, 7; traveled with, 148
bear: power, 20
Bear Runner, Oscar, 99
Bear Shield, Kermit, 174
Bellecourt, Clyde: and BIA (Bureau of Indian Affairs), 55, 143, 146; at Calico,

150; invited to Pine Ridge, 7; traveled with, 148
Big Foot: band, xxx, 139
Birgil, Kills Straight, 158
Bishop Hare School, 137
Black Bear, Ben, 48
Black Elk Speaks, xxxi
Black Hills, xvii, 27, 28–33, 147; Bradley Bill, 163–64; as illegal taking, 163; loss of, xxix
boys: test of courage, 122–23; traditional education of, 121–22
Bradley Bill, 163
Brotherhood Community, xii
buffalo, 127–28
Bull Bear, Royal, 93
bumblebee: power, 20–21
Bureau of Indian Affairs building takeover, 148, 159
butterflies, 26–27

cancega wanka (drum keeper), 53
Cante Tinza (Strong Hearts), 83
Carlisle Indian School, 79
celebrations: committee, 62
cepansi (older sister/cousin), 87, 89
ceremonies (*see also* Sun Dance; Sio Paha): 94; prohibited, 86
champion dancers, 100–01
chief song, 86
Chips, Ellis, 67, 100
circle(s): the center, xxiv

In the American Indian Lives Series

I Stand in the Center of the Good
Interviews with Contemporary Native American Artists
Edited by Lawrence Abbott

Chainbreaker
The Revolutionary War Memoir of Governor Blacksnake as Told to
Benjamin Williams
Edited by Thomas S. Abler

Chief
An Autobiography of Eugene Delorme, Imprisoned Santee Sioux
Edited by Inéz Cardozo-Freeman

Winged Words
Contemporary American Indian Writers Speak
Edited by Laura Coltelli

Life Lived Like a Story
Life Stories of Three Athapaskan Elders
Edited by Julie Cruikshank

Alex Posey
Creek Poet, Journalist, and Humorist
By Daniel F. Littlefield Jr.

Mourning Dove
A Salishan Autobiography
Edited by Jay Miller

John Rollin Ridge
His Life and Works
By James W. Parins

Singing an Indian Song
A Biography of D'Arcy McNickle
By Dorothy R. Parker

Sacred Feathers
The Reverend Peter Jones (Kahkewaquonaby) and the Mississauga
   Indians
By Donald B. Smith

I Tell You Now
Autobiographical Essays by Native American Writers
Edited by Brian Swann and Arnold Krupat